ADVENTUROUS DREAMS,

ADVENTUROUS LIVES

Other Books by the Author

ADVENTURE FICTION

Thai Gold (also published as *Nepal Gold,* and in hardbound as *The Bangkok Collection)*

Opium Dream

The Manila Galleon

NON FICTION

Westward from New Amsterdam: The Schoonover Epic, 13 Generations, One Branch, One Tree, One Forest (genealogical niche)

*Jason does what he writes about.
He lives his dreams. Jason is the real deal.
It will be hard to just sit on the beach
after you read this.*

DANIEL BENNETT,
PRESIDENT OF THE EXPLORERS CLUB, NEW YORK

*Many people have dreams.
The people in this book have fulfilled theirs.
And you? In the book of your life,
maybe there is still time!*

BERTRAND PICCARD,
BREITLING ORBITER 3 BALLOON

*When I was a boy I found there
were phrases in poems, books and songs
that kindled delicious imaginings inside
my childish heart:* Beyond the Blue
Horizon, The Royal Road to Romance,
Heart's Desire, *more than you know.
They were the dreams of others, but they
sparked and took fire in me. Robert Frost
wrote, "… And that has made
all the difference." Open this book
and read on.*

CAPTAIN NORMAN BAKER,
THOR HEYERDAHL'S FIRST MATE, NAVIGATOR &
RADIOMAN ABOARD *RA, RA II* AND *TIGRIS*

*Bravo, Jason Schoonover, for never
giving up on one of your dreams...that of
providing the world with this wonderful
anthology honoring the child in all of us! I
am proud to be part of it. We all have vivid
childhood dreams that often go unfulfilled.
Your book will show all that dreams
can assuredly come true!
Thank you.*

STRATTON LEOPOLD,
PRODUCER, *STAR TREK XI*; EXECUTIVE PRODUCER,
MISSION: IMPOSSIBLE III

*As a kid growing up in a small working
town, I gathered my inspiration to explore
from the pages of books.* Adventurous
Dreams, Adventurous Lives *is undoubtedly
the ultimate catalyst for any potential
explorer with adventure stirring
in their veins.*

COLIN ANGUS,
FIRST HUMAN-POWERED
CIRCUMNAVIGATOR OF THE GLOBE

*Jason Schoonover has beautifully
captured the power of youthful dreams
realized, through the words of those who
refused to let them die. His collection of
powerful vignettes must be read by all who
seek a life of fulfillment and happiness.
These inspirational writings are sure to spur
on many future explorers and adventurers
in life, regardless of age. The sentiments and
stories within these pages are timeless.*

SURVIVORMAN LES STROUD

*Perhaps the most wonderful thing
about this marvelous anthology is the fact
that the stories reveal the obvious, that
every great adventure begins with a dream,
and that every life well lived grows out of
a simple promise of hope. That such men
as Buzz Aldrin and Ed Hillary began as
ordinary mortals effectively suggests that
anyone has a chance to achieve a certain
immortality, based not on the ephemera of
celebrity, not on the essence of the hero, the
one who is not known for being known,
but known for the magnitude of his or her
deeds and achievements.*

WADE DAVIS, EXPLORER-IN-RESIDENCE
NATIONAL GEOGRAPHIC SOCIETY

*All great journeys start with a dream
and every great explorer started as a young
boy or girl looking at the sky and wondering
if their dreams would ever come true. Jason
Schoonover's* Adventurous Dreams *is a
touching yet refreshing look at the inner
thoughts of some of the greatest explorers of
the 20th century. Before anyone could take
"one small step for man" they had to take
one giant leap towards their own dream.*

RICHARD C. WIESE, PRESIDENT EMERITUS,
THE EXPLORERS CLUB AND HOST OF
EXPLORATION WITH RICHARD WIESE

*Anyone reading these thumbnail
autobiographies is bound to wind
up gathering tips and honing his own
techniques for bringing success to his
endeavors. (Besides finding a treasure
of biographical material on some very
interesting individuals.)*

HUGH DOWNS, BROADCASTER

Prepare to be inspired. Jason Schoonover's book reveals the spark which nurtured and sustained childhood curiosity leading to adventurous careers in exploration of the deepest oceans, remote tribes, obscure caves and outer space.

PAT AND ROSEMARIE KEOUGH,
CREATORS OF ANTARCTICA, INTERNATIONAL
PHOTOGRAPHIC BOOK OF THE YEAR, 2003

The dream of questing to new horizons of knowledge and new places began for many of us when we were children. Adventurous Dreams, Adventurous Lives captures our collective journeys and the sense of awe and thirst for knowledge that continues to fire our hearts and souls. Explore this book!

SEA HUNTER JIM DELGADO

Only Jason Schoonover could have pulled together 120 of the world's top explorers and drawn from them that moment when it all came into focus, that need to explore, to push the boundaries in pursuit of extending mankind's knowledge of our universe, even if it meant putting one's life on the line. An inspiring read into what sparks the physical expression of intellectual curiosity.

LIEUTENANT (NAVY) JOSEPH FREY,
CHAIRMAN OF THE EXPLORERS CLUB,
CANADIAN CHAPTER

Dreams can come true! Never before have I seen such a collection of influential adventurers divulge the inspirations that shaped their lives. Fantastic memories that will inspire young minds to go for the gold!

PHILIP CURRIE,
FORMER CURATOR OF DINOSAURS,
ALBERTA'S ROYAL TYRRELL MUSEUM
OF PALEONTOLOGY

"If you have a dream, begin it. Boldness has genius, power, and magic in it." The philosophy of Goethe realized in the lives of each of these explorers.

KEN KAMLER,
AUTHOR OF DOCTOR ON EVEREST

As a very young boy in south central Manitoba I read Jules Verne's books assiduously and dreamed of seeing "Far away places with strange enchanted names." This eventually led me to Ethiopia where I taught for two years but, far more importantly, to walk and dream as a research scientist on the tundra of northern Canada. Dreams are what adventures derive from—and that's what this remarkable book is all about.

DENIS ST-ONGE,
OFFICER OF THE ORDER OF CANADA

It's said that dreams can lead to high places. In my case, as a mountain climber, I had a distinct advantage in assuring this outcome. But having a youthful dream is one thing. Keeping it from being buried under an avalanche of daily travail is the hard part— sacrifice and compromise are needed to reach that personal summit. Jason Schoonover has garnered stories herein from exceptional individuals who have done just that.

PAT MORROW,
PIONEER OF THE
SEVEN SUMMITS QUEST

My adventurous dreams have always been so realistic that they inspired me to make them reality. The problem is, at 70, I'm still dreaming!

COLONEL JOHN BLASHFORD-SNELL,
AUTHOR OF SOMETHING LOST
BEHIND THE RANGES

Jason Schoonover's Adventurous Dreams, Adventurous Lives casts brilliant light on the great and mysterious human impulse to explore, capturing as if in amber that moment when individual dreams of discovery were born. It is at once a compelling, sometimes startling, glimpse into the minds of some of our greatest explorers, and an unrivalled catalogue of derring-do.

JOHN GEIGER,
AUTHOR OF FROZEN IN TIME:
THE FATE OF THE FRANKLIN EXPEDITION

Our dreams are tantalisingly just out of reach, our adventures are in stretching ourselves to touch them and our success reflects the degree of stretch we achieved. You'll find 120 such dreams realized between these very covers.

BRIAN JONES,
BREITLING ORBITER 3

Dreams open new vistas of possibility in all our lives. The dreams that led explorers to search out and discover the myriad wonders of the world make these men and women our lodestars as we walk into the future. The stories in Adventurous Dreams, Adventurous Lives *embody the power of dreams, a power that none of us should lose hold of.*

MILBRY POLK,
AUTHOR OF *WOMEN OF DISCOVERY*, CO-FOUNDER AND DIRECTOR OF WINGS WORLDQUEST

Are adventurers born or are they made by events? Here is a collection of short memoirs by explorers who went everywhere from deep sea to space, telling us that they were born with it and pursued it no matter what the odds. A great book for anyone who has a passion for exploration and hopes to inspire others to pursue a life of adventure.

ROSALY LOPES,
GUINNESS BOOK OF WORLD RECORDS "DISCOVERER OF MORE ACTIVE VOLCANOES ON IO (OR ON EARTH) THAN ANYONE."

The love of travel and exploration, and more importantly, the support and encouragement of my family and friends, allowed me to carry out my dreams as a field geologist. Jason Schoonover's book on the successful careers of 120 incredibly diverse adventurer-explorers should provide inspiration to anyone that has doubts that his or her dream cannot be fulfilled.

NAT RUTTER,
OFFICER OF THE ORDER OF CANADA, AND CO-AUTHOR OF *CLIMATE CHANGE AND LANDSCAPE IN THE CANADIAN ROCKIES*

I have travelled far, including both Poles, but the mind travels further. These fellow explorers will undoubtedly inspire us all to greater adventures. I go, I see, I write, I am.

NEVILLE SHULMAN, CBE,
AUTHOR OF *CLIMBING THE EQUATOR*

Everyone dreams and yearns for fulfillment. These personal chronicles are by those who faced adventurous challenges with passion, curiosity and persistence—and accomplished something of value. They are not only fascinating but also offer important lessons to all of us.

GEORGE B. SCHALLER,
WILDLIFE CONSERVATION SOCIETY

From the seafloor in the deepest part of the ocean to the surface of the moon, explorers have been there. No virtual reality, computer-generated, thrills here. It is all the real thing and told through the prism of what motivates men and women to do these things. Inside these two covers you will find that the spirit of exploration is alive and continuing!

DON WALSH,
COMMANDER OF THE BATHYSCAPHE *TRIESTE*, IN 1960 TO THE OCEAN'S DEEPEST SPOT

For most people, adventure involves experiencing something they have them-selves never done before. The adventurers profiled in this book have, for the most part, sought experiences that no one has ever done before. It is this willingness, this aspiration for the untravelled and unknown that sets these people apart and makes their stories both stimulating and slightly har-rowing for the rest of us. It may be a dream and it may be a gene, but something drives these exceptional people to pass over what is already recorded or recommended in fa-vour of what can only be discovered. Jason Schoonover has brought together their sto-ries for the first time and the result is literally marvellous.

STEPHEN INGLIS,
DIRECTOR GENERAL, RESEARCH AND COLLECTIONS, CANADIAN MUSEUM OF CIVILIZATION

Many people believe that to achieve great things requires brains and brawn but fail to recognise the true catalyst— a simple youthful adventurous dream.

ADVENTURER NEIL LAUGHTON

The idea for this collection is excellent: that moment of awareness, perhaps almost a calling in childhood, is a dream that stays warm for years. That key commitment to exploration stems early and very simply, perhaps from a book, a patchy map, a perplexing question, and then a long look in the bathroom mirror.

ROBERT L. FISHER,
SCRIPPS INSTITUTION OF OCEANOGRAPHY,
ONE OF THOSE WHO LED THE CHARGE
TO PLATE TECTONICS

It's truly amazing what you can dig up just by following your dreams. Think of Jason's book as a treasure chest of fascinating lives driven by an early dream of adventure and discovery—one that could be yours!

SUE HENDRICKSON,
DISCOVERER OF THE WORLD'S
LARGEST *T. REX*

Kudos to Jason Schoonover for his awe-inspiring gift, a glimpse into the mind and soul of some of society's most celebrated explorers. An illuminating journey into the magic of science, and its first creative spark!

KIRSTY DUNCAN,
AUTHOR OF *HUNTING THE 1918 FLU:
ONE SCIENTIST'S SEARCH FOR A KILLER VIRUS*

"Follow your dreams" may be the most important advice a young person can receive. Jason Schoonover presents the illuminating and inspiring stories of an incredible variety of prominent individuals who followed their youthful dreams to dramatic success.

LEE TALBOT,
AMERICAN ECOLOGIST, GEOGRAPHER
AND ENVIRONMENTALIST

If dreams are the blueprints for life then Jason Schoonover's book is the Architectural Digest *of lives well lived.*

JOHN LOVELACE,
HOST PILOT OF *WINGS OVER CANADA*

The spirit to explore gives humanity its vitality and dreams provide the motivation. These men and women dreamed big and those dreams motivated them to action. Their stories not only inspire but demonstrate that we all can be explorers in our own right.

CAPTAIN ROBERT "RIO" HAHN,
CO-CREATOR OF BIOSPHERE 2

I dream my dreams solo, sometimes afraid to share them for fear they will vanish, the way night dreams often do. What a happy surprise to be able to add my secret dreams to others whose dreams also shaped their lives. Thank you, Jason Schoonover!

ANN MCGOVERN,
AUTHOR

ADVENTUROUS DREAMS, ADVENTUROUS LIVES

Collected and Edited by
Jason Schoonover

Foreword by Meave Leakey

Rocky
Mountain Books

VANCOUVER • VICTORIA • CALGARY

Rocky Mountain Books
#108 – 17665 66A Avenue
Surrey, BC V3S 2A7
www.rmbooks.com

Rocky Mountain Books
PO Box 468
Custer, WA
98240-0468

Library and Archives Canada Cataloguing in Publication
Schoonover, Jason
        Adventurous dreams, adventurous lives / Jason Schoonover.
ISBN 978-1-894765-91-6
        1. Adventure and adventurers—Biography. 2. Explorers—Biography.
I. Title.

CT9970.S35 2007   920.02   C2007-902918-3

Library of Congress Control Number 2007931973

Edited by Colleen Munro
Text design by Frances Hunter
Front cover photo by Christine Balderas / iStockphoto

Printed in Canada

Rocky Mountain Books acknowledges the financial support for its publishing program from the Government of Canada through the Book Publishing Industry Development Program (BPIDP), Canada Council for the Arts, and the province of British Columbia through the British Columbia Arts Council and the Book Publishing Tax Credit.

The Canada Council | Le Conseil des Arts
for the Arts | du Canada

BRITISH COLUMBIA
ARTS COUNCIL
We acknowledge the support of the Province of British Columbia
through the British Columbia Arts Council

This book is dedicated to my
childhood friends, Huey, Dewey and Louie,
who took me on many a fabulous adventure.
And also to my mother, Linda, who bought me
my first typewriter and computer. And to my aunt
and godmother, Dot Symons, for mailing me
her stenographic book when I was 13 so
I could learn to type. They nurtured
another of the dreams.

There is always one moment

in childhood when the door opens

and lets the future in.

THE POWER AND THE GLORY, GRAHAM GREENE

ACKNOWLEDGMENTS

Sincere and deepest thanks to Richard Wiese, President Emeritus of The Explorers Club; current President Daniel Bennett; Lindley Kirksey Young, the Club's Book Committee Chair; Brian Hanson, Vice President for Chapters; Joseph Frey, Canadian Chapter Chairman; John Geiger, Canadian Chapter Awards Committee Chairman; and other officers for their keen support of this project.

Since virtually every international explorer of note is, or has been, a member of this fabled and exclusive club since its inception in 1904, its support was essential. Also appreciation to Michael Doyle, past Membership Director, for always so promptly providing contact information.

Always a warm and wonderful thank you to Su Hattori, the Imperial Dragon Lady, for enduring the unendurable into our third decade. Your unwavering support and intelligent advice, as well as your great legs, have always been immensely appreciated.

And a very special thank you to my adventurous dreamers. This book wouldn't have been possible without you, and it's as much yours as mine. From the overwhelming and passionate response, the theme reverberated with that child in you. It was great fun going out to play with you.

CONTENTS

FOREWORD

Dreams are the engines of exploration, the drive that makes people passionate about their goals. Dreams are with us every day. My passion is the search for fossilised remains of early human ancestors and the animals that lived alongside them. All those working on our field expeditions wake with the dream of finding an exceptionally complete fossil of a human ancestor, or a new species of mammal. This is what drives us all to keep searching for long hours day after day in the hot, dry dusty deserts of northern Kenya. We dream of the complete skull that will solve a long unanswered question, of a complete hand that will give us insights into the evolution of our manipulative fingers—or better still, a dream we hardly dare to contemplate, a complete skeleton which will reveal a wealth of new information.

It can happen; it did once when one of our team members, a particularly dedicated and persistent field worker, discovered a tiny piece of skull the size of a match box. This led to a discovery that surpassed all our wildest dreams and has revealed much about *Homo erectus*, a species on the threshold of becoming human and the first explorer to venture out of Africa. Was *Homo erectus* dreaming of what lay beyond when he began the long trek to Asia?

This book describes the dreams, drives and passions that have led a particularly adventurous group of people to achieve seemingly impossible feats and to make discoveries in extraordinary situations. These dreams have spurred people to lead lives that are an inspiration to us all. To have such dreams is to be obsessive about following a particular line of interest, to let no obstacle be too big to block one's goals.

Originally exploration was the journey to remote regions of the world; explorers planned expeditions to the North and South Poles, to the summits of the highest and most inaccessible peaks, to the depths of the oceans or to the immense vastness of outer space. But today exploration is more that this: today exploration has become a quest to understand all aspects of the world—its origins, its relation to the universe, its environments and its thin and fragile film of life supporting habitats on its surface. Exploration is thus often in the lab peering through powerful microscopes at the smallest particles of life or unravelling the mysteries of biology, physics and maths. Exploration is the path to discovery, and it can take place even in one's back yard. Discoveries are made every day by every one of us. Some lead to new inventions that touch all our lives, others are more personal and represent steps in a more complete understanding of ourselves. But these ventures are all driven by dreams—to be the first to solve a particular problem, to discover something unknown before.

A common theme through the many vignettes in this book is a shared regret. Places that many contributors first saw as "pristine" are now raped and razed and bear little resemblance to the untouched vistas that they originally set eyes on. This is particularly true for the oceans that cover 70 percent of the earth's surface. Because we cannot readily see what is happening under the sea, most people are unaware of the terrible devastation that human activities are producing. The planet holds an infinite well of undiscovered knowledge but sadly much of this is disappearing before we even know of its existence. There is now an urgency about exploration that was not appreciated before. We must know in order to conserve and to preserve; exploration today has a critical role in documenting the fragile ecosystems of which we are a part, in order to ensure their future for the survival of us all. The role of exploration in the modern world is not just to discover but also to spread awareness of the many facets of this wonderful planet and of the dangers it is currently facing, so that every individual understands the need to preserve what we have to ensure a future for our species.

Since we began to domesticate animals and to practise agriculture, we have been able to develop a reliable food supply. This has led to increasing numbers of people, so that today our population is multiplying exponentially. The current prediction is that by 2050 the human population will be 9.5 billion people (100 years before, in 1950, there were 2.5 billion).

Human population will continue to increase because we have found ways to thwart nature's natural checks and balances. Therefore we have to make a determined effort to develop alternative ways of control. Unfortunately humans are profligate and destructive; we over-utilize resources without thinking of tomorrow's needs. This is why the planet is in desperate trouble and increasing numbers of explorers are moving to conservation and education to spread awareness of the wanton destruction our species is wreaking on our planet. Today our most pressing dreams are to secure a future for our children, for our children's children and for all future generations, which will allow them to appreciate and to enjoy the wonders and bounties of the earth they live on and to follow their own dreams to explore.

Meave Leakey
Nairobi, Kenya
2007

PRE-EXPEDITION NOTES

This book is about dreams and dreamers. It's about a special breed who live their dreams, something few do. Specifically, it's about 120 international adventurer-explorers such as Robert Ballard, Meave and Louise Leakey, Buzz Aldrin, Sir Chris Bonington, Jean-Michel Cousteau and Nobel Laureate Charles H. Townes. Some famous, some not so famous. Most you've possibly seen on television: National Geographic, Discovery or Outdoor Life. In age, they range from 99-year-old Norman Vaughan, the remarkable last survivor of Admiral Byrd's Antarctic expedition of 1928–30, to 20-year-old Eve D'Vincent, the future of exploration. The explorers, all accomplished, vary from full- to part-timers with day jobs as varied as doctors, mail carriers and movie producers. Virtually all belong to that exclusive band of adventurers, The Explorers Club. Herein, all identify their greatest exploration discovery, achievement or experience—then that *Aha! Moment* when they experienced the indelible epiphany raising the sails on their extraordinary lives, with turning points leading to fulfillment of those dreams.

The dreams I'm talking about, of course, are the ones all of us invariably had when we were young. Most germinated during adolescence. You had one. You possibly remember the exact moment it burst into flower. Perhaps you dreamed of becoming a pilot, a police officer or a pediatrician, and perhaps you achieved it. It was adventurer T. E. Lawrence, a.k.a. Lawrence of Arabia, who commented, "All people dream, but not equally." This book is about people, cut from the same safari-suit cloth, if you will, who dreamed far beyond the familiar—who dreamed of castles in the air and then built them.

You'll meet those whose dreams led them to dive to the ocean's deepest point and to be first to walk on the moon; to sail across oceans in flimsy reed boats and to climb the seven continents' highest peaks; and to discover everything from the world's largest *T. rex*, to plate tectonics, to volcanoes on a Jupiterian moon. You'll meet "China's most accomplished living explorer," according to *Time* magazine, and one of their "top five contemporary explorers" from Canada, as well as the *Guinness Book of World Records'* "World's Greatest Explorer." It's a world filled with 'ologists'—paleontologists, archaeologists, anthropologists.

Dreams are powerful things. They can launch probes to the far wall of the universe, and, at their worst, they can kill. For a sad few there is the anguish of being so driven to follow a great dream that it destroys them when they fail—or perceive they failed. Witness Vincent Van Gogh, exploring the world through his art, his torment at not achieving his dream of success and acceptance, so painfully expressed in a letter to his brother Theo: "I as a painter shall never stand for anything of importance, I feel it utterly." He was only 37, still a young man, when he stood overwhelmed by hopelessness in that wheat field staring at the revolver in his hand. It was 1890—the Gay Nineties were about to kick off like a can can chorus line—and he well may have been swept up in them. Persistence is necessary to fulfill a dream, as Robert Ballard found while working towards his doctorate: "At times, the mental push-ups were fatiguing and I asked myself if I should go on, how strong was my dream?"

Indeed, most people's dreams die, which is sad. "Some people die at twenty-five and aren't buried until they are seventy-five," Ben Franklin observed. Malcolm Forbes, no small adventurer himself, was equally blunt: "When you cease to dream you cease to live." Don Walsh, who piloted the *Trieste* to the bottom of the Mariana Trench, further observes, "We are born with the exploration gene; most of us sublimate it by early adulthood." Although following dreams is the key to living a happy, fascinating, fulfilling life—making life worthwhile—the biggest killer of dreams, paradoxically, is life itself. It conspires to pick them out of our pockets. Carol Burnett (exploring comedy?) cautioned: "When you have a dream you've got to grab it and never let go." If that dream isn't strong enough to withstand the onslaught, or if the resolve isn't there, it'll early on wither and die. And enemies to dreams lurk everywhere. What kills them?

For a few, it's because that dream really was beyond their reach; I once knew a young woman who dreamed of becoming a singer ... but I could carry an armload of wet eels better than she, unfortunately, could carry a tune. Many never took their dreams seriously, which I really don't understand. Some claim they never had a youthful dream—but I think they've really forgotten—and pinball through life even more than those of us *with* a dream to guide us. True, some are faced with taking over a family business, effectively short-circuiting a contradictory dream ... think of your chances if you were born into India's caste system .... And, to be fair, many have dreams that, although small and everyday, *are* fulfilling.

For most though, it's the business of getting on with life itself that kills dreams. Nothing buries one under a granite headstone like the weight of having to pay rent and put food on the table. I don't think anyone dreams of becoming a plumber or an overhead-door executive. Both sacrifice dreams for money. There are many like that and, as Kahlil Gibran wrote: "The most pitiful among men is he who turns his dreams into silver and gold."

But for every one of these there are exceptions to the rule—rare individuals who break out of the moulds. My biggest surprise, pure serendipity, as I explored the explorers was how many of their lives were highly inspirational, reflecting come-from-behind stories! As Meave Leakey commented in the email in which she sent me her moving foreword: "I am sure many young people will be inspired reading how ordinary people achieve great things."

None was more ordinary than the icon we know today as Sir Edmund Hillary—arguably the most famous adventurer-explorer on Earth. At 86 and with more than enough recognition, he understandably declined to contribute to this project, but in his writings he has described a lonely childhood, partly because he skipped two grades and was the youngest in his class. Like many friendless kids, he found refuge in a make-believe world, roaming around his small New Zealand home-town with a stick in hand, imagining it was a sword and fighting great battles. He has also described how he was quiet and subdued in grade school—and how one teacher humiliated him by asking him to point out where Asia was on the map. He couldn't, and stood with a weak grin. How many of us have been in that situation? "Don't stand there like a laughing hyena!" the teacher barked. The class roared. He cringed. He never forgot. None of us ever does. His confidence took another hit at 16 when his gymnastics instructor eyed what Sir Ed described as his "scrawny physique." The muscular instructor not only muttered, "What will they send me next?" but went on cruelly to describe his ribs. I had a doctor do that to me too during a physical before a Boy Scout Jamboree in 1960. It stung, deeply. That same year of Ed's humiliation, though, he joined a ski party for the first time. They ar-rived at midnight and snow was everywhere, including on mountains—he'd never seen either before. Mountains. He spent idyllic days there. His dream was born. And look at the heights it swept him to ....

Another of my favourites is John Loret. Brought up by a widowed mother on the mean streets of Brooklyn during the Depression, at 10 he was shining shoes. But by 1955 he joined Thor Heyerdahl on an expedition to Easter Island. He subse-quently became a major explorer there, unravelling many of that quixotic island's tightly knotted secrets. John is now Professor Emeritus of Queens College, City University of New York, Executive Director of the Science Museum of Long Island and a past president of The Explorers Club.

Paleontologist Jack Horner and *Gossamer Albatross* inventor Paul MacCready faced dyslexia. Meave Epps, later Leakey, couldn't find a job in her chosen field—the then male-dominated field of marine biology—so she switched to paleontol-ogy, definitely that field's gain. Warren MacDonald—with both legs amputated at mid-thigh—not only climbed Mt. Kilimanjaro, but El Capitan in an astonishing 2,800 pull ups!

And then there's my favourite, Sue Hendrickson, who shot to international fame when she discovered the largest *T. rex* found to date, which stomped over to

Chicago's Field Museum. Sue—a high school dropout—now holds an honourary degree from the University of Illinois as well as several other honours. And she's renowned not just as a bone hunter; she's been the subject of several *National Geographic* articles and documentaries for her marine archaeological work, like the Manila galleon *San Diego* found off the Philippines; and has an international reputation in two other fields as well! Sue is a full-time adventurer-explorer.

Here you will find story after story of people who overcame obstacles and odds to follow their dreams and reap the greatest personal rewards imaginable.

By their nature, dreams are yearnings for distant realizations, for the seemingly impossible. Often the dreamer himself is surprised—as well as delighted—when that oh-so-remote goal is reached. That consummate gentleman Hugh Downs remarked in an email, "My dream is true as chronicled, but my aspiration was so distant I really never expected to have success either with media activities or with adventures. But they unfolded together out of that dream."

And that's what you can achieve when you dream the impossible dream. Even if you "fail" to fully realize it, you still win (Vincent aside) because, as in canoeing, the journey is the goal, not the destination.

What common denominators did I discover among these dreamers? Strikingly, they're the most positive, happiest, healthy-minded, energized, intelligent and fascinating group I've encountered. They share an excitement about life and unravelling its mysteries. Many have a larger-than-life quality. It's impossible to have a boring conversation with any of them. They're also the most thoroughly fulfilled group I've experienced.

If there was one spark that lit up most, it was *books*—and two authors in particular contributed to firing their respective generations. Richard Halliburton's five "true life" adventure books, published between 1925 and his disappearance in a typhoon in 1939, purportedly recounted his adventures travelling the world. They were highly romantic, colourful and didn't scrimp on imagination, let's say. A generation of impressionable kids hungry for adventure wolfed them down—and some followed in his footsteps. The other was Thor Heyerdahl with his 1950s *Kon-Tiki,* though it was the multimedia combination of his book, the 1951 Academy Award winning documentary and the dramatic pictures in *National Geographic* that contributed to the impact.

Thor really inspired several generations. He certainly inspired me as a baby of the boom—what a fabulous adventure! Only decades later would I learn that one of the unusual flags fluttering atop the mast was that of The Explorers Club.

To no surprise, movies were a powerful influence, and subsequently television. The Jacques Cousteau specials surfaced several times—he was the other major figure inspiring the boomers. A significant number were influenced by childhood visits to New York's outstanding American Museum of Natural History. The image is of awestruck kids staring slack-jawed at Carl Akeley's African mammals, the enormous dinosaurs and other exhibits. Some of those goggle-eyed kids grew up to be famous explorers making their own contribution to man's knowledge.

To no surprise also, *National Geographic* magazine holds a special, warm place in all explorers' hearts. Indeed, the relationship between this marvellous magazine and explorers is mythic. It's such a close one that almost 50 of the contributors in these pages have appeared in its pages. *National Geographic* certainly inspired me. I was attracted to it initially as an adolescent in a small town where *Playboy* wasn't for sale at the local Rexall drugstore and the raciest pictures could only be found in the lingerie section of the Eatons catalogue. Every issue of *National Geographic* seemed to have at least one great picture of a bare-breasted native girl! Whoopee! Then I peeked into the jungle behind her, and discovered a world that was just as enticing. I had read every dusty copy in the school library before I finished grade 12.

Each contributor was asked to give their definition of exploration and herein lay vital clues to shared traits. Sometimes definitions were in conflict, but two themes were repeated: the desire to satisfy one's *curiosity* by explaining the natural world; and, secondly, to live adventurously. As Sir Ed wrote, "Nobody climbs mountains for scientific reasons. Science is used to raise money for the expeditions, but you really climb for the hell of it." Many love the flash flood of adrenaline through their systems; all love facing huge challenges. These latter are obvious characteristics.

But *curiosity* stood out head and fedora above even adventure as a trait of an explorer—having it and following it. Don Walsh, again, said it well when he wrote, "Exploration is curiosity acted upon … this is the raw material from which explorers are made."

All are passionate about what they do, which isn't surprising. Is there a difference between a dream and a passion? No. Virtually all fell in love with nature at a young age. Virtually all had vivid imaginations that found expression in their childhood play. *All* are still children at heart—only now the toys they play with are rockets and bathyscaphes and towering balloons.

Sue Hendrickson: "Me? I'm just a kid who didn't grow up. I do all the things you wanted to do when you were young—digging for dinosaurs and diving for shipwrecks!"

Their differences also define them. For instance, many are academics with Ph.D.s, but many (like me, a high-school pool shark) hated school. An early picture of numerous explorer-adventurers is one of a bored student slumped at a school desk staring out the window, lost in daydreams of adventure (with the teacher about to whack the desk, and the student back to dull reality, with a yardstick).

A puzzle is that virtually all are white. I tried to achieve a balance of 'ologies,' as well as one internationally, but few emerged as Asian or Indian or black. Perhaps it's a reflection of economics, or America's and Europe's leading role in exploration in the last centuries. Interestingly, Poles emerged as especially vigorous explorers—clearly springing back after generations of oppression. Not surprisingly, Great Britain, with its dashing and often romantic history of exploration, throws up several major explorers, especially in the pure adventure category.

Did I find a difference between men and women? Yes. It didn't come as a surprise that many of the latter were tomboys, and there was a more "dreamy" quality to their dreams. Women seem more inclined to explore animal behaviour, especially social, such as Leakey's Angels—Birute Galdikas, Jane Goodall and Dian Fossey. Women's explorations, even their achievements, tend to be more internalized (though a significant number of men pointedly stated that the real fulfillment of exploration was what one learned about oneself).

This was perhaps best exemplified by Buzz Aldrin on a nostalgic return to Edgemont School in his home town of Montclair, New Jersey, in 2005. There, he was asked by a third-grade girl, "How did it feel to be on the moon?" "That is probably the most-asked question, and probably the most difficult for me to answer," he replied. After gathering his thoughts, Buzz continued: "Girls have feelings. Boys do things."

It comes as no surprise either that most explorers are male. The Explorers Club's ratio of 80:20, a fair sample, is similar to the mix here. Explorers do things. Boys do things.

Other common traits were the surprising number who formed charitable organizations to raise astonishing sums to help the disadvantaged—and keep the dream of exploration alive. There's innate altruism! Consider the Cousteau Society, the Jane Goodall Institute, George Bass' Institute of Nautical Archaeology, and the Sir Edmund Hillary Foundation and his Himalayan Trust, which has done so much for the magnificent Sherpa of the Solu-Khumbu, just to name a very few.

All lament the unprecedented deterioration of our planet, accelerating exponentially in step with our exploding population. Conservation is very high on everyone's list of priorities—as is keeping the dream of exploration alive by reaching young people and mentoring the emerging generation of explorers. This is not at all surprising, because the only thing separating seasoned explorers from the young is a skin leathered by sun and wind.

Why do explorers and adventurers keep their dreams alive while most others leave them behind with their childhood toys as they pass from Blakean Innocence to Experience? Why being riveted by a particular movie at 12 launched Robert Ballard on the path to becoming a world-famous oceanographer and not thousands of other kids who saw the same film can only be guessed at, but I believe it's because it triggered something latent in him, something that was more robust in his genes. Like several contributors, such as Don Walsh earlier, I subscribe to the view that both a sense of adventure and curiosity are part of our genetic makeup and directly stimulated our early ancestors to explore out of Africa and to every corner of the globe. Some people simply have it stronger than others. It's just waiting for the right conditions, like a seed awaiting rain.

I place myself in that category. I'm also a member of The Explorers Club, elected as a Fellow in 1986, which gave me access to mine these fascinating people, my colleagues (a very great number herein are recipients of Club awards but I didn't wish to clog the biographies with them and just noted a sample). Several are also members of the Royal Geographic Society, our British cousin, and other like clubs. The response I received was highly enthusiastic, the "dream theme" touching something, resonating deeply.

As an explorer, my credentials are modest. I'm an ethnologist whose area of interest is South and Southeast Asia. I've rummaged around the jungles and Himalayas of the region piecing together anthropological collections for major museums around the world, often under contract. It's been my goal to document and save the soft and hardware of many of these tribal and early belief systems before the steamrolling 20th—and now 21st—century flattens them. My own definition of exploration is in keeping with many others: the grand adventure of following one's curiosity to discover.

When was my dream born? I have a character, an adventurer named Lee Rivers, in an adventure thriller I wrote (another dream, another story, another time) called *Thai Gold* say it for me. Like me, Lee lives in Bangkok and collects for museums. He's taller than my 5'9", and is a bit more of a risk taker. People often call me an adventurer, but I'm nothing compared to Lee—he's a *real* adventurer! In my mind, I'm still merely a wannabe who writes about how I'd *really* like to live. Here's Lee thinking out loud about his early dream to be an anthropologist:

> I had a vague dream of what I wanted to do. It was a wild throw, but I had always believed in following my dreams. I could never understand people who didn't. I don't understand most people, in other words.

And I don't. My *Aha! Moment* came in the summer of 1958 when I was a skinny (that was even my nickname, or Skin for short) 12–year-old. Post-Jungle Jim, pre-Indiana Jones grade B adventure movies, titles long forgotten, had become my favourites on the square screen at the Marquis Theatre in Carrot River (go ahead and laugh; I find it funny myself), a then-rough frontier town, population 900, of mud, mosquitoes and muskeg backed into the Saskatchewan, Canada, bush. I longed for a life like that—that would elicit that exciting *emotion* of adventure—but "it" could only exist on celluloid, or on the pages of Walt Disney's *Huey, Dewey and Louie* comic books I so much loved, I was sure.

Then, one day, from either the *Star Weekly* or *Reader's Digest*, the only magazines outside of mom's *Redbook* we subscribed to, I learned of the existence of a club called … The Explorers Club! That such a club *existed*—and was filled with real-life adventurers—galvanized me! I remember to this day vividly thinking:

"*That's* a club I want to belong to!" Suddenly, living the *real* thing seemed possible! *Was* possible! I had another dream epiphany in my very next thought.

Again, I'd like to ask Lee Rivers to tell it for me. Lee and I also spring from similar backgrounds—while I'm from a small, backwater town in Saskatchewan, he's from a small, backwater town in North Dakota. In *Opium Dream* Lee and Maew, a Hmong lovely, are strolling one still evening in Afghanistan's Desert of Death. Later, as in all adventure romances, they'll share a camel blanket, but at this stage they're getting to know each other:

> "I've been meaning to ask you, Lee … how *did* you get interested in collecting?"
> "It was natural for me to study anthropology."
> A sheep *baaaed* in the distance.
> "That simple? Lots of people study anthropology, but they don't end up making a living out of the jungle. You have the most interesting life I know."
> "More than your Hollywood crowd? Come on."
> "Really. That's pretend, not real."
> I looked at her, impressed. "No, it wasn't that simple. It really goes back to the summer I was twelve. I remember standing on our front lawn with the summer breeze on my cheek. I mentally cast my mind around town, looking at all the bored, boring, wasted lives of so many of the adults … and it struck me at how many had dead eyes. I realized that the light of curiosity had gone out in them. I realized that once curiosity fades, a person may as well be dead. The walking dead."
> I paused. To this day I recall how vividly aware I felt at that moment.
> "And?"
> "And I made a vow to myself that I'd live the most adventurous, interesting life I could."
> "… And that's when your dream was born." Her eyes affixed mine. I had opened a window giving her a view to my core, she saw it clearly, and seemed comfortable with it.
> "I've always believed in following dreams. When you don't—"
> "You're a zombie."
> "Exactly. Without dreams, life would be a nightmare." I laughed. "Also, after all that forty-below crap, I headed for the tropics like a heat-seeking missile."

And that's exactly how it happened. Life as art. Born then and there on our front lawn, just across the gravel road and drainage ditch from the grain elevator, where the old steam locomotive idled all night, its deep, relaxed throb drifting in through my open bedroom window with mosquitoes the size of ravens. It was flattering some years later to discover that no less an explorer than Albert Einstein agreed with Lee: "The most beautiful emotion we can experience is the mysterious. It is the fundamental emotion that stands at the cradle of all true art and science. He to whom this emotion is a stranger, who can no longer wonder and stand rapt in awe, is as good as dead, a snuffed-out candle."

Did I have obstacles, like many, to overcome? With an alcoholic father too weak to cope with life who slid onto Skid Row, I'd be lying if I said otherwise. It took some effort to roll my apple away from the tree. I was raised by a grade two teacher who helped my sister and me through university (a Simon Fraser English and History B.A.) before finishing her own B.Ed. with marks worthy of high distinction. But following my dreams was a given, something I never questioned. They were what I wanted to do in life, I knew they would be *fun*, that they would make me happy, and it was as simple as that. Obviously there were low points, life's inevitable Dark Ages, when my dream's beacon faded to a mere, but always steady, candle flame on the far horizon of my mental vision, but I kept my eye on it. Eventually it led me through the wilderness until I re-emerged into the light of a personal Renaissance. I think we all took that same trek to some degree.

To have great dreams as a kid and then to go on to live them is the stuff of romance, and we "adventurers" are all romantics, kids at heart, as noted earlier. You've seen the images of astronauts on the moon hopping, singing—even playing games (golf)—just like kids. That's because there's a Calvin with his Hobbes racing around inside everyone one of us. Don't tell me that Neil Armstrong, while looking out the window at the receding moon, didn't think to himself: "Wow! This is way beyond my wildest dreams!"

I know because in 1982 when I was on assignment for the Smithsonian Institution and Vancouver's Museum of Anthropology in Sri Lanka exploring and collecting the ethnography of that beautiful island's Devil Dancers, I thought exactly the same way. "Wow! This is just like being in a movie—only it's *real*!" I *revelled* in it. I was *Living the Dream* ....

We all took different paths to get here. The academics had the most direct route; many others were more difficult. That's what makes this book such a statement on the power of following one's dreams.

By definition, adventurers live the most exciting, fascinating, remarkable lives on the planet. Here's when their dreams were born and how they fulfilled them, as recollected by these remarkable men and women themselves. For those interested in following dreams, hopefully there's a lesson herein ....

Jason Schoonover
Bangkok, Thailand

1 Early Dreamers

Twenty years from now you will be more disappointed by the things that you didn't do than by the ones you did do. So throw off the bowlines. Sail away from the safe harbor. Catch the trade winds in your sails. Explore. Dream. Discover.

—MARK TWAIN

Over Norm's shoulder is Mt. Vaughan, Antarctica, named by Admiral Byrd and which Norm climbed at an incredible 88 years of age. GORDON WILTSIE

Dream Big and Dare to Fail

My greatest exploration was taking part in Admiral Richard E. Byrd's 1928–1930 Antarctica expedition. He was the first to fly over both Poles. I was the dog handler and led 97 dogs pulling 650 tons of supplies to set up "Little America" where we wintered over. The next summer, we had a geological party of six who went out towards the South Pole so that we were in position in case the plane carrying Byrd to the Pole couldn't make it and he needed to be rescued. When they flew over us, they tossed out a package of letters from home and brownies, which we really appreciated!

I was brought up in Salem, Massachusetts, where my dad was a tanner. He created the process of tanning leather white for nurses' shoes that he manufactured as Vaughan's Ivory Sole Leather and sold to every shoemaker in the country.

I got the spark about dog sledding as a young boy when I read a book about Indians using dogs. I told my best friend, Eddie Goodale: "Let's do what the Indians did. You take your father's dog and I'll take mine and we'll make harnesses!" But

> *"Exploration is going to places that other people have not gone and declaring it, in our case, for the United States of America."*

we couldn't get them to go unless one of us went ahead and called them! I learned that the trick is to always go towards home and have your dogs hungry. And then give them the best food, which is raw meat. Raw meat sure motivates them.

I first dropped out of Harvard in 1925 to join my hero Sir Wilfred Grenfell who was bringing medical supplies by dog sledge to snowbound villagers in Newfoundland. Having honed my sledding skills, I returned to school to continue my meteorology studies. That didn't last long. While studying one night, I read in the *Boston Transcript*, "Byrd to South Pole!" I told my roommates then and there that I was going too. They said how could I if I didn't know him? I found out where Byrd lived in Boston and went to his house and knocked but a buxom housekeeper refused to let me see Byrd without an appointment. As I turned around, I had another idea: I looked up the journalist who had written the Byrd story. He saw my enthusiasm and spoke to Byrd on my behalf. My proposal was I would work for him for a whole year without pay if he would consider me at the end of that year. He signed me on. Later Eddie and another friend, Freddie Crockett, joined me to assemble, train and manage the dog sledding.

Byrd was a gentle, strong-willed man with good respect and love for his shipmates. He loved us all and wouldn't ask us to do anything he wouldn't. He was respected and admired because of that. After the huge tickertape parade in Manhattan (Freddie, Eddie and I were in the car right behind his), he told me that since he couldn't pay me, he would name a mountain in Antarctica after me. I thanked him and told him I would climb it one day—and I did. On December 16, 1994, three days shy of my 89th birthday, I reached the top of the 10,302-foot peak.

Ernest Shackleton's 1914 Antarctica expedition, and Robert Scott's attempt in 1901–04 and the other in 1912 (when he made it but he and his party froze to death), both ultimately failed because they didn't have anyone who was really good with dogs.

Roald Amundsen made it a month before Scott and survived because he knew dogs. After Byrd and Floyd Bennett were first to fly over the North Pole in 1926 and they set their sights on the South, it was Amundsen who advised him to take plenty of dogs. And, of course, he understood the part nobody talks about: you have to feed your dogs to the other dogs. It's a matter of survival. I hated that part, but it had to be done on our three-month, 1,500-mile geological expedition. Of course they know. I tied them to a stake with a very short leash and gave them a second bullet if they needed it. But I hated to do it.

NORMAN VAUGHAN is a living legend and the last survivor of the 42-man Byrd Antarctica Expedition. He was born in 1905 and still lives a life as big as his motto—the title of this piece.

He raced a dog team in the 1932 Olympic Games in Lake Placid. During World War II, he carried out numerous search-and-rescue operations, including commanding 209 dogs and 17 drivers in the U.S. Army in the Battle of the Bulge. His dog sledge ambulances later rescued 26 aircrew from the Greenland ice sheet, where he single-handedly saved a top-secret Norden bombsight. After the war, Norm became chief of search and rescue for the North Atlantic division of the International Civil Aviation Organization. In the Korean conflict he served in the psychological warfare department. In 1967 he rode a snowmobile from the Arctic Circle in Alaska to Boston. He's a veteran of 13 of the 1,000-mile Iditarod Arctic dog sledge races in Alaska and in 1997 organized the annual Norman Vaughan Serum Run commemorating the 1925 delivery of diphtheria vaccine by dog teams from Nenana to Nome. In 1981 he gave Pope John Paul II a ride in a dog sledge. He has been inaugurated into the Musher Hall of Fame and has received an honorary degree from the University of Alaska.

He's the author of *With Byrd at the Bottom of the World* and *My Life of Adventure*. He has also been featured in *National Geographic*'s *Height of Courage* video. He's been a member of The Explorers Club since 1931.

Norm lives in Anchorage, Alaska, and is married to Carolyn Muegge-Vaughan. His children are Gerard and Jacqueline. He still loves the outdoor life more than anything.

"Exploration is discovering parts of the world that are unknown until you get there."

Brad and Barb on the summit of Mt. McKinley, 1947.

It Started with a Sneeze

I guess my greatest achievement was at age 25 in 1935 leading the expedition that mapped 5,000-6,000 square miles of Alaska and the southwest Yukon, which includes Canada's highest peaks, dominated by Mt. Logan. The expedition produced the first published aerial shot of the mountain taken from the south.

I had terrible hay fever when I was a boy. But in 1921, when I was 11, I went to Squam Lake in New Hampshire and noticed that I didn't sneeze when I went into the mountains. So, naturally, I immediately liked mountains. I climbed Mt. Washington that year with my cousin Sherman Hall! But my dream of climbing and living an adventurous life really was launched one remarkable day when I was 16. Noel Odell—the last man to see George Mallory and Andrew Irvine alive on their 1924 Everest attempt—spoke at our school. I was riveted by his talk.

That very year while my father, Dean of Harvard's Episcopal Theological Seminary, was on sabbatical in Europe I started climbing in earnest. That summer I summitted Mont Blanc, the Matterhorn and Monte Rosa. While I was still 16, I wrote my first guidebook on the White Mountains.

My love of flying and photography was born at 13. On that birthday my parents took me for my first flight in a seaplane. That year my mother, an avid amateur photographer, also gave me a camera. Both led to my passion for photographing and mapping the world's great mountains. Aerial photography became my forte.

By 17 I had my second book, *Among the Alps*, which included my first aerial photos. The following year, 1928, Putnam published *Bradford on Mt. Washington*. I was off to an exciting start!

The most thrilling moment in my life took place on June 11, 1934—when, at Boeing Field in Seattle, I took the controls of a "Kinner Fleet" biplane and actually flew it alone for 20 minutes! I'm proud to say I have one of America's earliest pilot's licences—number 32898.

One adventure I'm glad I missed was in 1936. I was in discussion for the position of Amelia Earhart's navigator, but withdrew when I learned there would be insufficient radio support on the long Pacific leg from Lae, New Guinea, to San Francisco ....

Another of my most exciting moments was in 1999 when I looked through a telescope at Namche Bazaar and saw a bright ruby laser reflection dancing on Mount Everest's peak. We succeeded in measuring it at 29,035 feet—seven feet higher than believed.

BRADFORD WASHBURN—explorer, geologist, mountaineer, cartographer, scientist and photographer—is a living legend and a *National Geographic* icon. He was born in 1910 and brought up in Cambridge, Massachusetts, graduating from Harvard with a bachelor's degree in French history and literature in 1933 and a masters in geology in 1960. He was also an instructor at the university's Institute of Geographical Exploration from 1935 until 1942. For forty years beginning in 1939, he was the founding director of Boston's Museum of Science and built it into one of the world's leading institutions.

Most closely associated with Alaska's mountains and glaciers, Brad is well known for his photography there spanning six decades. He has made many first ascents of its peaks, including summiting Mount McKinley three times, once with wife Barbara in 1947, making her the first woman to reach the top. Among innumerable expeditions, he mapped Mt. McKinley, New Hampshire's Presidential Range and the depth of the Grand Canyon, pioneering the use of large-format film in aerial photography along the way.

Brad is the recipient of innumerable awards and nine honorary degrees, including one from Harvard. He is a Fellow of the American Academy of Arts and Sciences, London's Royal Geographical Society, and The Explorers Club, as well as The Alpine Club. In 1988, he and Barbara were honored with the Centennial Medal of the National Geographic Society.

The prestigious Bradford Washburn Award—named in his honor in 1964—is given annually to one who has made an outstanding contribution towards public understanding of science. Past recipients include Carl Sagan, Jane Goodall and Jacques-Yves Cousteau.

Brad is the subject of three biographies and the author of over 20 books, including his autobiography with Lewis Freedman, *Bradford Washburn: An Extraordinary Life*. He wrote the first of many *National Geographic* articles in 1935.

Married to Barbara since 1940, they have three children, Elizabeth, Dorothy and Edward, nine grandchildren and one great-grandchild. They live in Lexington, Massachusetts.

2 The Map-Makers

We must go beyond textbooks,
go out into the bypaths and
untrodden depths of the
wilderness and travel
and explore and tell
the world the glories
of our journey.

—SIR JOHN HOPE FRANKLIN

RICHARD BUTSON

Off the map in the Antarctic: Richard Butson on left in 1947 with Kevin Walton.
Robert Dodson

Poles Apart and in Between

In 1947 I was the medical officer on a team that crossed the 5,000-foot-high Antarctic Peninsula by husky dog team to map the last 1,000 miles of uncharted coastline in the world.

When I was 10, in 1933, I hung a London *Times* page of Mt. Everest in my bedroom. That launched my dream of climbing.

At Cambridge University the college gates were closed at 10 p.m. and many times I had to climb back over the walls with broken glass on top. This led to Cambridge Mountaineering Club camps—and I was hooked.

In 1946 after graduating and acquiring some experience in snow and ice climbing, glacier travel and skiing, I was privileged to be accepted as the medical officer with the British Falkland Islands Dependencies Survey, later named the British Antarctic Survey, for 16 months. That year, an American expedition led by Finn Ronne encamped 300 yards from the 10-man British base. Initial frosty relations

> *"Exploration is the discovery of the previously unknown, be it geographical, scientific or archaeological."*

developed into warm friendships, aided by the Royal Navy: we were supplied with alcoholic spirits whereas Ronne's expedition was dry.

Soon after arriving at the Stonington Island base in Marguerite Bay, I set off on a six-week reconnaissance to find a route across the peninsula, traveling by dog teams. It was on that journey that we heard by radio of Ronne arriving with 21 men and two women. Our reply was to request 19 more women!

During the next few months I participated in several short journeys, including one on the west coast sea ice. During that time, two near disasters occurred.

Two Americans who had had to evacuate their tent in the mountains were walking back to their base when one of them broke through a snow bridge and fell into a narrowing, 106-foot crevasse. I earned a measure of renown by going down to find him tightly wedged, head down. I had to remove some of my outer clothes and could feel the glacier move on my ribs. With great difficulty, I managed to get slings under his thighs and those above pulled him out without serious injuries. All this at night in the Antarctic winter, miles from the huts. The miracle was finding the small hole in the crevasse bridge in the dark.

The other near disaster happened to a small British reconnaissance plane with a pilot, co-pilot and surveyor aboard. They had been struck by a storm and while landing blind on the sea ice the plane flipped. None were injured but they had to walk 40 miles in eight days with each step breaking through the snow crust into two feet of brine. They only had a tiny tent and insufficient food and fuel. This was another miracle of survival.

After winter, the main journeys set off. I drove a dog team across the difficult mountains and glaciated valleys while the British surveyor led another team. Thus, I participated in the first 200 miles of what turned out to be a 1,200-mile round trip mapping the most inaccessible coastline in the world. One day I put on skis and climbed 2,000 feet up the escarpment to get a superb view of the coast for 80 miles to the south. It was a great thrill to realize that it had never been seen before. Descending, two crevasse bridges collapsed as I skied over them!

At the end of the year, five of us keen mountaineers took off climbing the local mountains. All were previously unclimbed, including a spectacular 1,200-foot rock pinnacle.

Forty years after hanging up that picture from the *Times*, I trekked to Everest. It was a great thrill and the fulfillment of the dream launched with that picture.

RICHARD BUTSON, MD, was born in 1922 in China of British parents. After being brought up in England, he immigrated to Canada in 1952 and established his surgical practice in Hamilton, Ont., and later taught surgery at McMaster University. He has published 22 scientific papers.

In 1957, Dick joined the Canadian Forces Reserve, trained as a parachutist and rose to the rank of colonel after reorganizing the reserve's medical services, and was called out for the first Gulf War. He was appointed Honorary Surgeon to Her Majesty the Queen in 1977-79, and made an Officer of the Order of Military Merit of Canada.

Dick was awarded the George Cross (the second-highest medal for bravery after the Victoria Cross), for gallantry in saving life, and also the prestigious Polar Medal. Butson Ridge in Antarctica was named after him. He led the 1978 Canadian Hindu Kush Mountaineering expedition and has climbed many European and Canadian peaks. In 1974, he spent a month climbing in Baffin Island where he made 12 first ascents.

Dick is married to Eileen and has three children, Sarah, Caroline and Richard.

Tom as a Martian Atlas: holding the Mars globe he mapped. BERYL DEE VREBALOVICH

"Explorers have the same goals as those of us who are research scientists: a conquest of Everest; the turbulence effect on the flow over a body; life on Mars or elsewhere in the universe. All who consider life an adventure are explorers!"

From Rubber Band Model Airplanes to the Moon and Mars

In 1971 I was Science Recommendation Team Chief on the Mariner 71 Mars Project at the Jet Propulsion Lab. As chief I was responsible for getting the Mars Science Team of 56 investigators to create a mission profile every day as the spacecraft orbited Mars. It arrived at Mars during a seasonal dust storm, so we could only take photographs of the peaks of extinct volcanoes and the polar caps for the first few weeks. Later we took over 7,000 photographs of the entire planet for nearly one year.

At the end of the mission I was given the task of getting a 16-inch globe of Mars made from the photographs. JPL Director William Pickering asked me to be sure that some major feature would be named after our very successful Mariner Mission. With the assistance of Ranger and Mars Mission Scientist Astronomer Gerard Kuiper, I named the large rift valley on the face of Mars "Valles Marineris"—Mariner Valley. I also named a crater for Theodore von Karman, founder of JPL and Caltech's Department of Aeronautical Engineering, and another for Russian Space Program Leader Sergei Pavlovich Korolev. Valles Marineris is a 4,000-kilometre-long valley created by tectonic activity and the largest on the planet. Our Grand Canyon is 140 kilometres long and would be lost in it. This was a pleasant conclusion to a very exciting mission.

When I was a kid in the 1930s and early 1940s my dad, an airplane "nut" and tool-and-die maker at Vultee Aircraft during World War II, took the family to see air shows at Mines Field (now LAX), where a biplane tried to set a new flight time endurance record by picking up cans of gasoline with a long rope and hook to refuel in flight. He took us to a parade in downtown LA when I was 12 celebrating Wrong Way Corrigan's 1938 round-trip flight Los Angeles to New York that ended in Dublin. And, in 1941, we watched the B-19, the then largest airplane in the world, take off from Douglas Airport in Santa Monica. These forays stimulated my interest in becoming an aeronautical engineer—a dream!

Byrd Wilmah Green, my high school math teacher, convinced me to go to Caltech and not UCLA as I had planned—she was the second greatest influence on my dream of becoming an aeronautical engineer. But my father was the spark plug to my career.

A lot of projects never got funded. The rocket that sent Buzz, Neil and Mike to the moon in 1969 was going to send two spacecraft to Mars, each with a rover, and I was going to be the Project Scientist. It was to have been launched in the 1970s at a cost of one billion dollars! Glad we waited for the 2004 rovers—they are really doing well on Mars.

TOM VREBALOVICH was born in 1926 and graduated from Caltech in 1954 with three degrees, including his Ph.D., in Mechanical and Aeronautical Engineering. He was with the Jet Propulsion Lab 1952–1975. After the 1958 success of the first American Earth-orbiting spacecraft, *Explorer I*, JPL focused on planetary research. From 1952 to 1961 Tom researched unsteady flow in supersonic and hypersonic wind tunnels. From 1961–1965, he was on the Ranger Project, including being Project Scientist on 1964–1965's *Rangers 6* to *9*, examining the moon for manned Apollo landing sites, taking 40,000 photographs. After being Associate Project Scientist on 1966's *Surveyors 1* and *2*, testing landing techniques and continuing to seek landing sites for Apollo, he was Project Scientist on 1967's *Surveyor III*. After returning to JPL in 1970 after a two-year hiatus teaching at the USAID-sponsored Indian Institute of Technology in Kanpur, India, he was assigned to the Mariner 71 Mars Project.

From 1975 to 1988 as Embassy Science Counselor, Tom lectured in India, Egypt, Indonesia, Hong Kong, China, Dacca, Bangkok, Singapore, Afghanistan and Yugoslavia on the Lunar and Martian Programs and remote sensing. He kept in touch with the JPL Space Program with visits by Bill Pickering and other JPLers to his overseas posts.

Tom is married to Beryl Dee and they live in Marina Del Rey, California. They have a son, Todd, a daughter, Lisa, and one grandchild. Katie Marie is the "smartest one in the family," having graduated from high school with an A+ average. Tom tried, he jokes, to convince her to go to Caltech, but she opted for Santa Cruz and liberal arts.

3 Exploring Space

That's one small step for man,
one giant leap for mankind.

—NEIL ARMSTRONG

Say cheese: Neil reflected in Buzz's visor during the first moon landing, 1969. You can bet they're both grinning. NASA, BY NEIL ARMSTRONG

Moon over Newark

July 20, 1969, after I landed *Apollo 11's* Lunar Module on the Sea of Tranquility, and while Mike Collins orbited in the Command Module, Neil Armstrong and I became the first humans to walk on the moon. My first thoughts, expressed to Houston, on stepping down were, "Beautiful, beautiful. Magnificent desolation." *Magnificent* for the achievement of being there, and *desolate* for the eons of lifelessness.

I come from a family of aviators. My aunt was one of the first stewardesses for Eastern Airlines and my father was in the Army Air Corps from 1917 to 1928 and an aide to the immortal General Billy Mitchell. He flew in and out of Newark Airport and associated with all sorts of other early aviation pioneers, people like Amelia Earhart and Charles Lindbergh. So, really, my wanting somehow to get into the flying airplane business was just an accepted fact. Those were my role models.

Moment of epiphany? I'm sure it was approaching World War II in December of '41. I don't recall the exact age, I think 11 going on 12. My father took me up

> *"Exploration is human contribution to building on the vast knowledge of the world around us in new and unexplored areas that adds significantly to the basic understanding of the world that is around us."*

for a ride. (It was not the first I ever had—I was way too young at age two for my first one to influence me greatly, since I could hardly look out the window as our family flew in one of the company planes down to Florida. But I remember being airsick!) I do remember the other flight though, from Newark airport around the local area. I was able to look down and see cars moving along, and that just seemed to me to be the place I wanted to explore the very most in my life. It was not like something every weekend after school that I went out flying with my father. It was a fairly rare occurrence. It was probably in a Lockheed Vega, the same plane I took my first ride in at two.

It remained for me to get a little bit older. Where do I go to school? What prepares me best? That's what led to the decision to go into the military.

BUZZ ALDRIN was born in Montclair, New Jersey, in 1930. Prophetically, his mother's name was Marion Moon. His father, Edwin Eugene Sr., was an aviation pioneer and a student of rocket developer Robert Goddard. Buzz graduated from West Point with honours and third in his class in 1951. He flew Sabre jets in 66 combat missions in the Korean Conflict, shooting down two MIG-15s, and was awarded the Distinguished Flying Cross.

Returning to his education, he earned a doctorate in astronautics from MIT in Manned Space Rendezvous. Techniques he devised are used on all NASA missions, including the first space docking with Russian cosmonauts.

Buzz joined the astronaut program in 1963 and in 1966 performed the longest spacewalk of the Gemini program—five-and-a-half hours. Three years later, he and civilian test pilot Neil Armstrong were handed the space program's Holy Grail: *Apollo* 11. In arguably the most heroic and important exploration achievement of the 20th century, the moon landing was witnessed by the largest television audience in history.

Buzz was presented the Presidential Medal of Freedom, the highest among over 50 other distinguished awards and medals he has received. He has logged 4,500 hours of flying time, 290 in space, including eight hours of extra-vehicular activity.

Buzz is retired from NASA, the Air Force, and command of the Test Pilot School at Edwards Air Force Base and now travels and lectures around the world, pursuing and discussing the latest concepts and ideas for exploring the universe. He has authored five books: an autobiography, *Return to Earth*; an historical documentary, *Men from Earth*; two science fiction novels; and a new children's book, *Reaching for the Moon*, which describes his trip to the moon and his unique perspective on America's space program.

Buzz and wife Lois live in Los Angeles. Their combined family is comprised of six grown children and one grandson. Their leisure time is spent exploring the deep-sea world of scuba diving and skiing the mountain tops at Sun Valley, Idaho.

JOHN ALLEN

Inside Biosphere 2. GILL KENNY

Under the Big Top

My biggest exploration was the several years required to design and build the biomes of the Biosphere 2 project in Arizona. On September 1, 1991, four men and four women carrying The Explorers Club flag entered the Mission One closure experiment to test the first physical model of Earth's biosphere. Millions watched worldwide. Biosphere 2 set a number of records in closed life systems, including degree of sealing tightness, 100 percent waste and water recycling, and duration of human residency (eight people for two years). We learned a tremendous amount that has been applied to everything from housing to future colonization of the moon and planets.

My interest in the natural world was sparked years before. When I turned nine in 1938, my father gave me an old flintlock musket from about 1775 used by my ancestor in the Revolution. I could hardly hold it straight out from my shoulder it was so heavy. Then he told me a saga of moving further west in every generation, trapping and hunting. As he spoke I fell in love with the idea of exploring. Knowing no frontier existed any longer in America, I dreamed of exploring the planet

"I think of exploration as entering from the known into the unknown, intentionally moving past some previous limit of knowledge, seeking exciting and useful experiences that might add to science, art, technics and history."

both alone and with a small group of like-minded free and easy pals who could get along anywhere with anybody.

I really fell in love with being out there in 1948 when I was 19 and walked alone along the North Canadian river from El Reno, Oklahoma, to its source in New Mexico. Then I decided to study the west coast and went from Calexico to Hungry Horse, paying for it by doing logging and agricultural work here and there. A friend and I made three expeditions into the Four Corners Rio Grande area in the 1950s, staying with tribal medicine men. From 1963 to 1964, I made a lone expedition around the world by freighter and steerage that's covered in my *Journey Around an Extraordinary Planet*.

In the early 1960s, I worked on regional development projects in the U.S., Iran and Ivory Coast. Before that I headed a special metals team at Allegheny-Ludlum Steel Corporation that developed over 30 alloys. Eventually, in 1974–1975, my friends and I built the conceptual design for an ocean, coral reef and big river ship—the research vessel *Heraclitus*. It has done numerous expeditions over 30 years to the Antarctic, up the Amazon and around the tropic world. From the '70s on, I led several land expeditions studying ecology and ancient civilizations, from Peru and Bolivia to Turkey, Persia, India and Kathmandu. I have also led remote area expeditions to Nigeria, Iraq, Iran, Afghanistan, Uzbekistan, Tibet, India and Belize.

A special moment came during the Biosphere experiment when, on March 22, 1992, our crew spoke to the crew at the Amundsen-Scott South Pole Station by ham radio. It was a unique link between teams isolated in different manners.

And that old flintlock? It's still in the family but when I started traveling, I passed it on to a cousin and his son now has it.

JOHN ALLEN of Santa Fe, New Mexico, was born in 1929 in Carnegie, Oklahoma, and is the conceiver, inventor and co-founder (retired) of the Biosphere 2 project. He is the former Executive Chairman and Director of Biospheric Research, Development and Engineering for Space Biospheres Ventures. John began the first manned Biosphere Test Module experiment in September 1988, residing in a closed ecological system environment for three days and setting a world record at that time.

Currently the Chairman of Global Ecotechnics Corporation, he helps design the second generation of closed biospheric systems. John is also a co-founder and Chairman of The Biosphere Foundation and its division, the Planetary Coral Reef Foundation. The foundation is a non-profit corporation devoted to mapping and monitoring the health and vitality of coral reefs and exploring the origins of human cultures.

He's also a Fellow of the Royal Geographic Society who has over two dozen publications to his credit. Most are scientific, while the rest are poetry, drama, prose and films written under the pen name Johnny Dolphin.

John has a long-time companion, Deborah Parrish Snyder, and a daughter, Starrlight, living in France.

PAUL P. SIPIERA, JR.

"Exploration is the plain and simple discovery of new ideas, information or places. "To go where no man has gone before" is often quoted, but it is not limited to space exploration. I find as much satisfaction in classifying a new meteorite as the mountain climber does in reaching the summit."

A meteoric career: Paul hunting for specimens in Antarctica. WILLIAM J. GRUBER.

Reaching for the Stars

My greatest exploration moment occurred in January 2000 on the windswept blue icefields at the Moulton Escarpment, Antarctica. I was the leader of Antarctica 2000, a privately funded scientific expedition searching for meteorites. Previously only government funded expeditions had the capability of taking on this challenge.

In 1983 I had been a member of a National Science Foundation meteorite recovery team and I had a very good idea of the risks involved. There was certainly no guarantee that we would find any. Two years earlier, on our first expedition to Patriot Hills, we found no significant meteorites. I hoped we would have better luck this time. On our first day of searching, former NASA astronaut and fellow Explorers Club member Owen K. Garriott found the first one. It was later classified as one of the rare acapulcoite-type meteorites. With that one meteorite in hand all my expectations were fulfilled (though I found two more and the team total was 20). We had traveled over 9,000 miles to that spot on the ice where that little meteorite was waiting for us, and that moment of discovery was worth it!

My dream of becoming an explorer was born on a late 1960 summer's evening when I was 12 in Chicago. While standing in our backyard with my parents and several neighbors, I witnessed the *Echo I* communications satellite streak across the sky. Everyone stood in silence as that little point of light passed overhead. I knew from that moment on that I had to learn as much as possible about astronomy and the space program.

Formal education was never easy for me and I struggled through both elementary and high school. Two subjects—science and the space program—really held my attention. Like most children at that time, I dreamed of becoming an astronaut but knew it would probably never happen. I knew I would have to find some other way of getting involved in space exploration. It was during my last semesters of undergraduate studies that I found the courage to pursue studies in meteorite research. This seemed quite natural since I was always either looking up at the stars or looking down for rocks. This decision led to a master of science degree and a career teaching undergraduates astronomy and geology.

My big break came in 1983 when I was invited to participate in the National Science Foundation's Antarctic Search For Meteorites Program. That experience changed my life since it galvanized my interest and introduced me to the beauty of Antarctica. Once Antarctica gets into your blood it is hard to stay away and I am always looking for ways to get back. In addition, my experiences in Antarctica and meteorite research finally rewarded me with a Ph.D. relatively late in my career. This achievement was not just the fulfillment of a dream but an opportunity to set new goals and explore new frontiers that never seemed possible for me.

So far I've found over 50 meteorites, the largest about a kilogram, all from the asteroid belt. The 55 found during the three expeditions are part of the Planetary Studies Foundation's James M. DuPont Meteorite Collection in Crystal Lake, Illinois.

PAUL P. SIPIERA, JR., PH.D., M.S., was born in Chicago in 1948 and makes his home in Galena, Illinois, with his wife, Diane, and their daughters, Paula Frances and Caroline Antarctica.

Paul received his B.A. in Ancient History in 1971 and an M.S. in Earth Sciences in 1975 from Northeastern Illinois University in Chicago. He was a graduate student at Argonne National Laboratory and a summer research associate at the Center for Meteorite Studies at Arizona State University. Following his studies, Paul accepted a teaching position in 1976 at William Rainey Harper College in Palatine, Illinois, where he taught undergraduate courses in astronomy and geology. Over his 30-year teaching career, Paul achieved the rank of professor and received numerous teaching and research awards, including the United States Antarctic Service Medal. In May 2004, he was awarded his Ph.D. in Natural Sciences from the University of Innsbruck, Austria. He has written over 150 professional publications, including 29 biographical and science books targeted primarily at children.

Other explorations have taken him to Egypt, on solar eclipse expeditions to Mexico, Aruba and Turkey, and on geological studies to the High Arctic, Iceland, Chile, New Zealand, Australia and Hawaii.

4 Up, Up and Away

Curiosity is natural to the soul
of men and interesting objects
have a powerful influence on
our affections.

—DANIEL BOONE

BERTRAND PICCARD

"Exploration is a state of mind in the unpredictability of the winds of life."

Days of epiphany: young Bertrand with his father, Jacques, in front of the Ben Franklin *submarine, 1969.* PICCARD FAMILY ARCHIVES

Around the World in Twenty Days

After captaining three attempts, on March 21, 1999, I succeeded with Brian Jones in the first-ever non-stop, round-the-world balloon flight in *Breitling Orbiter 3*. We captured seven world records, among them achieving the longest flight in both duration and distance in the history of aviation: 45,755 kilometres in 19 days, 21 hours and 47 minutes.

In July, 1969, I knew already that my life would never be the same again.

Four weeks beforehand, in the early morning, I could still see very far away on the horizon a tiny yellow spot contrasting with the dark blue of the ocean. The *Ben Franklin* submarine, towed by a U.S. Navy minesweeper, was carrying my father and his five crew members away for a one-month drift mission in the Gulf Stream. As they left Palm Beach harbour for open seas, I had run along the side of the inlet, together with my mother, my sister and my little brother, to stay with him as long as I could. Then, with a walkie-talkie in my hand, I heard my father's voice progressively disappearing as the crackle of interference took over. During the previous two years, he had build this Mesoscaphe submersible in Switzerland, for Grumman Aerospace Inc., who wanted to open an oceanographic department, and I had painted a small part of the hull. At 11 years old, I therefore considered that it was also *my* submarine! But now, it was leaving me alone on the Florida shores.

Every day with my family, we followed the track of the *Ben Franklin* in the Gulf Stream on a map of the East Coast right up until July 15, when I headed with my mother to Cape Kennedy for the launch of *Apollo 11*. The evening before the liftoff, I was invited by Grumman and NASA to the traditional cocktail party attended by all the astronauts who had already flown or were about to do so. There, with my child eyes wide open, I was dreaming of exploring unknown territories—like them, like my father, like Charles Lindbergh, whom I met that evening. I could only have an explorer's life—it was the life of all the people I met.

That evening, Wernher von Braun invited me to spend the night in his family's hotel suite, in order to arrive early the following morning on the launch pad with his son Peter. Can you imagine that? The night before the take off to the moon, I had the chance to sleep in the suite of the father of the American space program. This man who was about to fulfill the dream of his life still had the time and the inclination to take care of a little boy because he was a friend of my father and wanted to encourage me.

The next day, with the *Ben Franklin* drifting off the coast of Cape Kennedy, I witnessed the most fabulous moment in the entire history of aviation: the liftoff for the moon!

A week later, Neil Armstrong, Buzz Aldrin and Mike Collins were back. I noticed there was an incredible light in their eyes: the look of those who have experienced what no one else had experienced before. My father was still underwater and when he surfaced 10 days later, I found in his eyes exactly the same light, the same smile. He was standing very tall on the deck of his submarine, together with his crew, welcomed by the fountains of the firemen's boats in New York harbour, under the watchful eye of the Statue of Liberty. If I remember the pictures of my grandfather, he also had this same intense look when, in 1931, he landed after the first-ever flight in the stratosphere, having been the first man to have seen the curvature of the earth with his own eyes.

I was hooked. I wanted to have this very special light in my eyes—this intense look of those people who have seen what nobody before them had ever managed to see. On July 31, 1969, I knew I would become an explorer, even if I had no idea of what could still possibly be explored. With the naivety of a child, I wanted to be the archaeologist who would discover the lost Atlantis Continent or the medical doctor who would first understand the keys to the human soul. I had a conviction. Absolutely everything was possible, achievable, using the three qualities I had learned from the heroes of my childhood: curiosity, without which we never try anything new; perseverance, without which we are never successful in what we try; and respect, without which our successes have no value.

Thirty years later, when I came back with Brian Jones from the first-ever around-the-world, non-stop balloon flight, it was my three children who ran into my arms in front of thousands of enthusiastic spectators, exactly the same way I had dashed into my father's arms. I had not only circumnavigated the Earth, I had gone through the circle of life. And I had fulfilled my dream of going where no one before had ever gone. So many people had told me it was impossible. I knew everything is worth trying, especially if you believe you can end up with that special light in your eyes.

BERTRAND PICCARD was born in 1958 in Lausanne, Switzerland, into a family of explorers and scientists and seemed predestined to carry on the legacy of family adventuring.

After a classical education, he studied medicine and became a senior consultant in a psychiatric hospital. Always interested in the study of human behavior in extreme situations, he was one of the pioneers of hang-gliding and microlights in the 1970s and became European champion in hang-glider aerobatics (1985). He won, with Wim Verstraeten, the first transatlantic balloon race (Chrysler Challenge, 1992) and then initiated the Breitling Orbiter project.

After the successful circumnavigation—considered by many to be the last great adventure of the 20th century—Bertrand and his partner Brian Jones were decorated with the Olympic Order and the gold medal of the French Ministry of Youth and Sport. They also received, among numerous other awards worldwide, the highest distinctions of the Fédération Aéronautique Internationale, the National Geographic Society and The Explorers Club.

Bertrand's name figures in the *Larousse Encyclopedia* alongside those of his father and grandfather. Together with his co-pilot and their sponsor, the Breitling watch company, he created the Winds of Hope humanitarian foundation to fight forgotten and neglected sufferings on Earth. His two books on the flight, including *The Greatest Adventure*, have contributed to Bertrand becoming known as "Le Savanturier," someone who is endeavoring to combine the scientific background inherited from his family with his desire to explore the great adventure of human life.

Bertrand is married to Michèle and they have three children, Estelle, Oriane and Solange. They live in Lausanne.

At the Breitling Orbiter 3 *gondola entrance.* BILL SLY

"Curiosity is the initial vital ingredient in exploration, followed quickly by the question 'Why shouldn't I?' We know that knowledge dispels fear, but it also invites opportunities that need to be grasped with both hands, an open mind and a grand desire. This is the stuff explorers are made of."

Taking a Flier

My highest achievement was undoubtedly the first balloon flight around the world in 1999 that established seven world records for me and flying partner Bertrand Piccard. We took off in Switzerland and landed in Egypt 20 days later after flying over 29,000 miles.

As a boy I was the outdoor type—hiking, cycling, rock climbing, caving and sport in general. The trouble was that I wasn't very good at any of it.

My 'Eureka' moment came when I was 13, in 1960, in the front seat of a glider. The previous five minutes had seen the usual trepidation at one's first flight: the safety briefing, the clumsiness and fumbling with the seat harness, the sudden and violent snatch of the winch cable, followed by a seemingly uncontrolled acceleration and ridiculously steep ascent before the world stopped on the pull of the cable release lever. There we were, floating at 1,200 feet, and for the first time in my life I felt that inner peace. I knew now that the air was my medium; it was in this place that I would be at one with myself and my God.

I had to fight to fly. Most spare time was taken up with part-time jobs to pay for weekend trips to the gliding club. On leaving school I succumbed to the unworthy promises of Royal Air Force recruiters who suggested that being a pilot was one small step away once one signed on. Whilst applying three times for pilot training before becoming too old at the grand age of 25, I joined a flying squadron as a loadmaster and then as a helicopter crewman. It was naive of me to think that without a university education (or 'background' as the discreditable English class system would describe it) I might gain a flying commission.

On retiring from the RAF at 30, I went into commerce, ultimately setting up my own business. Now the glass ceiling was removed and naivety had given way to maturity and financial independence. I was gliding again, this time teaching youngsters to fly, watching for that rare but magical moment I had experienced at their age.

My love of flying turned into a passion when I found ballooning in 1986. Balloons are fun, unpredictable and immensely demanding when one takes up the challenge of crossing mountains or oceans. This passion, combined with the joy of teaching, is a typical recipe for success: from professional balloon pilot to instructor, to examiner and then to my country's chief flying instructor. Invitations to join exciting boundary-breaking projects followed.

One such project was the *Breitling Orbiter 3* mission to be the first to fly a balloon non-stop around the world. Our flight capsule now stands proudly in the Milestones of Flight exhibit in the Smithsonian National Air & Space Museum in Washington, D.C., along with *Apollo 11*'s command module, the *Spirit of St. Louis*, the *X1* and the *Wright Flyer*.

BRIAN JONES, OBE, D.Sc, M.A. was born in 1947 and educated in Bristol, England, where he still lives. He's married to Joanna, and has two daughters and four grandchildren.

Following the Air Force, he joined the U.K. pharmaceutical industry and eventually started his own company supplying catering equipment to the hotel and restaurant trade. He sold the main trading division in 1999 in order to take up ballooning full time, specializing in setting up new ballooning companies. He was chief pilot for four such companies. In 1993, the Civil Aviation Authority appointed him pilot examiner and in 1994, training officer for the British Balloon & Airship Club, where he was responsible for the training and appointment of all British balloon-flying instructors.

In 1997 Brian joined the technical team producing the *Breitling Orbiter 2* round-the-world balloon. In 1998 he was appointed project manager and reserve pilot, assuming the role of second pilot later that year. He co-authored the story of their milestone success in *The Greatest Adventure*. With the million-dollar prize from the flight, he co-founded the Winds of Hope charity foundation, which works to help children suffering in unreported or forgotten circumstances.

His other ballooning ventures include being part of the team making the first successful balloon flight to the North Pole, in 2000, and an attempt on the altitude record of 118,000 feet in 2003. Brian holds almost 30 honours and awards, including The Explorer's Club Lowell Thomas medal.

He finally got his fixed-wing pilot's licence in 2002, but describes it as a formality rather than a trophy.

5 Twelve O'Clock High

Your hopes, dreams and aspirations are legitimate. They are trying to take you airborne, above the clouds, above the storms, if you only let them.

—WILLIAM JAMES

Paul launching his career in the late 1930s. Paul MacCready Collection

Doing More With Less

I take the most pride in having won the 18-year-old Kremer Prize for being first to demonstrate significant human-powered flight.

In 1977, my giant, ultra-light *Gossamer Condor*, built from balsa wood, aluminum tubes, cardboard, Mylar plastic and piano wire, was successfully pedaled by Bryan Allen around the figure-eight course. The £50,000 reward (then about $100,000 U.S.) was appealing to me because I had a $100,000 debt acquired in financing a friend's company that did not succeed. Unfortunately, the project had cost $65,000.

Subsequently Henry Kremer initiated another reward, with twice the money, for a human-powered flight 22 miles across the English Channel. An improved vehicle, our *Gossamer Albatross*, performed this amazing prize flight in 1979—and

"Exploration isn't about dealing with problems, but challenges. Things aren't barriers. If there is a barrier or a stone wall, you walk around the end, you leap over it."

finally covered my debts. Nevertheless, the *Gossamer Condor* provided me with the most excitement.

It was books that really got me going when I was the age of 11 growing up in New Haven, Connecticut: J. Holland's 1903 *Moth Book* and 1935 *Butterfly Guide*, C. M. Weed's 1917 and 1926 *Butterflies* and the Comstock's 1904 *How to Know the Butterflies*. I got hugely involved in collecting butterflies and moths and learned the scientific names of all the big ones. Then, when I was 13, in 1938, I remember a newsreel showing a sailplane flying over a slope. Just this big, graceful machine flying along—it still sticks in my mind as an early memory. The newsreel also showed a crash a few minutes later, but that didn't bother me. No one was hurt. It was such a great kind of flying. And I found that it was a wonderful, addicting hobby. In summers I lived on a lonely peninsula in Branford, Connecticut, building model planes—ornithopters, autogyros, helicopters, gliders and indoor and outdoor powered planes with rubber and gasoline engines.

In high school, besides being dyslexic (which I didn't realize then, of course), I was always the smallest kid in the class, not especially coordinated or athletic, socially kind of immature, not the comfortable leader type. And so, when I began getting into model airplanes, getting into contests and creating new things, I probably got more psychological benefit from that than the typical school things. And once you're into model airplanes, you learn about thermals and you hear a little bit about sailplanes.

Back at college for two years after World War II, and then in graduate school, I flew sailplanes and powered aircraft as hobbies that led to business. The sailplane flying—I was National Champion three years; International Champion in 1956 in France; and in 1947 I developed the Speed Ring, which tells a pilot what speed to fly in down currents to the next thermal—including climbing in thunderstorms. This sort of flying launched me into cloud seeding (weather modification), which was my main professional activity from 1948 to 1960. My company, AeroVironment Inc., started an aviation division after the human-powered flights and, with DuPont support, initiated a solar-powered airplane program.

In 1980 a three-quarter size version of the *Gossamer Albatross* had its pedals removed and the propeller connected to a motor powered by a small solar panel. It introduced solar flight, piloted by my 13-year-old, 80-pound son Marshall. In 1981 our final piloted solar plane, the *Solar Challenger*, carried pilot Steve Ptacek 163 miles from Paris to an airport in England at 11,000 feet.

Now, pushing the idea of "doing more with less" is my main goal. The *Gossamer Condor* project really set the stage for this philosophy by providing the guide for all subsequent work on very efficient air, ground and water products. Such devices are essential as we look at huge overpopulation, decreasing water levels, loss of forests, and releasing CO_2 from consuming oil, natural gas and coal. We must learn to live on Earth's interest, not her capital.

Time Magazine's 20th century feature The Century's Greatest Minds listed PAUL B. MacCREADY as one of the world's 100 most influential people. Born in 1925, he was educated at Yale and then at Caltech where he received his Ph.D. in Aeronautics in 1952.

Paul has received many awards for his pioneering work in soaring, human-powered flight, thinking skills, instrumentation, environmental topics and low-energy vehicles. The 45 awards include: Caltech's Distinguished Alumni Award; the Collins Trophy; the Reed Aeronautical Award; Ingenieur of the Century Gold Medal (American Society of Mechanical Engineers); the Lindbergh Award; the Guggenheim Medal (AIAA, SAE and ASME); the Cole Award; the Hughes Memorial Award; the Heinz Award; and the Bowers Award. He's also been featured in *National Geographic*.

His work on high-flying aircraft, tiny drones, battery-hybrid cars and very efficient electrical devices continues.

He's been married to Judy since 1957 and they live in Pasadena. They have three technologically proficient sons: Parker, Tyler and Marshall.

Solving the Henry Hudson mystery: Ron with his Norseman in northern Canada, 1956.
KAYE CRAVEN

"Exploration has two meanings to me. The first is the search for things that were accomplished in the past. However, the more important one is the search into the unknown for things we are not aware of. We must explore the unknown to move forward."

Soaring with Eagles

After flying World War II bombers, I became an Arctic and bush pilot in Canada. From the late 1950s to 1967 I serviced all the Inuit and Cree communities around Hudson Bay, mostly out of Moose Factory on James Bay. Flying gave me lots of time to feed my curiosity about the North's fascinating history—especially documenting the Henry Hudson survival saga.

History books say that after the mutiny at an island in James Bay in June, 1611, Hudson, his son and seven others were set adrift and never heard from again.

Well, maybe not by white men! The story of Hudson's survival until either the fall of 1611 or 1612 with Indian help has been handed down by word of mouth from generation to generation among the Cree. In Canada, because of the fur trade, Indians were business allies of white men. You see, they helped them, which isn't surprising when you think of it.

Father Steinman, the Catholic priest at Povungnituk, high up on the east side of the Bay, and Bill Anderson, the factor at the Albany Hudson Bay Trading Post, also did research at the same time and we agreed on many things. Bill was married to a Cree and she had lots of information about the "big white ship" that had so impressed her ancestors. Sometimes the oral tradition was in conflict, such as which island the mutiny took place on. But it agreed that Hudson stayed at Cabbage Willows on the edge of Rupert Bay in the bottom of James Bay after the mutiny.

Oral tradition also says one man died, and that Hudson built a signal cairn but when no ship came to rescue them, they tried to make their way to Quebec along the Rupert River. Here, they disappear, even to the Natives. It's believed they were massacred, along with their Indian allies, at a long portage about 40 miles inland from James Bay.

There are cultural memories of Hudson at many communities along the Bay because of the *Discovery*'s many stops and meetings with Inuit and Cree. It was always easy for me to ask about Hudson because he was still known as "the white man with the red beard." His story must be told. He was a fellow pilot too, of sorts.

My dream was flying and it started in a single, exciting moment when I was 5 in 1925. I was brought up on a farm near Bath, Ontario, and was coming home from school when I heard a strange, guttural sound coming from the sky. Looking up I saw the British Airship R100—the English competitor to the Graf Zeppelin—coming over! I had never seen anything like it! It passed over me on its way to a mooring spot in Kingston, 20 miles away. It was huge and so close, just 500 feet, that I could see markings on it very clearly. I was very impressed by its size and thought it would be *wonderful* to fly a machine like it.

I loved being outside and was curious about everything. I loved studying birds and how they flew. I built many model airplanes out of tissue paper and wood and perfected them to the point of stable flight. My launching point was a window in the top of our barn. I cannot count the number of times I climbed the ladder to launch my models. My fascination with flying stayed with me all through my teenage years. After I graduated, I naturally joined the Royal Canadian Air Force, and flew 28 missions in a Halifax bomber called *Vicky* with Bomber Command. I led a raid on Cologne and participated in two on Hamburg, including the firebombing (we could see it burning for 400 miles behind us on the way home; it looked like the glow from a sunset!). Most of my missions, however, were over "Happy Valley"—the Ruhr.

My childhood perfecting aircraft didn't stop then! *Vicky* was painted with a flat, dull finish, but the crew and I found that after waxing the aircraft with floor wax, we cruised 10 mph faster! The commanding officer wondered why we arrived back 20 minutes before the others. When I explained, all the aircraft in 6 Group were varnished!

After the war I flew everything from Beavers to Otters but mostly Norsemen. I flew all over northern Canada, supplying everything from the Distant Early Warning (DEW) Line to ferrying the first drilling rig into the mining town of Thompson, Manitoba, in 1957. The population there is now over 13,000. I also flew scientists to study Chubb Crater (now New Quebec Crater).

RON CRAVEN was born in 1920. In a career logging 27,000 hours, Ron flew the Arctic and knew it better than anyone. He has owned his own airline and was the CEO of another. He has been honoured with an Award of Excellence by the Poetry Institute of Canada. Craven Lake is named after him for rescuing a stranded family of Indians from nearby Wabowden, Manitoba.

Ron's documentation of the Henry Hudson saga, complete with maps, is ensconced in The Explorers Club Archives in New York where it is available for researchers.

He still makes model airplanes, and to that hobby he's added an old ship, Nelson's *Victory*. He and wife Kaye live in Stratford, Ontario, Canada.

A Small Poem

In a small town where I went to school
With poetry, as a pastime, I used to doodle
After graduation I did leave
To defend a country where my help was in need.
I soared with the eagles as a career
And went to lands far and near,
So now once more I take up my pen
And have the joy of writing poetry again.

A plane life, but hardly a plain one: Tim easing into the cockpit of a Spitfire. Bob Fassold

Into the Eye

Flying into the eye of my *second* hurricane, Karen, in 2001, was undoubtedly one of my greatest moments as a research pilot. Why not the first, Michael, in 2000? Well, frankly, because I was somewhat nervous … okay, too damn scared to register the enormity of the event. I was so focused on just surviving that I missed so much of the beauty and wonder that was literally off the tip of my nose.

On the second hurricane, unburdened by silly thoughts of my imminent demise, I was able to focus on the absolute beauty of the cloud formations as we spiralled clockwise inward toward the eye. As we closed in on the wall, the clouds darkened and thickened from eerie tendrils of gold and brown to a thick and ominous dark grey. A sharp "BAM" reverberated throughout the entire aircraft and I once again found myself within the eye of a hurricane; the noise was caused by the sudden change in the wind to absolute stillness in the eye. And what a sight! Without being vulgar, it reminds me of the swirl of a toilet flushing. Looking up through the "tube" one sees blue sky and sunshine. Looking down reveals an oddly calm,

> *"Exploration is being at the edge where the known meets the unknown. It is all about taking measured risks that open new pathways."*

bluish-grey ocean. I am privileged to have seen one of nature's most fascinatingly devastating machines from the inside. Few get the opportunity.

It's hard to ascertain exactly when I decided my calling was to be a test and research pilot. It was an amalgam of golden experiences: a friend taking me fishing in his father's Super Cub; the first time I saw a Voodoo screech by at the North Bay, Ontario, air show; as a curious 12-year-old hiking in the woods when a loud bleating cracked through the air and flattened the treetops. I followed the noise toward a clearing and saw a camouflage green, twin-rotor helicopter (a Chinook) settle onto the beaten-down grass. It was the most amazing spectacle I had ever witnessed … it left me trembling with excitement. It might as well have been an alien ship. In hindsight (having flown helicopters), I suspect one of the crew was answering the call of nature.

The Apollo missions came along just as I was hitting my most impressionable years. Though I hate to admit it, the original Star Trek TV series also played a role in the formation of my dream. It sounds corny as I think back, but the opening line, "To boldly go where no man has gone before" rang as loud as "That's one small step for man, one giant leap for mankind." Somewhere between fact and fiction, I decided my future lay in flight research.

How does one get here? Had somebody told me early on what it would take I think I would have turned my back on my dream … far too much work and sacrifice for a poor kid from the North. But, taken one step at a time, I am proof positive it can be done. Paramount in any worthwhile achievement is the insatiable desire to learn. Thirty years after my first solo I still bring flight manuals home from work to study after dinner. The only way one can truly excel in research flying is to allow the lines between work, hobby and family to blur. An understanding wife certainly helps.

Not being afraid to take chances is another important aspect of pursuing one's dream. I joined the military wanting to be a pilot. I shipped off to basic training, did survival training, completed a math and geography B.Sc., and then attended primary and advanced pilot training. A few operational tours, more studying, and then the luck of seeing a job vacancy being advertised by the National Research

Council … and *voilà*, a career flying through hurricanes, measuring ice thickness at the poles, studying pollution in mountains and valleys and doing freefall flights in support of the Canadian Space Agency. There were numerous other fascinating projects that took one to the limits of ability and imagination. I am lucky … but then, luck is nothing but preparedness meeting opportunity.

MAJOR (retired) TIM LESLIE was born in 1963 and raised in Baysville, Ontario, attending school in Huntsville. Tim joined the Canadian Armed Forces in 1980 and was commissioned in 1983. After several tours flying helicopter, jet, and multi-engine aircraft he retired from the military in 1997 to join the Flight Research Laboratory of Canada's National Research Council as Supervisor of Flying Operations and Training.

Tim slips his kayak into the Ottawa River from the home around Arnprior-Braeside he shares with wife Carolyn and Tim and Alexandra.

6 The Adventurers

Man wanted for hazardous journey.
Small wages, bitter cold, long
months of complete darkness,
constant danger, safe
return doubtful.
Honour and
recognition in case
of success.

—SIR ERNEST SHACKLETON

DAVID HEMPLEMAN-ADAMS

For Queen and country: David at the South Pole heading towards the Explorers Grand Slam.
DAVID HEMPLEMAN-ADAMS

The Explorers Grand Slam

The highest achievement for me was in May 1998 when, after three attempts, I reached the North Geographical Pole on foot. In doing so I completed 20 years of trying to be first to achieve the Explorers Grand Slam: becoming the first person to conquer the North and South Magnetic and Geographical Poles and climb the highest mountain in each of the seven continents.

I was brought up in Moredon, England, until I was nine when my parents divorced. I stayed with my mother, but we moved to the tiny village of Stoney Littleton, near Bath. I had been transformed from a boy from a railway town to a country lad. I loved getting dirty, working hard and forever being in the fresh air. Without that move, I well may never have become an explorer, for when I was 13

"Adventure and exploration are closely linked and sometimes merge. Pure exploration is, by definition, going somewhere where no one has been before. But you can start on an adventure and you quickly find out you're in a big exploration. Exploration is not just physical but mental as well. I think Browning's quote 'A man's reach should exceed his grasp or what's a heaven for?' personifies that quest for understanding."

I was able to embark on The Duke of Edinburgh's Award scheme. I remember doing the bronze award and being dropped off in Brecon Beacons National Park in mid-Wales with a map and compass with three other boys and told to climb to the other side of a mountain. This was the first time I had ever been away from home, been to the mountains or the wilderness. It was cold, wet and miserable; the fog was so thick we couldn't see further than six feet in front of us. I kept wondering what I was doing there. As we climbed higher and higher we slowly walked out of the mist and as I looked back all I could see was a vast expanse of cotton wool bouncing up against the mountain peaks. It was at that exact moment I decided I wanted to continue in adventure!

By 16 I had won the gold award and conquered many Welsh peaks. While in college at Manchester studying business, I spent all my spare time learning about mountaineering. At 23, in 1979, I visited Mt. Everest for the first time and saw enough of the spectacle that I *had* to go back.

I am very luck that I have one foot in commerce and one in adventure. Over the years, I have been able to take holidays and do adventure, slowly getting experience from climbing in the Alps to the Himalayas and from small Arctic trips to bigger solo expeditions.

I'm also fortunate to hold several other firsts. I was the first Briton to fly a hot-air balloon across the Andes and the first person to fly a balloon to the North Pole. In 2003 I crossed the Atlantic on my own in a balloon with an open wicker basket. I also hold the absolute world altitude record for a balloon at 41,287 feet. In 2004

I became the first person to fly a single-engine Cessna the entire length of North and South America from Cape Columbia to Cape Horn.

I'm passionate in my belief that every individual can achieve extraordinary things, and I regularly share my 25 years of experience as an adventurer with global business audiences.

DAVID HEMPLEMAN-ADAMS, OBE, DL, was born in 1956 in Swindon, Wiltshire, England. He is a uniquely talented British adventurer with over 30 major expeditions to his credit. He also holds 33 FAI world aviation records.

David is the author of four books, including his autobiography, *Toughing It Out*. He has made eight documentaries about his expeditions. He has several awards from around the world.

With wife Claire and daughters Alicia, Camilla and Amelia, he lives in Box, near Bath, England.

David is a director of three companies and co-founder of The Mitchemp Trust. By providing adventure camps, the charity helps vulnerable youth improve their confidence, self-esteem and ability to take responsibility for themselves. He is also still closely associated with The Duke of Edinburgh's Award scheme.

SIR RANULPH FIENNES

> *"I go on expeditions for the same reason an estate agent sells houses—to pay the bills."*

Sir Ran at the Banff Mountain Book and Film Festival, 2005. JASON SCHOONOVER

Look for a Brave Spirit

Of various projects over the past 40 years, perhaps the most satisfying was the 26 years of on-and-off searching for the legendary lost city of Ubar in Oman's Rub al Khali Desert, which disappeared around A.D. 300 and was Ptolemy's frankincense centre. I launched seven major four-wheel-drive expeditions before finally locating the ruins—through sheer good luck in 1991.

My wife and I were sitting in the shade and overheard two government officials posted to our archaeological dig saying that my team had been out there for six weeks and hadn't dug and the American film team that were with us were filming everything everywhere, which was disallowed. If they told their bosses—the Ministry of Heritage—we'd be out! I literally immediately rushed to the archaeologist, Dr. Yuris Zarins, and said, "Get your toothbrush and start right away!" He said, "We haven't found anything worth digging yet, it's a big country." I said, "Well, there's rubble 300 metres over there." He shrugged, "All right, we'll get some practice in for the team."

Within three or four days, about nine inches down, he unearthed a 2,500-year-old chess set! Within six weeks the outline of the city wall! And this within sight of our base camp, from which we had roamed hundreds of kilometres! Now it's the biggest active excavation in Arabia.

As a schoolboy I was very mischievous and often climbed up on our school's roof. I was frequently caught but it was good fun nonetheless. That may have launched my interest in climbing. Since childhood my mother brought me up on stories of my father's wartime exploits. He was the Commanding Officer of the Royal Scots Greys cavalry regiment, which he was commanding when he was killed in World War II. One memorable story stirred my sense of adventure: when he forgot to pack his pistol, he used a pipe to ambush enemy in Palestine in 1942. I dreamed of following in his footsteps.

But in 1960 I was forced to change from one set of "my life's dreams" to a very different alternative. This was due to the realization that I had been badly designed since birth for the passing of A-level exams. At that time it was not possible to become a Regular Army officer without two key A-levels. I could not make it to Sandhurst Officer Cadet School as a result of this unbendable requirement. This all meant switching to civilian life after eight years in the Royal Scots Greys. In order to make a living, my only path lay in using my "adventure training" experience. I moved into planning and organizing international expeditions. And all as a direct result of this intellectual shortcoming....

The Guinness Book of World Records describes SIR RANULPH TWISLETON-WYKEHAM-FIENNES, 3rd Baronet, OBE, as "the world's greatest living explorer." Born in 1944 in Windsor, Berkshire, England, he spent part of his childhood in South Africa before the family returned to England when he was 12. While in the elite SAS, he became the youngest captain in the British Army. He spent eight years there before being dismissed following a prank in which he blew up the movie set of *Doctor Doolittle*. He then moved to the Middle East as a member of the Sultan of Oman's forces. In the fighting there in 1968–1970 he was awarded the Sultan's Bravery Medal.

Since 1969 his astonishing feats of physical and mental endurance have claimed 10 expeditionary world records on over 30 expeditions. He led one up the White Nile by hovercraft, recalling the days of the great British Victorian explorers; another on the first polar circumnavigation with Charles Burton, an expedition of three years and 52,000 miles; and the first unsupported crossing of the Antarctic continent with Dr. Michael Stroud, pulling a 500-pound sledge for 97 days, making it the longest polar journey in history.

Ran was also shortlisted to replace Sean Connery as James Bond. In 1993 Queen Elizabeth awarded him the Order of the British Empire (OBE) for "human endeavour and charitable services" because, on the way to breaking records, he raised over £5-million for charity.

He is the author of numerous books, including his autobiography *Living Dangerously*. He holds honorary doctorates from the universities of Loughborough, Central England, Portsmouth and Glasgow; the Polar Medal with Bar; the Royal Geographical Society's Founders Medal; and the Polar Exploration Millennium award from The Explorers Club, British Chapter.

Ran lives in Exmoor, West Somerset, England, with wife Louise, 200 cattle, and dogs Thule and Pingo. *Look for a Brave Spirit* is the family motto.

"An explorer goes out to find out about people, fauna, flora, geography, geology and the world, whereas an adventurer is often trying to discover something about themselves."

The full safari: the very picture of a romantic explorer/adventurer. NICK WILCOX-BROWN

A Life of Adventure

My greatest sense of achievement was following the first descent of the infamous Blue Nile in 1968. After two gun battles with bandits, a wild escape at night by raft in enormous rapids in which one raft capsized, and fending off giant crocodiles, I was thankful to be alive. But my life of adventure had started years earlier ....

Clutching the Maori war spear, Jacko and I worked our way through the long grass, still damp with dew. The great cat must be very close and we hardly dared to breathe. Inching the spear forward and with the sun rising behind, I lifted my head very slowly over the stalks. There, only ten feet away, our quarry crouched, his evil green eyes fixed on me. Changing my grip, I rose and hurled the heavy weapon with all my strength. But the killer leapt sideways and the blade thudded into the ground. In a trice, Jack, my pet monkey, was in hot pursuit. Alas, the enormous ginger tomcat that had so recently devoured one of my mother's rabbits escaped.

The spear had come from New Zealand, where my parents spent their early married life. Jacko was an ex-regimental mascot whose tail had been shut in the canteen door, making it permanently crooked, and thus he detested anyone in khaki. We had much in common: like me Jacko was mischievous, loved eggs, hated cats, pulled little girls' hair and screamed with rage when he couldn't get his own way. Together we went on safari through the 'jungle' of orchards and rose gardens. The long grass behind the church became our Serengeti in which lurked a fearsome lion, obligingly played by the overfed tom. On sighting our prey, Jacko would chatter excitedly and with Tarzan-like whoops we would give chase. Sometimes we both got too near and got badly scratched for our pains.

At this time my family lived in a Herefordshire rectory in England. My blissful life as an eight-year-old in 1944 was full of excitement. World War II was raging, my father was an army chaplain, and our house was always full of British and American soldiers with tales of derring-do. This and the long seafaring heritage of my family combined to form my dreams of adventure and exploration—but in a way that would help people, fauna and flora.

I was educated at Victoria College, Jersey, and the Royal Military Academy Sandhurst and served 37 years in the British Army. As a Royal Engineer, I established links for adventurous training with the armed forces of many countries. Under the patronage of the Prince of Wales I organized and led Operations Drake and Raleigh, involving over 10,000 young men and women in the largest youth leadership expedition ever. Being appointed by the Army to lead that Blue Nile Expedition was the turning point into my life of adventure.

As Chairman of the Scientific Exploration Society, I now organize expeditions for more mature people concentrating on archaeological, environmental, medical and wildlife projects.

After some 80 expeditions in 50 years, I have no regrets at having led such a fascinating and hopefully worthwhile life, thanks to a great many kind and patient friends. I wanted to be an explorer rather than an adventurer, though adventure comes with the territory.

COLONEL JOHN BLASHFORD-SNELL, OBE, FRGS, of Dorset, is one of the world's most seasoned and legendary explorers. Fascinated by early civilizations, he has explored the sites of ancient harbours off Cyprus and Libya, discovered forgotten settlements in the jungles of South America and deep in the Kalahari and Sahara deserts. While leading the first expedition to descend Ethiopia's Blue Nile he developed inflatable boats that revolutionized river exploration. John has tested the theories of the late Thor Heyerdahl using traditional reed boats to show how ancient people could have navigated the rivers of South America and voyaged around the world. In Nepal, his teams have discovered giant "mammoth-like" elephants.

John was awarded the Segrave Trophy and the Livingstone Medal. The Royal Geographical Society, with the approval of Her Majesty Queen Elizabeth II, presented him with their Patron's Medal for "encouragement of exploration by young people." The Institute of Royal Engineers awarded him their Gold Medal.

Author of 15 books, he also finds time to work with underprivileged youngsters in Britain's inner cities, and chairs the Liverpool Construction-Crafts Guild, which is encouraging the training of skilled craftsmen.

He married Judith in 1960 and they have two daughters, Emma and Victoria. His account of the Blue Nile adventure can be found in *Something Lost Behind the Ranges*.

"Exploration can be looking in a microscope, climbing an obscure mountain peak or probing the depths of the atom as one reaches out to go where no man has been before. I try to light a fire in our young people in hopes they too will take up the flag of exploration."

Gerry traded in the cockpit of an F-4D for this log house. COL. RAYMOND GIRARD

Night of the Black Bird

I was on a moonless night trip with two canoes loaded with naked Amazon Indians when we hunted a large black bird that was on a small island. One group went to one end as drivers. I remained with the others awaiting the bird that we shot out of the trees with a bow and arrow. All night not a word was said. The next morning when I realized we had been communicating by mental pictures (ESP), the hair stood up on the back of my head! I realized how little we know about what's out there.

I was a child of the Depression, brought up on a truck farm in southern Illinois. We made it to town once a week to shop, sell eggs and produce and pick up a 20-pound block of ice and kerosene for the lamps. We grew the rest. While some might consider that life to be one of hardship, it was to me just the opposite. I spent hours in the woods with my grandfather trapping coons, possums and muskrats. We also dug roots and my grandfather taught me which mushrooms I could eat, along with a plethora of knowledge about the natural world. My half-Indian uncle, Jewel, taught me how to make a bow and arrow and hit a rabbit on the run.

Later Jewel moved to Crescent City, California, to work with his brother salmon fishing. The year was 1942 and World War II had just begun. I left with my grandmother Anna and grandfather—"Uncle Frank" to everyone—to be with Frank's half-Indian children there. Away we went in our new 1941 Ford pickup with me in the back with my dog, Wimpy. We only averaged a few hundred miles a day while roughly following the Lewis and Clark trail. The roads were mostly rock and sometime dirt. I sat in the back for over three wonderful months. We caught fish and shot rabbits with our .22 rifle, and camped out every night, eating beans, hominy and side pork, all cooked in a big black iron kettle. At 10 I was like a great sponge. We passed giant fields of prairie dogs and saw herds of antelope and mule deer. Wildlife was everywhere.

Somewhere on that grand trip while walking in the woods with my grandfather, a fire was lit within me for knowledge of the natural world that has never extinguished. This adventure left an undying hunger in my soul to want to know what was over the next ridge.

After I completed high school in 1950 with great marks, my teachers urged me to go to college, but my family didn't have the resources so I joined the Air Force. I flew B26s in Korea and 100 missions in F4Ds in Vietnam.

I also flew with the Brazilian Air Force and it was then that my interest in the natural world really reared up. Flying over the Amazon, I'd spot untouched Indian tribes. With the brothers Villas Boas, we'd trek in and leave presents, then return later to make contact. I spent weeks with the Indians and became knowledgeable about their culture. On some trips I collected rare atlatl throwing sticks still in use!

GERRY BASS of Miami advanced from private to full colonel in 28 years, along the way picking up a degree in business management. He also attended the Air Command Staff College and the Armed Forces Staff College.

Expert in Portuguese, while stationed in South America, he acted as a translator for the Brazilian Command, Staff College and Brazilian War College on trips to the U.S. where he interpreted for President Johnson in the White House. On these trips he met five future Brazilian presidents. He has visited all the Latin American countries except Cuba, and his travels encompass over 60 countries.

He has led expeditions to Alaska and several to Amazon tributaries, where he flew in some of the first surveyors for the Trans Amazon Highway. In Indonesia and Guatemala he studied relationships between Polynesian and Mayan temple construction. He received the Sweeny Medal from The Explorers Club, and is a Royal Geographic Society Fellow.

Upon leaving the Air Force, Gerry had a successful career at Eastern Airlines. He went on to become Executive Vice-President at Ryder Corporation in the Aviation Sales Division. He also served as President of Ryder Accessories Company for 11 years until he retired.

He and Carol Rae have a son, Mark, a daughter, Mary, two granddaughters and one great-granddaughter.

MACIEJ KUCZYNSKI

*"When exploring,
do not conquer, seize,
capture, defeat, fight,
beat ... just walk, climb,
enter, crawl, cross, go, sail,
navigate. Those who were
thinking they are fighting
nature—are dead...."*

*In the Sudety Mountains of southwestern
Poland.* BARBARA KUCZYNSKI

The Architect of Dreams

Exploration is a disease. The discoverer is ill; flaming brain, driven by the hope of discovery.

The helicopter hovered at the edge of a natural well in the Venezuelan Amazon. After rappelling down I realize I am the first man ever to step here. Our team slid to the bottom, where a gallery led to the interior. We stopped at the edge of a giant underground hollow valley. Each square inch was shining with colourful crystals. Bewildered, eyes flooded by sweat, we stared at the world biggest—and probably oldest—quartzite cave. Four billion years after Earth solidified from the cosmic debris, we were accorded the privilege of discovering this wonderful and awe-inspiring part of nature.

For me it began in 1938 in the sitting room of my parent's apartment in Warsaw, Poland. I was kneeling on the carpet playing a geographic board game called "Flight Around the World" presented to me by my father's friend, Capt. S. Skarzynski, who was the first to fly solo across the South Atlantic. While moving my game piece across the map of the world I was fascinated by exotic names like Valparaiso, Kamchatka, Mombasa. I wanted hungrily to see these places. At the same time, over my head, on the big table, my father worked developing the first

Polish airline to connect Central Europe with South America. But World War II exploded upon us and for years I forgot about the faraway world.

However, the dream returned with a vengeance after the war when, as an architect, I had to travel by train to boring construction sites. Looking through the window at the moving landscape a powerful conviction arose that one day, free of all obligations, I would travel to discover and explore exotic, mysterious, faraway places.

Then came teasing dreams at night: I was moving in some kind of vehicle across vast spaces—plains, savannahs, deserts ....

Then the miracle happened. As a mountaineer and cave explorer with experience only of the Polish Tatra Mountains, I was appointed by the Polish Academy of Sciences as technical manager of The Polish Polar Spitsbergen expedition in the 1956–57 International Geophysical Year. I had no idea whatsoever that I would never return to the drawing board. In preparing for this expedition I read several books and among them 1935's *Arctic Adventure,* by Peter Freuchen, who, at the beginning of the 20th century, spent several years amongst Greenland's Eskimos. I was impressed by his account of how he was invited to be a member of, for him, an almost mythological organization—'The Explorers Club' (which I had never heard of) and how he was welcomed at their splendid headquarters in New York where he met many famous explorers. All of this, for a young man like me, living behind the Iron Curtain in the time of the Cold War, was like a fairy tale that I could only dream about.

Then a few years later, I received unexpectedly a new sign when I was given an Explorers Club Bulletin: this was the first tangible evidence for me that The Club really existed. From that time onwards the Bulletin, with the Club's sign and flag on its cover, was on my desk as a constant reminder that there was something to achieve. The realization of what had become another dream arrived when my friend the great mountain and polar explorer Richard Schramm sponsored me. And in 1982 I became a member.

MACIEJ KUCZYNSKI of Warsaw is an architect, author, speleologist, alpinist and explorer. Born there in 1929, he commenced mountaineering and caving in 1949 while a student at the Krakow Institute of Technology. His life is one long, unbroken sequence of expeditions to exotic locations worldwide. He's been leader on untold expeditions to caves, many virgin, including descents of the world's deepest in France and Mexico. He was the manager of several Polish Academy of Sciences expeditions to the Gobi Desert, where he discovered skeletons of new species of dinosaurs. He's also led an expedition to the Andes, making several ascents, including the first of Cerro Sólo (6120 metres). He's participated in expeditions to the Himalayas, Uganda's Ruwenzori Mountains and Alaska. He led a joint Polish-Venezuelan expedition to Tepui Sarisariñama in the Amazon.

Maciej is the author of over 30 books published in four languages. He is included on the List of Honour of UNESCO's Board on Books for Young Men. He's published hundreds of articles, as well as radio scripts; and directed and photographed TV travel and animated films.

NEIL LAUGHTON

Yippee! I made it! The first ascent of Mt. Olivia, East Greenland. STEPHEN JONES

"There is much debate as to what is or isn't exploration. As the world gets "smaller" it becomes less easy to establish geographical or geophysical "firsts." However, we still have much to discover, learn and understand about our fragile planet. Anyone who seeks knowledge and enhances our understanding of our world, be it a first mountain ascent or discovery of a new species of plant can rightly claim to have participated in exploration."

Thin Line

I had been preparing for this final, daunting, exhausting 24 hours of climbing for the best part of ten years. Would my body hold out? Would my mind function properly? Would the gods favour me? Waiting and waiting for the clock to tick round to the appointed hour before eventually it was time to don the heavy boots and crampons, twist the bezel of one's head torch, and gingerly slide out of the orange tent at 8,000 metres on the South Col of Mt. Everest. In my 10-year quest to scale the highest peak on each of the seven continents, I had been here twice before. On reaching the South Col in May 1996, a terrible storm had pulverized us from dusk till dawn and round the clock again. Dreadful scenes played out in the ensuing chaos … the sad, shocking and public loss of Rob Hall, whom I had chatted with only the previous day; the desperation of not being able to get help to Scott Fischer; the look of exhaustion on the face of Anatoli Boukreev as he set off on another heroic foray into the maelstrom in search of his missing colleagues; the utter exasperation when my request to borrow a radio to assist with the rescue effort was turned down for selfish reasons; the horror and relief of watching a disfigured but determined Beck Weathers return to camp having been given up for dead.

Then, two years later, as my party descended from The Balcony at 8,500 metres following another failed summit attempt, I witnessed the horrific sight of two friends, roped together, slip and tumble down the mountain. They came to rest some 300 feet below me, unconscious, their path and certain death shortened by a snowdrift. Then I saw the best in human spirit, the welcome sight of fellow mountaineers abandoning what they were doing to offer assistance and aid a slow but successful evacuation off the mountain.

One week later, my body was in shape, my mind in sharp focus and the gods were smiling. I reached the mystical summit of Mt. Everest with a mixture of awe, tears and relief. I embraced my climbing partners and radioed our Base Camp: "We've run out of Earth!" I squatted for a moment to reflect on the 10-year journey I had undertaken. It had had its share of ups and downs, joys and frustrations, triumphs and tragedies. Ultimately, we explorers and adventurers are at the mercy of circumstances: some are within our control; many are not. It is a very thin line between success and failure.

In 1975 I was an unremarkable, sports-mad but exam-shy 12-year-old heading for an unremarkable life when I witnessed an event that was to change my life. A troop of Royal Marine Commandos demonstrated how to fast-rope down from a helicopter whilst it hovered above the deck of an aircraft carrier at sea. Seven years later I was presented with the coveted Green Beret, having learned the techniques of cliff assault and helicopter abseiling, a precursor to the lure of the mountains and my love of mountaineering.

NEIL LAUGHTON was born in Woolwich, London, England, in 1963 and raised in Somerset. He attended private schools in Sussex and then Westminster University, receiving a business diploma. Following the Royal Marines and U.K. Special Forces, he founded Office Projects Ltd., a commercial interiors company.

Besides the seven summits, he has made 12 first ascents in Greenland, completed an expedition to the North Pole, jet-skied around Britain, recreated Sir Ernest Shackleton's voyage in South Georgia and helped Glenn Shaw, a brittle-bone disease sufferer in a wheelchair, realize his dream of reaching Everest Base Camp.

His most bizarre sporting challenge, however, was his Awesome Eight Extreme Golfing Expedition completed in 2002—playing the eight most extreme golf courses in the world within one calendar year: the highest, lowest, hottest, coldest, most northerly, southerly, toughest and greatest! (The coldest round was played in -27°c and in two feet of snow; the hottest in +53°c and two feet of sand!)

Neil has been presented with the Ness Award by the Royal Geographical Society. He lives in the more temperate parts of Putney, London, with wife Caroline and son Oscar Ronnie Laughton.

"Exploration is the overriding passion of mankind. Explorers are risk-takers who push the boundaries of knowledge in the quest to experience the infinite."

The Desert Song: in North Africa hot on Alexander's trail. MILBRY POLK

Dreams of Adventure

In 1979 I fulfilled a long-time dream in retracing, by camel caravan, Alexander the Great's probable route across Egypt, supported by *National Geographic*. But my dreams of exploration began much earlier ....

I didn't have much time. My *Hopalong Cassidy* record had just finished and soon it would be dinnertime. I put two packages of baloney in my blue bandana, knotted the points, and stuck it through the end of my stick. I cinched my gun belt, and filled my pockets with Fig Newtons, a pocket knife, caps and matches. For a bedroll I took the sofa blanket. After donning great-grandfather's Civil War hat I was ready. I slipped out the back door, ran across the meadow and climbed over the stone wall, making sure to make lots of noise so any rattlers in the rocks would slither away (Hopalong, I was sure, had done that, too). I wasn't sure how far I had to go or how long it would take, but I hadn't reached our nearby village before I had eaten all my Fig Newtons. Soon I would have to make camp and then I could eat one pack of baloney. But then a car passed, stopped and backed up. It was my Dad on his way home from teaching at Harvard University. "And just where do you think you're going?" he inquired. I replied proudly, "Out west to find Annie Oakley but then I will come right back." He just opened the side door. I climbed in and we drove home. Thus ended my first expedition, age 5.

A few years later he gave me a book. He had actually given me lots of books, taken me camping and spent hours in our woods searching for Indian sites while telling me endless stories about growing up on a ranch in Texas. But this book was special. It was JRR Tolkien's *The Hobbit*. He told me he had known the author while he was a student in Oxford. So I felt connected to the book before I started reading—and I was mesmerized! *The Hobbit* was the grandest adventure quest story I had ever read! The next morning I could not put it down, so I put my forehead on the radiator and when I could hardly stand the heat I stumbled to my mother and told her I was ill. She felt my sweltering forehead and said, "O.K. No school." I rushed to my room and back to the mines of Moria. For the next few years I read and reread all of Tolkien's books. I wanted nothing more than to lead a life of quests.

But I had to find real quests. And in high school I did. It began with Sir Richard Burton. Again Dad supplied the books and Burton the dream of exploration. I tacked Burton's portrait on my bedroom wall next to a map of Asia with his travels highlighted. Those wandering lines became my dream quests.

Then my dream *idea* was born. In my high-school sophomore year I wrote a paper on Alexander the Great. Again, as with Tolkein and Burton, I immersed myself. As I went on canoe, kayak and mountaineering trips and began photographing for magazines, Alexander stayed in the back of my mind. I was 23 and finishing up two years of working at the American Museum of Natural History, trying to decide if I should go on for my Ph.D. Margaret Mead said to me: "You know what you want to do—just go out and do it."

And I did!

MILBRY CATHERINE POLK was born in 1954 in Oxford, England, and was educated at the University of London and Harvard, receiving a B.A. in Anthropology. She has ridden horseback through Pakistan's Northwest Territories, lived with Bedouin tribesmen, surveyed Arthurian sites in Wales, sailed the Mediterranean, rafted above the Arctic Circle, photographed rock carvings in Saudi Arabia and trained for the first Chinese-American canoe expedition.

She is the founder of the Margaret Mead Festival for the American Museum of Natural History as well as being a founder and director of the non-profit Wings WorldQuest—one of its programs is the WINGS Women of Discovery Awards, which celebrates female explorers. She won a Gracie Award, a woman of the 21st century award from Women's eNews, received an honorary fellowship from the Royal Canadian Geographical Society and the Environmental Leadership Award from Unity College. She's an advisor to the George Polk Awards for Journalistic Excellence, is on the Council of the New York Hall of Science and the Boards of The National Arts Club and The Children's Shakespeare Theatre.

She's written and edited 10 books, including *Women of Discovery* and *The Looting of the Iraqi Museum*. Her photojournalism has appeared in numerous magazines.

Milbry lives in Palisades, New York, with her husband, Phillip Bauman, and their daughters, Elisabeth, Bree and Mary.

7 The Modern Margaret Meads – the Anthropologists

Only barbarians are not curious about where they come from, how they came to be, where they are, where they appear to be going, whether they wish to go there, and if so, why, and if not, why not.

—ISAIAH BERLIN

WADE DAVIS

"Exploration is the pursuit of knowledge."

National Geographic *Explorer-in-Residence Wade in Borneo.*
Jeff Gibbs

Yes

In an attempt to make sense out of sensation, I identified a possible ethnopharmacological basis to the zombie phenomenon and in doing so opened ethnographic, historical and political vistas that offered a new understanding of the essence of a practice that had been exploited in an egregious manner.

I was raised in Pointe Claire, Quebec, which was surrounded by a larger English community, mostly commuters working in Montreal. It was an era, the 1950s and early '60s, famously remembered in Canada as the two solitudes, when French and English rarely interacted. There was a road, Cartier Avenue, which ran between the two worlds, forming both a literal and metaphorical divide that was never spoken about but never forgotten. As a young boy this chasm fascinated me. Across a narrow ribbon of asphalt lay another culture, another religion and language, a different way of being. So distant and yet so close.

Fortunately I had a somewhat wild older sister, Sandra, who fell in love with a wonderful boy from the village. As she slipped across that daunting social barrier, I followed and was introduced to the warmth of Latin culture. It was that opening to another culture and the wonder of what it revealed that kindled my dream of becoming an anthropologist.

A second opening occurred in 1968 when a Spanish teacher from Montreal took six students, including me, to Colombia. The teacher was English by birth, dapper, with a scent of cologne that gave him the fey veneer of a dandy, an impression betrayed by scars on his face and a glass eye that marked a body blown apart in war. His name was John Forester. At 14, I was the youngest and most fortunate, for unlike the others, who spent a sweltering season in Cali, I was billeted in the mountains. It was a typical Colombian scene: a flock of children too large to count, an indulgent father half the size of his wife, a wizened grandmother muttering to herself on a porch overlooking cane and coffee fields, a protective sister who more than once carried her brother and me home half drunk to a mother, kind beyond words, who stood by the garden gate, hands on hips, feigning anger.

For eight weeks, I encountered the warmth and decency of a people charged with a strange intensity, a passion for life and a quiet acceptance of the frailty of the human spirit. Several of the Canadian students longed for home. I had finally found it.

Each Sunday, there were dances and wild moments when horsemen raced over parched fields and along dusty roads where women offered food and teased the riders with their beauty. Though school was out for the summer, one teacher convened classes in his house, and discreetly introduced themes that could not be embraced in the open: the plight of the poor, the meaning of a phrase of poetry, the fate of Che Guevara, recently killed in Bolivia. And there were darker moments: the beggars, and armed soldiers beating ragged children, feral as alley cats, as they scattered into a black night cracked by gunfire.

Life was real, visceral, dense with intoxicating possibilities. I learned, that summer, to have but one operative word in my vocabulary, and that was *yes* to any experience. Colombia taught me that it was possible to fling oneself upon the benevolence of the world and emerge not only unscathed but transformed. It was a naive notion, but one that I carried with me for a long time.

WADE DAVIS is a *National Geographic* Explorer-in-Residence who has been described as "a rare combination of scientist, scholar, poet and passionate defender of all of life's diversity." An ethnographer, writer, photographer and filmmaker, he holds degrees in anthropology and biology and received his Ph.D. in Ethnobotany, all from Harvard University. Through the Harvard Botanical Museum he spent over three years in the Amazon and Andes as a plant explorer, living among 15 indigenous groups in eight Latin American nations making some 6,000 botanical collections. He has also lived among the nomadic Penan in Borneo.

Wade's work took him to Haiti to investigate folk preparations implicated in the creation of zombies, an assignment leading to *The Serpent and the Rainbow*, a bestseller turned into a movie. He is the author of nine other books, as well as being the recipient of numerous awards, including the Lannan Foundation $125,000 prize for literary non-fiction and has published 140 articles. His film credits include *Light at the Edge of the World*, *Phantastica*, *One River* and *The Lost Amazon*.

A research associate of the Institute of Economic Botany of the New York Botanical Garden, he's also a board member of the David Suzuki Foundation, Ecotrust, Future Generations and Cultural Survival, all dedicated to conservation-based development and protection of cultural and biological diversity.

Born in 1953, he's married to anthropologist Gail Percy. They divide their time between Washington, D.C., Vancouver, British Columbia, and their lodge in the Stikine Valley of B.C. They have two children, Tara and Raina.

JOHN OLSEN

With a Buddhist stele in Tibetan script, northern Mongolia. OVADAN
K. AMANOVA

Mongolia Dreaming

Unequivocally, the most important and durable contributions to knowledge in
which I will likely participate is our increasing ability to narrow down and
test comprehensive explanations for how, why and when our Ice Age ancestors
came to occupy marginal environments such as the Gobi Desert and the Tibetan
Plateau. I am always aware of the direct linkages that tie what may ultimately prove
to be my own greatest achievements with those early eye-opening and mind-ex-
panding experiences, surrounded by giant squids, dinosaurs and Haida canoes in
the American Museum of Natural History.

"I really do consider exploration to be humankind's noblest venture; one that links us across cultures and through time. The experiences of Ice Age foragers following game east across the Bering Strait; 19th century polar explorers crossing open leads on their way to bleak and transient spots at the ends of the Earth; biomedical researchers investigating the human genome at the molecular level, and a host of other superficially unrelated activities are, in my mind, integrally linked by the human passion for exploration."

It's always been clear to me that I owe much of what I am as a scholar and explorer to my father's benign influence and the equally unconscious persuasion of the AMNH in New York. Long hours spent there with him provided me the emotional, if not intellectual, perspective necessary to eventually think outside my own disciplinary box as an archaeologist and seek to articulate disparate information from many sources to understand complex phenomena, such as prehistoric human behavior.

As a child of only 5 or 6, I remember accompanying my Dad, Stanley J. Olsen, a vertebrate paleontologist and zooarchaeologist, on summer research visits to the AMNH. There, I would watch quietly over his shoulder as he compared and measured bones of animals in the Frick fossil collection ranging from mammoths to musk oxen.

In those days—the early 1960s—academic visitors were accorded the privilege of working in the museum after hours with very little supervision. I remember holding Dad's hand as we walked alone through semi-darkened exhibition halls, looking up all agog at Northwest Coast totem poles, Carl Akeley's gorilla group in the Hall of African Mammals, Charles Knight's murals and, of course, the dinosaurs! I suspect I'm not the only archaeologist who must admit my lifelong career pursuing the pathways of prehistoric human cultural evolution began as a childhood fascination with dinosaurs! As we walked, Dad told me stories of Roy Chapman Andrews discovering *Protoceratops* in Mongolia. After returning with Dad to the Paris Hotel, I would lie awake in bed for hours, my head reeling in wonder.

My course into anthropology was as straight as an arrow and 40-odd years later, I find myself camping in the Gobi. I now live in a very dry environment inhabited by pernicious wool-loving insects (among other, more pleasant things, I hasten to add). Cross-cultural and time-transgressive aspects of human cognitive behaviour are rare and fascinate me.

To this day, one whiff of moth crystals and dust takes me straight back to the AMNH and I'm reminded—more often than most, I think—of the seminal experiences in my formative years that set me on the course that has defined my life.

JOHN W. OLSEN of Tucson is Regents' Professor of Anthropology, Head of the Anthropology Department, and Director of the Je Tsongkhapa Endowment for Central and Inner Asian Archaeology at the University of Arizona. John received his Ph.D. in Anthropology from Berkeley. He joined the University of Arizona in 1980 and from 1982 to 1984 was a Research Associate at the Institute of Archaeology, London. From 1990 to 1992 Olsen represented the U.S. National Academy of Sciences in Beijing and spent a year conducting research in Kazakhstan as a Fulbright scholar.

John has conducted archaeological fieldwork in the now independent Central Asian republics of the former Soviet Union, and in Russia, China, East Turkistan, Tibet, and Mongolia. He has been awarded academic titles by the Mongolian Academy of Humanitarian Sciences (Academician, 1998) and the Mongolian Academy of Sciences (Doctoris Scientiae Honoris Causa, 2003).

He and wife Ovadan live in Tucson, Arizona.

On an Explorers Club flag expedition to the Sacred Cave of Death and Spiritual Power, Irian Jaya, Indonesia, 1989. BUD HAMPTON

"Exploration is exploring-and-discovering (a powerful symbiosis), fuelled through millennia in each explorer by an inherited explorer gene (or genes) and prompted into action by a pervasive curiosity to explore."

A Multifaceted Explorer

During ten expeditions (1982–1999) I put together the jigsaw puzzle that gives a complete picture of behavior surrounding the use of stone by an entire Neolithic culture in the Highlands of Irian Jaya (now Papua), Indonesia. I documented the entire inventory and use of sacred and secular stones, from utilitarian stone tools to profane symbolic stones and spirit stones, power stones with multiple functions, and medicinal power stone tools. The resulting book, *Culture of Stone: Sacred and Profane Uses of Stone Among the Dani*, was nominated within the Society for American Archaeology as a book "expected to have a major impact on the direction and character of archaeological research."

I was born an explorer, and being raised near the Colorado Mountain Club and The Denver Museum of Natural History had an immense effect furthering that direction in my early life. As a youngster of about six I accompanied my parents to the museum for a nature talk. But the talk was boring for me! I'm a visual person and wanted to see and experience things so I slipped away and explored the museum. Wow! I was awed by *Brontosaurus* rex and much intrigued by the rows of displayed rocks, fossils, projectile points and the exciting dioramas. After that I looked forward to what became regular Sunday visits when I would explore over and over again those same displays, making new discoveries each trip.

I came from a loving family that supported my passions for athletics, academics and exploring—searching for things in nature such as rocks, plants, fossils, Indian artifacts, small animals, reptiles, insects and who knows what else. By 12 I had put together such huge rock collections I had to bury some of them next to the house because there wasn't enough room inside!

From age 10-16, I learned to climb by taking lessons from the Colorado Mountain Club, another nascent passion.

Museum archaeologists and geologists, recognizing my intense, wide-ranging interests, invited me to their labs, and then on field expeditions. What I learned made geology and archaeology credible as possible careers. When I was about 11, Dr. Nininger, the renowned meteorite expert (and a Denver neighbor), fascinated me with stories of meteors and meteorites. He had tons of meteorites at the museum. From Dr. Nininger I learned how he and his team would triangulate "falling" meteorites and then search them out. This sparked another youthful epiphany. I wanted to do that too!

And all this time, I was also fascinated by climbing! By 16, I knew that I wanted to be a climber—but also to explore all of nature. You see, my overall "epiphany" for exploration wasn't for just a single academic discipline, but rather a plethora—heightened by the "wows" of exciting field discoveries and nurtured by adult explorers. The focus of my exploration as an adult has been as a pluralist—a mountaineer/climber, naturalist, geologist, geomorphologist, paleontologist, geographer, oceanographer and archaeologist.

By the time I entered college in 1946 I planned to be a geologist first and then an archaeologist. Everything unfolded from there.

O. WINSTON "BUD" HAMPTON, born in 1928, is Adjoint Curator, Anthropology, University of Colorado Museum and holds five degrees with multiple honors, including a doctorate of archaeology/anthropology from Texas A&M University and a masters in geology from the University of Colorado. He is a retired Lt. Colonel, U.S. Marine Corps, and retired President of Amoco Indonesia Petroleum Company and five other Amoco exploration companies after a 27-year international career. He has lived and/or explored in 21 U.S. states, lived in Africa, Japan and Indonesia and led or participated in 66 expeditions in 36 countries.

Bud has taught climbing at the University of Colorado and climbed, spelunked and dived all over the world. He was a charter member of the Texas Running Club and member of the Philippines and Indonesia Running Clubs, and was awarded a gold medal from President Suharto at Indonesia's Proklathon Olympic Games in 1982. His photography has won many awards, the highest being judged "Best of Show" by the Editor of Photography for National Geographic.

His twelve publications include eight scientific papers and two articles in The Explorers Club Journal. Bud is a lifetime member of Sigma Xi, a Fellow of the Royal Geographic Society and a member of the American Alpine Club. Numerous other affiliations encompass his wide-ranging professional affiliations and personal interests.

Bud lives with his wife Fleur in Estes Park, Colorado. They have three adult children, Virginia, Winston and Hollis, and 10 grandchildren. He's pleased that many of them have inherited his robust curiosity gene and are following his path into exploration.

ERIC KJELLGREN

Eric with acclaimed Aboriginal artist Billy Thomas, Kununurra, Western Australia, 1996. ERIC KJELLGREN

"For me exploration has as much to do with perception as with geography. Seen from a novel perspective, even familiar places can appear entirely new. Many Aboriginal painters who I work with have traveled widely and it is as fascinating to listen to their impressions of Paris or Tokyo as to hear Western explorers talk about remote corners of the world."

From Manhattan to Australia (and Back)

The day had been hot but now, as the dancers gathered for the ceremony, the night was clear and cold. They were elders of the Gija, one of several Aboriginal peoples of the East Kimberley, a remote region in Western Australia's outback. I had worked with Gija painters and other Aboriginal artists for nearly a year and they often referred to me as "Jangala," a kinship term. Their bodies painted a ghostly white with ochre, some dancers carried paintings on their shoulders as they began to move. Their bodies swayed to the drone of the didgeridoo and beat of wooden clapsticks that accompanied the sacred songs. Leading the singers was Sandy Thomas. The lyrics had been revealed to him decades earlier in dreams by beings from the Dreaming or creation period—a revelation of such intense supernatural power it had nearly killed him. Now a grey-haired, wiry old man, he moved with youthful ease, at once singer, master of ceremonies, owner of, and commentator on, the performance, eerily lit by improvised spotlights. Cautious of intruding, I asked him if I could make recordings and photographs. "We know you, Jangala," he replied. "You are always welcome."

My path to that outback night began with dinosaurs. Whether at home in Manhattan, where I was born in 1964, where tiny plastic giants fought for domination of trackless expanses of carpet, or in the old dinosaur halls at the American Museum of Natural History where I was as much frightened as fascinated, at the age of three I became obsessed with them. My childhood interest in paleontology did not last, but it awakened in me a passion to explore the wider world, which has never wavered. My parents did two things that, unknown to them, set me on the path of exploration. They brought me to the AMNH, and they hung a map of the world on the wall next to my bed. As I awoke each morning, I saw Australia and the vast expanse of the Pacific. I knew nothing about them, but remember feeling certain that one day I would go.

I got to the Pacific by a convoluted route. At 16 I volunteered at the AMNH and spent a hot summer cataloguing minerals in an airless storeroom, and later went to an ornithological research station where the only showers were provided by flocks of angry terns. As a Harvard undergraduate, I began studying anthropology, specializing in archaeology, and worked on excavations in England and the Alaska interior. I worked on the Native American gallery at the Peabody Museum and, after graduation, got my first job at the Museum of Science in Boston. I later returned to Harvard and spent two years studying invertebrate zoology.

My interest in the Pacific was rekindled by chance in 1989 when I read Herman Melville's *Typee*, set in the Marquesas Islands. Fascinated, I began reading further and visiting museums and other exhibits on Pacific art and culture. Later that year I went to an exhibition of New Guinea art at a Boston gallery. Together with *Typee*, that exhibition was the turning point. Scarcely a decade after I walked into that gallery, I became the curator of the Pacific collections at The Metropolitan Museum of Art—ironically, not half a mile from where that world map hung on my childhood bedroom wall.

ERIC KJELLGREN is the Evelyn A. J. Hall and John A. Friede Associate Curator for Oceanic Art at The Metropolitan Museum of Art in New York. He received his B.A. *summa cum laude* in Anthropology and M.A. in Organismic and Evolutionary Biology from Harvard. He holds a second masters and doctorate in anthropology from the University of Hawai'i, Manoa. A Fellow of the Royal Geographical Society and former Fulbright scholar, Eric has worked extensively in Australia and the Pacific. He has done field research in Australia, Indonesia, Vanuatu, and Rekohu (the Chatham Islands) and participated in archaeological excavations in England, Alaska, Louisiana and the Marquesas.

Eric has written extensively on Australian Aboriginal art, and also on the arts and cultures of Easter Island, the Marquesas, Borneo, Rekohu, Rotuma, Vanuatu and Hawaii. At the Metropolitan he has curated exhibitions on the arts of Borneo, Easter Island and the Marquesas Islands.

WILLIAM THOMAS

*"Exploration:
expanding our
understanding of
the universe by
acting on our
wildest dreams."*

Gone bamboo in New Guinea.
WILLIAM THOMAS COLLECTION

Better Late Than Never

I have spent much of my adult life exploring the minds of the people living in one of the most remote regions of the world—the unexplored mountains of New Guinea's Central Range. I am determined to conserve New Guinea's magnificent wilderness and the cultures of the people who inhabit it. Most particularly, I have spent my time roaming the forests surrounding the headwaters of the Strickland River with a people known as the Hewa. They were supposed to be cannibals, but they haven't eaten me. Instead they have become my teachers.

My greatest discovery has been that although the Hewa are the stewards of tremendous biological diversity, they make no attempt to live in balance with their natural surroundings. Instead, they describe their lives as a series of small-scale disturbances, continually cutting the forest to plant gardens. By so doing they create a shifting mosaic of open space, grassland, secondary forest and old-growth forest. Since Western science now recognizes the role of disturbance in the promotion of biological diversity, the Hewa were ahead of the curve in understanding the relationship between traditional life and biodiversity. Many attempts at involving native people in conservation have been failures. I believe this is due to our notion that indigenous people have evolved differently than Westerners, i.e. they have developed sophisticated techniques to conserve biological diversity by balancing their needs with those of other creatures. Like many new ideas, this one does not sit well with many people. Yet, it reflects the Hewa perspective on the relationship between tradition and conservation and I may be part of a real breakthrough in conservation.

My *Aha! Moment* came later—in appearance—than most. On Christmas Eve 1988 I was 44 and sitting on a log outside my hut on the hillside above the Urubwai River. I was sipping homemade brew from a tin cup, watching for shooting stars and enjoying the cool, mosquito-free breeze. After tramping around these mountains for over four months, I needed a break. I had reams of notes, but no idea where it would all lead. I had embarked on my graduate degree rather late, was broke, and though I knew what I wanted to do with my Ph.D., I was not sure that the conservation community would ever embrace an anthropologist. In the midst of one of those "What am I doing here?" moments, I was overcome with a wave of nostalgia. Floating up into my consciousness, like newspaper headlines from a film noir, came memories of watching elephants in a parade from my grandfather's shoulders … my mother teasing me as I butchered Chingachgook's name from my favorite TV show, Last of the Mohicans … my friend John, the one-eyed boat-builder, telling me to be patient and my path would appear… and the endless stacks of *National Geographic* magazines. Suddenly it seemed that my entire life had been pointing to this moment. This was what I was meant to do. How and where would remain a mystery for some time, but I finally became comfortable with the notion that mine would be a life of exploration.

The events that had led me here, the prospect that it might never come to more than the privilege of getting to know the Hewa, became my rite of passage. Alone on Christmas Eve with the stars falling, I finally let it go. Exploration became my art. Accepted or not, whatever would be would be. I was doing what I was supposed to.

WILLIAM THOMAS was born in 1954 and raised in Youngstown, Ohio. After spending a few years working in the steel industry, Bill packed it all in and moved to the beach. There he was "adopted" by the Van Duynes, who nurtured his love for adventure, employed him and enabled him to travel. He spent 15 years working with John, Sam, Dave, Tom and John Jr. as a carpenter and travelled around the world. Eventually, he returned to Arizona State University to earn a Ph.D. in Anthropology. His work with the Hewa has been recognized by UNESCO as a "Best Practice" in the use of indigenous knowledge.

Bill is currently working with Conservation International and the National Geographic Society to conserve the watersheds of New Guinea's four great rivers through a program called the Forest Stewards. The Forest Stewards partner the area's cultures with museums, universities and NGOs, granting management rights to these institutions for the limited use of each culture's traditional knowledge. In this way, the conservation of traditions will become the key to their development and the source of a sustainable income.

Bill is married to Patricia Durante, they have a daughter, Theadora, and live in Branchville, New Jersey.

8 The Drifters

Following the light of the sun,
we left the Old World.

—CHRISTOPHER COLUMBUS

Thor Heyerdahl's right-hand man shooting the sun aboard Tigris. CARLO MAURI

Heart's Desire

There is no doubt in my mind that reaching, with Thor Heyerdahl, across the Atlantic in 1970 on the reed boat *Ra II* was my greatest achievement. Two thirds the size of the first *Ra*, and sunk to only 12 inches of freeboard two weeks out of Safi, Morocco, we were dejected at the imminent failure of this second voyage far short of our first attempt. We decided to sail into the Cape Verde Islands another week away and quietly quit. We jettisoned all the weight we could, not even keeping enough food and water for sailing much farther. But the lightening caused her to stabilize, so we tacitly decided to sail on and see if we could at least make a reasonable showing. We reached Barbados in two months with decks awash—suffering salt water sores and severely dehydrated—but we had made it!

I was born in 1928 in Brooklyn. At Boy Scout age I frequently bicycled down to the sea past farms that, at that time, comprised almost all of southern Brooklyn. Sometimes I went alone, sometimes with friends. The target was Floyd Bennett Field, where we were enthralled watching military airplanes take off and land.

*"Exploration is venturing into
the unknown hoping to drive back
the frontiers of ignorance."*

But I had an additional dream that I didn't share. My gaze recurrently wandered from the airfield to the sea and noted ships outbound to the horizon. I watched as the hulls disappeared over the curve of the sea's surface, followed by the superstructure, the masts finally sinking into the vast ocean's blue. A secret phrase I loved was "heart's desire" and what my heart desired was that, just as those ships disappeared from my sight ashore, someday I would sail so far out to sea I could turn 360 degrees around and be completely out of sight of land.

Well, the United States Navy took good care of that! I first went to sea on a destroyer as assistant navigator. Standing on the bridge the ship began to roll under my feet and I had to concentrate on my navigation instead of thrilling to my boyhood dream coming true. But off Korea, deeply sleep-deprived, all four destroyers of my division hit by shore batteries, I told an ex-sailing ship radarman how different I found this from the romance and adventure I'd pictured! He said, "What you need is not a steel ship run by steam but a wooden ship driven by wind!"

Homeward bound, we stopped in Hawaii in time to catch the Transpacific Yacht Race rounding Diamond Head at night. As I watched the brilliant schooner turning the black sea white with bow wave and wake I understood what he meant. The next race was in two years and I was on it!

Months later, at 26, I was the captain sailing her back to Seattle. My next berth was navigator with a marine biologist on an expedition to the South Seas on a 36-foot ketch. The biologist introduced me to Thor Heyerdahl in Tahiti, where his Easter Island expedition was replenishing. The introduction was almost embarrassing as the biologist described me as an excellent celestial navigator, able scuba diver and a strong sailor. Thor obviously filed that description away because in 1969 he invited me to be his first mate, navigator and radioman aboard *Ra*, the first attempt to cross the Atlantic Ocean on a reed boat replicating those used 4,000 years ago. The expedition was to see if those craft were capable of crossing the ocean to communicate the Mediterranean civilizations to Americans then living in a stone age culture. *Ra* broke up 500 miles short of land. Eight days elapsed between radioing Mayday and being rescued.

We tried again the following year on *Ra II*, correcting our mistakes and making it. In 1978, again with Thor, we sailed the reed boat *Tigris* 4,200 miles in over five months from Iraq to the Red Sea via Pakistan around the Horn of Africa. Next my family and I rebuilt *Anne Kristine*, an 1868 Norwegian fishing boat, and sailed her in the 1986 Tall Ships Parade in New York. She was lost at sea nine years later, my insurance cancelled because, for the first time, I wasn't aboard. I was devastated. I replaced the vastness of the sea with the endless sky. I returned to another of my earliest dreams: flying. My Cessna Skyhawk is named *Anne Kristine II*.

CAPTAIN NORMAN BAKER attended Cornell University in Ithaca, New York, for a Bachelor of Civil Engineering. He co-authored, with Barbara Murphy, *Thor Heyerdahl and the Reed Boat Ra. Ra* was covered by *Life* magazine; *Ra II* resulted in a *National Geographic* cover story, and *Tigris* was an inside story.

He also does whitewater canoeing, scuba diving, horseback riding, served on the National Ski Patrol and as an instructor of oceanography with the Naval Reserve.

Norm and Mary Ann's children are Daniel, Elizabeth and Mitchell. Home is Windsor, Massachusetts.

Aboard the Viracocha II *reedship, 1,200 miles off Chile on the way to Easter Island.* ©THOM POLLARD, PHOTO TAKEN BY PHIL BUCK

"The ultimate definition of exploration is the process of diving deep within oneself to discover our own intimate truths. For me, this is catalyzed when taking part in explorations to little-understood regions of the planet."

Born on the Edge of a Mountain

I was a filmmaker for the National Geographic channel on the 2003 *Viracocha II* expedition. Our international team, led by Phil Buck, built an ancient-styled ship of two million totora reeds. It sailed from Chile to Easter Island, shedding light on ancient migration routes, and became only the second ancient-styled reed vessel to reach Easter Island in modern times.

As the youngest of three I was naturally drawn to my big brother, Jeff, the oldest and six years my senior. He was a major influence in everything I did including ultimately defining my life's ambitions of becoming a documentary producer and adventurer-explorer. In my mid-twenties I was working discontentedly as a television reporter in Massachusetts. In 1987 Jeff, a successful graphic designer/illustrator, invited me to join him for ice climbing lessons in New Hampshire's White Mountains. I was completely unsuspecting that this trip would transform my life.

I recall a cold and misty morning. Clouds clung to the sides of the mountains revealing glimpses of perilous rock outcrops and treacherous slopes. What dangers lay hidden behind those clouds? This ice climbing would surely kill me, I thought. I nervously affixed my crampons, wrestled with my ice axes and looked upward tentatively to the icy ramparts of Mt. Willard. Our guide disappeared through a steep chimney. The rope soon tightened on my harness and he called me to follow. I leaned slowly into the ice and front-pointed my first step. I felt the satisfying bite of cold metal on ice pulse throughout my body. A grinding THUD. The tinkle of ice chips sliding beneath me. A rush of excitement. And, a sudden laugh. Jeff looks up and says, "Have fun, buddy."

Suddenly, I feel something I'd never known before. There's no words to describe it. It just feels right. Any adventurer or explorer knows it. We live our lives trying to recapture it, looking to new and distant peaks, wilder and more dangerous rivers, denser jungles, deeper caverns, more treacherous ocean passages. That wonder-filled day catalyzed the beginning of a new 'career' path for me. Everything from that day on was geared to melding my vocation with the world of adventure and exploration.

During that weekend I befriended Marc Chauvin, with whom I would film and produce two documentaries on ice and rock climbing routes of New England. A couple of years later I accompanied Marc as assistant guide on a technical ascent of Mt. McKinley's West Rib route. A severe storm destroyed our tents at over 16,000 feet. We barely survived, three of us cramped into an inadequate snow cave. Realizing that I could handle the extremes without losing my mind, I continued filming. Right then and there, I set my sights on greater goals.

Seeking mentors, I was fortunate to develop a friendship with Bradford and Barbara Washburn. Over the years Brad and I have poured through his films, photos and maps dating back to the 1920s. With both I've filmed dozens of hours of interviews. In 2001 we spent two weeks filming aerials throughout the Alaska Range.

Another defining moment was as high-altitude cameraman for PBS and the BBC on the 1999 Everest expedition that discovered George Mallory's body. Being the only person to have peered into the face of Mallory offered me a chilling look into the final moments of one of our greatest explorers. This experience opened my eyes to how grace and tragedy often walk hand-in-hand.

From months of climbing in the French Alps to a gripping epic on Denali that nearly claimed my life (I lost my toenails) to equally harrowing attempts on 8,000-metre peaks in Pakistan, I always carried still and video cameras.

I have yet to recapture exactly that feeling I had on Mt. Willard. But, if I can instil in my children that same sense of wonder given to me by my now, sadly, late brother, I'll have succeeded.

THOM POLLARD, born in 1961 and brought up in Wilbraham, Massachusetts, is an award-winning documentary producer, director of photography and editor. He has filmed in the most extreme situations around the world, including producing, filming and editing the Emmy Award winning documentary, *Orphan Orca: Saving Springer* for PBS, and *Orca Man* for the National Geographic channel.

Thom travels nationwide presenting motivational and inspirational programs about his adventures. His photographs have been featured in *National Geographic* and dozens of publications and books.

He and wife Kris with boys Will and Sam live in the Mount Washington Valley near Bartlett, New Hampshire.

GENE SAVOY

"Exploration is an unpredictable, tremendous challenge with an opportunity to make a contribution to mankind."

People Magazine's *"Real Indiana Jones"* at the ruins of Gran Pajaten. COURTESY AEFOSC

Lost City of the Incas

Vilcabamba, where the Inca retreated after Cusco fell in 1533 to Francisco Pizarro and his conquistadors, had been abandoned for centuries when I pushed through the rain and jungle in 1964 to discover stone terraces littered with broken pottery. My heart pounded as I wiped away sweat and my mind flashed back in time. I could hear the battle, the clashing of swords. The city had been burned by the Incas and ransacked by the Spaniards. Now flowers grew through charred ceramic tiles—it was surreal.

Men dream of adventure and I'm no exception. I can't remember *not* wanting to be an explorer—I was born in Bellingham, Washington, in 1927 with that dream. I hated school when I was a boy in the 1930s. I would sit listening to our history teacher drone on about the Roman Empire, stressing dates, names and places, and I would gaze out the window, daydreaming back in time and wishing I could visit the antique temples to see for myself. I longed to break away and fly to strange and wondrous places.

The best part of school was vacation when my dad took me to the forests of Oregon and Washington. He taught me how to be patient and to observe. I fell in love with animals. Those were my first adventures. Much later, my brothers and I would explore the Columbia River Gorge and meet with Indians. That I was one sixty-fourth Cherokee was hugely romantic to a boy. It was natural for me to become fascinated with the history, legends and folklore of American Indians.

During World War II, I served on an aircraft carrier and flew as a gunner. When I went to work for the *Peruvian Times* in 1957, I transferred my fascination to the Inca and pre-Inca peoples. I visited the Moche Pyramids of the Sun and Moon, where Indians showed me how to enter secret chambers. I began to develop my own theories—and to use my flying experience with my good friend Mirko. The Incas built roads along river valleys, which we'd follow by air. They had to be there for a purpose! They would lead to ruins! This technique led to discoveries I then explored by foot.

I taught myself archaeology, anthropology and history from reading, study and practical field experience. I simply call myself an explorer and let it go at that. No one explores without a motive and mine was a love of mythology and science. Call it a love of adventure—or manhood wanting to find expression. I became an explorer because of the unpredictable and tremendous challenge. I was disenchanted and bored with an age in which our technology is conquering space and turning civilization into a mechanized mass society, where the individual gets lost in the charge for material gain. To me, South America was the last real frontier, the true Dark Continent untamed. There, a man could get his feet on the ground. There, was an opportunity to make a contribution to man's knowledge.

GENE SAVOY, *People Magazine's* "Real Indiana Jones," achieved international fame in the 1960s with a series of daring expeditions into the Peruvian jungles that led to the discovery of numerous ancient stone cities and settlements. He came to these discoveries as a result of his unique theory that pre-Inca and Inca civilizations originally occupied the tropical rain forests. Gene followed the Vilcabamba discovery later in 1965 by documenting another site, which he named Gran Pajaten. He discovered over 40 additional ruins in the area.

In 1969 Gene built and captained the *Kuviqu*, or *Feathered Serpent I*, a totora reed raft of ancient design, along 2,000 miles of ocean coastline from Peru to Mesoamerica following natural currents. This proved that ancient Peruvians and Mexicans could have maintained contact and the legendary cultural heroes of Peru and Mexico—Viracocha and Quetzalcoatl—were one and the same. From 1977 to 1982 he captained the 60-foot schooner *Feathered Serpent II*, exploring possible sea routes used by ancient civilizations between the Orient and the Americas.

In 1985, he made a startling discovery in Peru's Amazonas—a vast metropolis he named Gran Vilaya that may prove to be one of the largest and most unique cities discovered in the history of archaeology.

From 1977 to 1998 he captained the *Feathered Serpent III-Ophir*, a catamaran of ancient design, from Callao to Hilo, demonstrating that ancient Peruvians could have sailed in large seagoing vessels across the ocean.

In over 50 expeditions in over 40 years, he has made an outstanding contribution to exploration and sailing. He is the author of dozens of books, produced numerous documentaries, belongs to scores of societies, and is the recipient of untold medals, trophies and awards.

Gene resides in Reno, Nevada. He was formerly married to Sylvia Ontaneda Bernales and they have three children, Gene Jr., Sean and Jamila.

CAPTAIN ROBERT "RIO" G. HAHN

Just don't write 'Kick me': the woman is doing a traditional painting with dye from the genipa plant, Darien province, Panama. Pascale Maslin

Necessary Adventure

It is not necessary to live, It is necessary to travel. Ancient Proverb

My most intense exploration moment lasted 36 days. Starting in 1983, I led a 40-month multidisciplinary circumnavigation expedition on board the research vessel *Heraclitus*, an 82-foot, 120-ton, ferro-cement Chinese junk, built by my friends and me in the mid-1970s.

We set out to test the legend that the Chinese had sailed the globe in their junks. We did finally succeed, accomplishing the first, and to date only, around-the-world voyage on the *Heraclitus*. Less than six months into the expedition, the ship nearly sank after running aground in Western Samoa and circumstances forced us to depart prior to completing repairs. Once at sea, the damaged hull began to leak; the engine froze up; all diesel, gasoline and fresh water became

*"My definition of exploration is best exemplified by
Sir Richard Burton, whose "real passion was not for
geographical discovery but for the hidden in man, for
the unknowable, and inevitably the unthinkable." I have a
metaphor I call the Explorers Sword, with one edge in
the external world and one edge in the explorer's. The
sword points to a synergetic goal—of adding to
humanity's store of knowledge, with the hope
of making new discoveries about one's self."*

contaminated with sea water; the three sails were not yet rigged; the ship's radio went dead after sending a distress call; the hydraulic steering failed; and our captain resigned at sea! Thirty-six days later, with only one attempt possible, our seven-person crew made landfall at Vanua Lava Island in the Banks Islands, north of Vanuatu. All were in good health and the ship and our spirits were intact.

The philosopher Heraclitus said, "Out of strife, all things" which aptly describes the birth of my thirst for exploration. The summer I turned 10, my father organized a two-week, 250-mile wilderness canoe trip, starting from Hudson Bay, Canada. Six of us, including our Indian guide, set out with two canoes that we carried, along with all our gear, when making portages. At the end, crossing a lake to rendezvous with our pickup plane, a strong storm blew up, nearly sinking our canoes. Unlike my comrades, who swore off such dangerous endeavors, the experience left me exhilarated and filled with a sense of life. I wanted more!

As my life unfolded, I continually found myself undertaking unconventional adventures with like-minded friends. After sailing the *Heraclitus* from San Francisco to Marseilles, we set off overland across Europe, Turkey, Iran, Afghanistan and Pakistan to India, and later Iraq, always taking the "road less travelled," relentlessly testing our capacity for survival. Annually circling the globe, I developed the ability to be at home in a multitude of cultural and geographical regions. In 1979 I jumped at the opportunity to head up an Amazon expedition. Motoring the R/V *Heraclitus* 2,200 miles up the Amazon, we investigated the use of medicinal plants by shamans, who opened my mind to a new way of experiencing the world. From there my exploring spirit brought me back to the ocean, and later to the mountains of Nepal, where a Hindu Swami initiated me into the sacred use of the deadly *Datura* plant.

It is the exploring spirit that makes us human, that gives us hope and preserves our access to the unknown, from which all our futures emerge.

CAPTAIN ROBERT "RIO" G. HAHN has been referred to as a Renaissance man. Born in 1948 and with approximately 50 expeditions to his credit, he's a Fellow of the Royal Geographical Society; a founding and life member of the Rainforest Club and a Fellow, two-term Director and a past Ombudsman of The Explorers Club. He is a licensed sea captain, a diver, a founding member of the International Society of Ethnopharmacology and was awarded the title of High Chief of Western Samoa.

Rio is also a co-founder, fellow, director and past president of the Institute of Ecotechnics, whose research led to the Biosphere 2 Project, which he co-initiated. He has a B.A. from the University of Pennsylvania with an individualized major in communications, including studies at the Annenberg Graduate School of Communications. He has carried out post-graduate work in microbial technology at Penn and in communications at the University of Arizona. He became an apprentice-in-residence and assistant to Prof. Minor White, founder of the photography department at the Massachusetts Institute of Technology.

He lives in Bonsall, California, a rural area of north San Diego County, with his wife Teresa Fiske, where they track the international adventures of their daughters, Sky, Rachel and Zodiac. There, Rio operates an organic avocado orchard, publishes from his extensive photographic archive and prepares for future explorations.

9 The Easter Islander

If you can dream it, you can do it.
Always remember this whole
thing was started by
a mouse.

—WALT DISNEY

JOHN LORET

The first of many expeditions to Easter Island was with Thor Heyerdahl in 1955. PROPERTY OF
JOHN LORET

When Dreams Were Born

On Easter Island, through pollen analysis, scientific teams I led identified
changes in forestation and climate for 75,000 years; and from coral cores,
past El Niño episodes. We have unearthed evidence of possible cannibalism and,
using C-14 and thermal luminescence, determined when the *ahu* were constructed
and the *moais* overturned. I take great pleasure in pointing out that the current
Chilean government's Chief Archaeologist, Sergio Rapu, is an Easter Islander who
was six when I first arrived in 1955.

My dreams were born in a series of expanding experiences. My most persistent
childhood memories involve an urge to escape from the tiny apartment I shared
with my widowed mother; my father, a fisherman, was lost at sea when I was sev-
en in 1935. By ten, I was on Brooklyn's crowded streets shining shoes, but I felt
hemmed in. I took the subway to the end of the line and would walk back, stopping

*An explorer must contribute
new information to the
human pool of knowledge.*

at bars. My profits increased as did my horizons. At twelve, I worked in a bowling alley setting pins. On weekends I carried blocks of ice, coal or two five-gallon cans of kerosene up as many as four flights to customers. These experiences developed, in me a solid work ethic, a feeling of freedom and strong self-confidence.

As a teenager during World War II, I wondered what exotic ports Liberty ships were bound for. How I wished I could be aboard! A dream! I would also see fishing vessels coming and going; soon I was a deckhand. At sixteen, I changed my birth certificate, dropped out, and enlisted in the navy. I was sent to deep-sea diving school—a skill that impacted my future in ways I couldn't foresee.

After the war, I joined the Coast Guard and was assigned to the icebreaker *Eastwind* that served research scientists. My duties on the bridge allowed me to consult with them. Influenced, I began reading adventure books, raced through Peary, Byrd, Nansen, Amundsen and became fascinated with their commitment to explore the unknown. A dream was born to become one of them. The highlight came in 1948 when we broke into the Lincoln Sea, part of the Arctic Ocean, achieving the farthest northerly point ever navigated. We were also first to circumnavigate Baffin Island. I realized that if I wished to live the adventurous life of an explorer, I had to continue my education.

On completion of my B.S., with the assistance of my friend Leif Strand, I received a summer school scholarship at the University of Oslo. There, I was fortunate to study with outstanding professors including explorer and oceanographer Harald U. Sverdrup and Fredrick Bear. I enjoyed my experience so much that I sought a graduate degree in Oslo. During my studies, I volunteered to go to the Canary Islands to collect algae. In Las Palmas, I set up camp on a beautiful beach. The next day while diving, my money and equipment were stolen. How would I complete my assignment? Fortunately, I knew that Thor Heyerdahl was vacationing there. Since his legendary *Kon Tiki* expedition, Heyerdahl and his crew were my idols. I asked him for help.

This tall, gentle, soft-spoken man, with the iciest blue eyes I have ever seen, showed real interest in my work. He gave me money to rent a room. The next day while we were snorkelling together, a shark visited us. Later, Thor revealed that this was his first underwater encounter with one.

In the summer of 1955 I learned of his upcoming expedition to Easter and the Society Islands. This was what I had been waiting for! A telephone call to Oslo confirmed that the one spot he had to fill—a seaman/diver—was mine! I was about to realize my dream as a member of the Norwegian Archaeological Expedition.

JOHN H. LORET, PH.D., is a marine biologist. He is Professor Emeritus of Queens College, City University of New York. John is currently Executive Director of the Science Museum of Long Island and past president of The Explorers Club, 1993-96.

He served as associate scientist aboard the Norwegian research vessels *H.U. Sverdrup* and *H.H. Gran* in 1961–1964, and was a research scientist with the Norwegian Institute of Water Research. As a member of the 1968 CEDAM expedition, he dove in the sacred well at Chichen Itza, Mexico, which was covered by *National Geographic*. John has developed more than 35 expeditions. In 1995, he served as chief scientist aboard the M/V *Itasca*, sailing the Northwest Passage, the first private yacht to do so, west to east, in a single season. For the past ten years, he has led scientific teams to Easter Island.

He and his late wife Elisa have three children, Erik, Leah and Mary.

10 Keeping Up with the Indiana Jones – the Archaeologists

The important thing is not to stop questing. Curiosity has its own reason for existing. One cannot help but be in awe when he contemplates the mysteries of eternity, of life, of the marvelous structure of reality. It is enough if one tries merely to comprehend a little of this mystery every day. Never lose a holy curiosity.

—ALBERT EINSTEIN

GARY ZIEGLER

Overlooking Peru's Apurimac Canyon. AMY FINGER

Temple of the Sun

Inti, the great Inca sun god, rises golden from the distant peaks of the cordillera over Machu Picchu several kilometers away. From our position at Llactapata, where Machu Picchu's sun temple observatory is, solstice sunlight races precisely down the long corridor before us, illuminating the carefully aligned stone walls of the temple. We stand transfixed, realizing the significance of our find!

Although my earlier years were influenced by travels and outdoor life with mineral-collecting and bird-studying parents, my dream began while studying at Colorado College in 1962. I remember the moment—one of those rare flashes of inspiration that can change lives. While daydreaming in a boring literature class, Robert Service's poem *Call of the Wild* was introduced: "Let us probe the silent places, let us seek what luck betides us … and the wild is calling, calling let us go." Something clicked … this moment inspired visions of lost civilizations and great summits to be conquered. That became my life's focus.

*"Exploration is an ongoing quest
to reveal secrets and mysteries—and
in my case, of the Inca."*

That year, I was recommended by the American Alpine Club for a job with the fledgling Peace Corps at the new training camp in Puerto Rico. A few weeks in the Washington, D.C., office with dynamic personalities like Patrick Moynihan and Bill Moyers, followed by survival training and cliff hanging in Puerto Rico, sent me off on bold new adventures fuelled by the positive "can do" idealism of those times. Later, with a fresh philosophy degree in hand, head full of Hegel, Jaspers, Heidegger and existential self-determination, a climbing friend and I hitchhiked to Peru—launching a lifelong odyssey of adventure, exploration and discovery.

Returning to Colorado, I purchased a ranch, learned cowboy ways, roped cows, packed horses and guided for Outward Bound. As outdoor adventure vacations became cool, I formed an adventure travel service, Adventure Specialists, which became the means of funding ongoing expeditions and explorations.

I've been poking around Peru's rugged Vilcabamba region for decades, finding and studying forgotten ruins. Each season's explorations found something significant but the crowning achievement may be Llactapata. I believe in teamwork. The old adage "the sum of the whole is greater than its parts" is true. My successes are largely due to combining skills, talent, drive and energy with positive, like-minded others to achieve a common objective. It is just such a team that rediscovered the lost Inca complex almost a stone's throw from famous Machu Picchu.

Conquest historian John Hemming and the Royal Geographical Society supported our expedition. British author/historian Hugh Thomson did the research. Colorado archaeo-astronomer J. McKim Malville identified astronomical alignments. British Cusco resident ornithologist Barry Walker and railroad owner Nichlas Asheshov handled logistics. Australian John Leivers led the field crew. Inca scholar Tom Zudemia helped with interpretation. I contributed management, archaeological and surveying skills. Together, along with a strong team of enthusiastic machete-swinging helpers, we uncovered and charted an unknown, large complex of ceremonial buildings, roads and an extensive urban settlement closely associated with Machu Picchu.

Each new season brings a return to Peru. The wild is calling. Let us go!

Explorer, archaeologist, mountaineer, sailor, cowboy and sometime philosopher, GARY ZIEGLER was born in 1941 and grew up on skis in Colorado. He ran the first Pikes Peak Marathon in 1956 and again 50 years later in 2005. Graduating from Colorado College, he led an American Alpine Club expedition to Peru in 1964, later climbing 14 peaks above 20,000 feet, including seven first ascents over 18,000 feet. He completed graduate studies in archaeology at San Marcos, Peru's national university, and served with Army Special Forces and the Australian SAS in Vietnam, leaving as a Captain.

He and Amy Finger operate the 3,500-acre Bear Basin Ranch near Westcliffe, Colorado. Gary has served as County Sheriff, volunteer fireman, trained the local search/rescue unit, and volunteers as commander of the Sheriff's Mounted Horse Patrol. He is an experienced ocean sailor, having crewed on a square rigger and sailed his own chartered boats around South and Central America, the Caribbean and the Aegean.

Gary's explorations in Peru include discoveries of the Inca ruins of Lisascayhauana, Cota Coca and Llactapata. He led part of the National Geographic team that located and excavated Corihuayrachina. He has co-directed and is featured in films for the Discovery and National Geographic channels, BBC, Reader's Digest, Lonely Planet and has been a guest expert on National Public Radio's Science Friday program. He is published in numerous publications and has written a book, *Beyond Machu Picchu*. Gary is a Fellow of the Royal Geographical Society of London, The Explorers Club and a sometime lecturer at Colorado College.

GREG DEYERMENJIAN

"To go beyond what you've done before, to go beyond where you've been, to go beyond where anyone is known to have been—and to come back and tell about it—that's exploration!"

At the Petroglyphs of Pusharo.
GREGORY DEYERMENJIAN

A Quest for Paititi— Farthest Reach of the Incas

During the past 24 years, I have sustained the search for Paititi, and other Incan sites lost in the mountains and jungles beyond Cusco, Peru, documenting more sites in those remote areas than had previously been known to exist. I reached legendary sites for the first time, such as the peaks of Apu Catinti (1986) and Callanga's Llaqtapata (1995), the Pyramids of Paratoari (1996), the Lago de Angel (1999), and the farthest reach of the Incas directly north of Cusco, the Ultimo Punto (2004). I maintained firm friendships and brotherhood with my Peruvian expedition partners, be they highland Quechua-speaking descendants of the Incas, Machiguenga tribal Indians of the jungles or Spanish-speaking explorers and researchers from cities like Cusco, Arequipa or Lima.

The road that led me to become an explorer was not born of a single epiphany, and really began with a feeling that just developed within me, a process. From as far back as I can remember—as a three-year-old in 1952 in Watertown, Massachusetts, watching sunrays streaming mysteriously through a window, illuminating dust particles suspended magically in the air; or, as a pre-adolescent in Boston, obsessed with collecting stamps from archaic semi-autonomous territories—some atavistic impulse had been at work, making me long for the ancient and the exotic. Ongoing fortunate circumstance—my mother's affection for archaeology, my father's love of history, my years at Boston Latin School with its emphasis on the ancient world—nurtured this impulse.

But subsequent fortuitous events gave dramatic form and direction to this generalized proclivity towards things far away and long ago. One fine day my assigned roommate during my first year at the University of Massachusetts unfurled a map of South America and launched into an oration on the continent's unique history so impassioned that I distinctly remember the map shimmering before my eyes! I was instantly infected with his geographical obsession.

And another epiphany came when I was in Cusco in 1981, having just returned from a journey to the site of Vilcabamba, the redoubt of Manco Inca in the tropical forests northwest of Machu Picchu. The area was first touched upon by Hiram Bingham but not definitively located and identified until its rediscovery 50 years later by Gene Savoy and Antonio Santander Caselli. A jungle guide wished to make me aware of the possibility of other sites still hidden in the jungles far to the east. He placed before me an old copy of a book about Paititi, the legendary ultimate Incan refuge. The name just struck me, and I can still conjure in my mind exactly how the weathered cover of the book looked and felt. The ongoing quest to find and identify lost Incan sites further into the eastern jungles then became the latest addition to that continuous thread begun so many years before.

GREGORY DEYERMENJIAN'S specialty has been investigating tropical forest areas of South America to see what ancient civilizations lie there. He has organized and led over a dozen expeditions into the jungle-covered mountains and hills of southeast Peru, where he and his team are seeking the farthest reach of the ancient Incas and investigating the legend of Paititi. This quest has also included following an unmapped Incan stone road farther into the cloud forests than anyone since Incan times; the discovery of the large highland lake now named Lago de Angel; and identifying the farthest reach of the Incas beyond that. His team was the first to reach, film and fully document the true nature of the Pyramids of Paratoari—large pyramidal formations in the Manu jungle first identified by a NASA satellite photograph 20 years before.

Additionally, in 1992 he was a participant in an expedition investigating the true route of the conquistador Francisco de Orellana through eastern Ecuador, and in 1997 he was co-leader of an expedition into northernmost Brazil, seeking the origin of the El Dorado legend. He has carried The Explorers Club flag on 10 expeditions.

Greg's day gig is as a psychologist for the Massachusetts Department of Mental Retardation. He is blessed with a beautiful and wildly perceptive Peruvian wife who accompanies him in the exploration zones, and two wonderful young children who make him laugh heartily when not on expedition. They live in Everett, Massachusetts.

PAULINO MAMANI

"For me, this is exploration: following what you feel in your heart, going and seeking what your heart tells you must be sought...."

Jungle buddies: With a Machiguenga native, Río Sinkibenia, soon after leaving the Petroglyphs of Pusharo, 1991. GREGORY DEYERMENJIAN

In Search of the Lost Realms of his Incan Ancestors

My greatest achievement would be the series of "firsts" and "farthests" I've made as principal pathfinder within the mountains and jungles of remote southeastern Peru: the first ascent of the tropical peak of Llaqtapata in the Callanga jungle; reaching the Pyramids of Paratoari in the Manu rain forest; discovering the Lago de Angel in the high Meseta de Pantiacolla; and discovering the farthest reach of the Inca directly to the north of Cusco at Último Punto.

I was born in 1964 and grew up in the shadow of the high peaks of the Andes of Peru. My father, Sr. Victor Mamani, was a *campesino*, a man who worked his farm, growing his potatoes and grazing his cattle, on his *chacara*, his cultivated settlement. He went blind at 50, some say because of a curse from a thief he had castigated, but he could always play hauntingly beautiful music on his simple Andean flute. We were way out in the lonely mountains of the Paucartambo mountain range that overlooks the high-altitude jungle of the Amazon basin. From as early as I can remember, I always heard tales of the legendary lost city of Paititi that lay beyond where my family lived, toward the jungles below. I listened to my father tell these stories of what lay beyond the perpetual mists of our highland world, and I listened to the tales told him by other campesinos who visited him when passing through our little settlement at Umapata.

These stories, of gold and mystery and an enchanted city of stone, were a part of my daily life. The things left by the Incas—their pottery and metal ornaments and the vestiges of their stone roads—were all around, too. Even my dreams came to be filled with images of that magical world described by my father! How could I not grow up to be an explorer, to seek this Paititi?

So, when two explorers, American Gregory Deyermenjian and Englishman Michael Mirecki, came to my family when I was 20 seeking horses and people to accompany them on a journey towards the jungles, to seek Paititi, my opportunity had come. I went along, and we've been exploring my beloved mountains and forests ever since. We haven't found Paititi yet, but each expedition we get closer. Someday ....

PAULINO MAMANI is a Peruvian descendant of those who were part of the Incan empire in southeastern Peru. He has been chief pathfinder for many expeditions into the Amazon jungle, and has made a multitude of solo reconnaissance journeys into lonely areas where none but the ancient Incas preceded him. His exceptional skills include those of machete man, cook, navigator, cartographer, boatman, mechanic, healer-medic, shaman, linguist (Quechua, Spanish and Machiguenga) and hunter.

He was elected a Fellow of The Explorers Club in 1996, the year he was principal guide for Gregory Deyermenjian's expedition to the famous "Pyramids of Paratoari"—the pyramidal formations in the jungles of Peru's Manu region which they were first to reach, explore and report upon. In 2004 their expedition found and documented the farthest reach of the Incas directly to the north of Cusco.

Paulino lives with his wife and three kids beyond the reach of electricity or road at his *chacara* in the valley of the Rio Mapacho, in the province of Calca.

He has the rural Peruvian equivalent of high school.*

*(Editor's note: translated from Spanish by Gregory Deyermenjian.)

11 Curse of the Mummies

I long to set foot where no man has trod before.

—CHARLES DARWIN

Flushed with excitement while exiting the tomb of vizier Merefnebef (ca. 2300 B.C.E.) after its discovery. Zbigniew Kosc

Born Archaeologist

The discovery of the rock-hewn tomb of vizier Merefnebef (Fefi) at Saqqara, in a place where no scholar ever expected to find anything else than an ancient rubbish heap, was my greatest discovery. I can't describe the thrill! The tomb turned out to be a masterpiece of Egyptian art and a unique historical source of the period when Pharaohs' power first started shaking things up.

"I learned that exploration is like the main concept of medical treatment: primum non nocere, first do no harm—to monuments or to people. The most important thing is a feeling of responsibility for nature, for whatever you may have excavated."

My audacious explorer's dreams were born together with me. Perhaps even slightly earlier! My mother gave me life one year before the end of World War II in a poor family living in a small village in southeastern Poland. I am sure it was in her womb that I developed my taste for drama and mystery. A few months after I was born, the region was abandoned by the Nazis and taken over by the Red Army. This event may, though subconsciously, have tremendously contributed to my interest in history. The "transfer" was accompanied by the defeated players expelling the entire population of the neighbouring town, burning down one building after another.

I will never forget the enormous field of ruins as the stage of our plays during my first school years. We organized ourselves into clandestine gangs or squads, and loved crossing forests playing partisans, but we did not share the passion of our contemporaries looking for mines or bombs. Many never returned. Our command was headed by a brave girl who swore she was going to become a sea captain. She eventually became a housewife (trained in geography, though!), but her exuberant, adventurous spirit left indelible traces in my consciousness.

We held meetings in cellars, the only remaining rooms of the ex-houses. This inspired my imagination. I tried to reconstruct the life of those who just passed away out of the scanty remains of their belongings. Their personalities started emerging from the darkness. Each object found was becoming a page of history.

Would the artifacts left by ancient Egyptians, and later covered with sands, allow a similar reconstruction?

However, the stronger I dreamed, the weaker were the chances to go anywhere. Crossing any border was unthinkable in Poland under Stalin. His death surprised everybody, because we could hardly believe he would not be living forever. The first travel abroad then became possible! Unbelievable, a dream was coming true! I was fourteen. Today, travel to the moon would not impress me as much as stepping on the soil of our neighbour in those days. I decided when I first heard the news that travel was possible that the world must belong to me!

But that question born in those World War II ruins continued tormenting me for years until I read the name of professor Kazimierz Michałowski in Polish newspapers. The founder of what used to be called the "Polish School of Mediterranean Archaeology" had discovered a temple of a pharaoh in a place much explored by various archaeologists before him. Looking for another pharaonic temple in Sudanese Nubia, he found a medieval cathedral with marvelous paintings decorating its walls. This permanent play between imagination and reality fascinated me enormously. I never looked back.

PROFESSOR KAROL MYSLIWIEC is Director of the Research Centre for Mediterranean Archaeology in the Polish Academy of Sciences and a professor of Egyptian archaeology at Warsaw University, where he studied Mediterranean archaeology. His field experience started in 1969 in Egypt, where he subsequently lived for nearly ten years, participating in various excavations in Alexandria, Deir el-Bahari and the Qurna temple of Pharaoh Seti I. He also excavated in Palmyra, Syria; Qadero, Sudan; and Nea Paphos, Cyprus. He was a fellow of the Alexander von Humboldt-Stiftung in Munich, Germany, for two years.

After returning to Poland in 1979, he started teaching, both in Poland and in other countries, particularly in Vienna, where he is a frequent visiting professor. From 1985 to 1995 he directed the Polish-Egyptian rescue excavations at Tell Atrib in Lower Egypt, discovering part of the town built in the time of Alexander the Great, including artists' and artisans' workshops. In 1987, Karol initiated Polish-Egyptian excavations at Saqqara, west of the world's oldest pyramid, explorations he annually continues to this day.

Among his sensational discoveries in Saqqara, documented on the Discovery and National Geographic channels, are rock-hewn, superbly decorated tombs of the highest noblemen from the late Old Kingdom (circa 2300 B.C.E.). He is the author of approximately 300 scholarly publications, including 15 books in seven languages, including his highly acclaimed *Eros on the Nile*. Karol has lectured all over the world. Since 2004, he has been a corresponding member of the Polish Academy of Sciences.

Holding mummified brain material.
Lou Scaglione

"Exploring is the state of human physical and intellectual endeavours that discover the myriad unknown secrets of the universe. Thus my childhood dreams of discovery unlocked an even more interesting Pandora's box, leading to ongoing investigations in the history of mankind and biological evolution."

Dreams, the Nectar of Adventurous Brains

There I was, suddenly confronted with a mummified hand of an ancient Egyptian girl who had died about 2,500 years ago. I had no experience whatsoever in the examination of such specimens. However, at the time, I was examining human tissues at very high magnifications using an electron microscope. I took a snippet of skin, softened it with various solutions, and embedded the material in resin. When the thin sections were examined under the electron microscope—I was absolutely amazed to note that most of these ancient skin cells were beautifully preserved with intact nuclei and cellular components!

I just could not believe that the wonderful preservation of these tissues were hundreds of years old! I was overcome with a generalized excitement of orgiastic proportions, and rushed from one colleague to another with the photographic evidence of my discovery—the first time ancient Egyptian cells had been so well visualized! From these observations I knew at least in part some of the chemistry of the cells was intact, like proteins and genetic components, and that this would revolutionize not only the investigation of ancient mankind, but also ancient animals, plants and micro-organisms.

That was really the second epiphany leading me on the path to becoming a medical archaeologist. The first one was equally dramatic. I was born in Jerusalem, but grew up in Alexandria, Egypt, where I lived from 1939 to 1953, and where I was surrounded by the remains of ancient Egypt's glorious past. As a 12-year-old boy in the fall of 1947, while exploring an old Greco-Roman cemetery in Canopus near Alexandria, I suddenly slipped into a hole in the sandy rubble that led to a darkened underground chamber. I was gripped with utter excitement accompanied by sweaty palpitations at the thought that I may have found an ancient Egyptian royal tomb, filled with golden treasures, even more splendid than that of Tutankhamen!

Alas, it turned out to be an already desecrated catacomb with the floor covered by potsherds, a few bones and an occasional funerary lamp. However this memorable event so stimulated my subconscious mind, I kept having flashbacks of finding untold ancient treasures.

Time went on, I left Egypt to study medicine in London, England, and then on to Toronto. It was there in 1966, while a research fellow in pathology at the Banting Institute of the University of Toronto, that I was contacted by the Curator of the Egyptian Department of the Royal Ontario Museum. She had heard about my interest in Egyptology, and felt I might find interesting pathology in that specimen. Well, I sure did!

But the story doesn't end there. My seminal paper was published in the British scientific publication *Nature* and was quoted not long after by Dr. George Poinar, who extracted DNA from insects embedded for millions of years in amber. Dr. Michael Crichton then used Poinar's work as the basis of his bestseller *Jurassic Park*, which was subsequently made into the blockbuster movie of the same name.

DR. PETER LEWIN is a pediatrician at the Hospital for Sick Children, Toronto; Assistant Professor in Pediatrics at the University of Toronto; and has a private practice. Besides performing the first electron microscopy of ancient Egyptian mummified tissues, he pioneered the latest radiological imaging (two and three dimensional CT scans) in archaeology. He is a founding member of the International Paleopathology Association.

Peter has published many scientific papers, particularly on his pioneering work with infectious proteins that cause neuro-degenerative disease in animals (Scrapie and BSE) and humans (Kuru, Creutzfeld-Jakob).

Honours include being appointed the personal physician to Queen Elizabeth, the Queen Mother, during her 1974 visit to Canada. He also received the 1998 History of Medicine Spaulding Certificate awarded by the Associated Medical Services of Canada; the Canadian Decoration with Clasp; the Order of St. John of Jerusalem (Serving Brother); and the Canadian Order of Military Merit, in the rank of Officer (O.M.M.). He is a retired colonel in the Canadian armed forces.

12 Raging Rivers, Gorgeous Gorges

Of the gladdest moments in human life, methinks, is the departure on a distant journey into unknown lands, shaking off, with one mighty effort, the fetters of habit, the leaden weight of routine, the cloak of many cares, and the slavery of home ....

—ZANZIBAR, SIR RICHARD FRANCIS BURTON

JERZY "YUREK" MAJCHERCZYK

"An explorer is the first, the conqueror, the discoverer. To be where no other has stepped foot."

Yurek, front left, shooting the Colca Canyon. Zbigniew Bzdak/Canoandes '79

Embraced by the Colca Canyon

I was part of the expedition that first conquered Peru's Colca Canyon—believed to be the world's deepest at that time. *National Geographic* and the 1984 *Guinness Book of World Records* featured the canyon and used us on its cover.

In 1979 the Polish Student Kayaking Expedition Canoandes '79 embarked on a journey lasting almost three years. We followed our dream to run virgin rivers in the Americas, conquering twenty-five. The most challenging was the Colca. On May 18, 1981, we descended in pursuit of our passion for exploration, conquest, and to challenge our kayaking and survival skills. And we did it for the Polish Pope, who on that day was shot in Rome. We carried his picture on our truck and believed it protected us.

We began on furious waters running between vertical walls over 3,000 metres tall, dropping 50 to 100 metres for each kilometre. We had two old fiberglass kayaks, a 14-foot raft with dozens of patches, and food for only seven days as we had no money. We believed in ourselves as a team of six experienced friends, in our destiny and in God. The first 11 days we advanced only 44 kilometres, running what we could while portaging around 21 Class VI rapids. Day two our raft flipped. We barely managed to save it and our scant provisions. For me as raft captain this was crushing. Later we lost a kayak and our raft floor broke. We were mentally and physically drained when, on day 11, we came across an Indian oasis—Canco. After a 10-day recovery we resumed, fighting the most difficult rapids ever. Seven days later, we emerged, completing the impossible and marking my greatest exploratory achievement.

I was told I swam before I walked. As a baby, my siblings left me in my carriage and went swimming. I rattled it—and sent it downhill into the river! Through some miracle I floated until rescued! This was only a foretelling of my love for water. It was my father, a barrel maker and farmer, who instilled dreams of going beyond the horizon. I grew up in the small historic town of Siewierz in communist Poland, where my family sometimes went days without food. My father hunted illegally, bringing back not only food but wild stories of surviving in the forest for days while avoiding the militia. This fed my imagination for adventure. He taught me to be unafraid and to cross all barriers if I believe they are not correct.

My fervent dream of exploring culminated when Polish explorer Stanislaw Szwarc-Bronikowski came to school when I was 12—showing us pictures of the Amazon that until this day I remember. He concluded with: "I plant within you the seeds of exploration, and I hope that within one of you they will grow." Thirty years later, I sponsored him into The Explorers Club.

I first saw a kayak as a student in Krakow. On my way to university, I crossed over a bridge and looked down into the river. I was captivated—frozen!—to see them manoeuvring. That rush, along with my love for water, made up my mind to become a kayaker. My first navigation on a very easy Class I river was a disaster. My friend Janusz and I broke a two-person kayak in half. All night we reglued it to avoid being expelled from the sports club we initially joined.

JERZY "YUREK" MAJCHERCZYK of Wallington, New Jersey, was born in 1952. In 1972, he co-founded Krakow's "Bystrze" (Rapid) Academic Kayaking Club. He ran dozens of European rivers, and organized the Canoandes'79 expedition, one of the longest of the 20th century.

Canoandes'79's 33-day odyssey shooting Colca Canyon was named by *Paddler* magazine as one of the "World's Top 10 River Expeditions," and Yurek as one of "20 Legends of Paddling" as well as being listed in the magazine's "Paddlers of the Century" article in January, 2000.

In 1981, he co-organized the Office of Solidarity in Lima. In 1982, dangerously ill with typhus, he escaped Peru's Maoist guerrillas (later the Shining Path), arriving in New York with $44. After receiving political asylum, he continued his campaign.

Yurek is a founder of the Polish Chapter of The Explorers Club, member of the Polish Institute of Arts & Sciences of America, and president of the Polish American Travelers Club. In 2003 he was decorated with the Knight Cross of Polonia Restituta by Poland's president. As well, he was granted Honorary Citizenship from the City of Arequipa.

He has authored hundreds of articles and three books, including *The Conquest of Rio Colca*. With wife Margaret and sons Paul, Peter and Michael, he runs a travel agency in New Jersey.

EUGENE BUCHANAN

Competing in the FIBArk event on the Arkansas River in Saleda, Colorado. Jeff Moab

"As a paddler involved with exploration, it's not as important to me to be the first to dip my paddle somewhere as it is to personally explore something for the first time (we call it a personal first descent) —and to go with an open heart and itinerary towards people, cultures and respect for the environment."

The Song my Paddle Sings

Using the winnings from W.L. Gore & Associates 1992 Shipton Tilman Grant, we ran Siberia's Bashkaus River, billed as the most difficult run in the former Soviet Union. That 28-day trip with a team of 10 Latvians on homemade catarafts was probably my greatest achievement in river running. But exploration of water-ways by watercraft started years before one beautiful day ....

"Go ahead, kiss the wall."

"Now?" I asked.

Wait, wait a sec ... okay, now!" said the guide behind the oars, spinning our raft at the last moment until my lips aligned perfectly with Tiger Wall on Yampa Canyon of Colorado's Yampa River.

Holding onto my dad's lifejacket with one hand while standing on the tube for balance, I leaned over the churning water and puckered up. My lips felt the cool wall, streaked black with stripes of desert varnish, and the coarseness of its sand-stone, before the moment quickly passed and the current carried us away.

It wasn't my first kiss. I had kissed my parents, siblings and other relatives, and even Eleanor Roller at recess in second grade. But at just nine years old, it was my first amorous act toward a rock. It was only a split second during a five-day trip through the towering walls of Dinosaur National Monument, but I remember it to this day. Not because my tongue still bears blisters, but because it launched a deep appreciation, deeper than the gorge we were traversing, of canyons and the rivers that carve them—and a dream. The year was 1972, the rest of the country was in the Class v whitewater of Vietnam and the hydraulics of Watergate. But that kiss sealed a future that would revolve around rivers.

Fast forward 13 years to my first year out of college when working as Sports Editor for Colorado's *Telluride Times*. *River Runner* magazine's annual *River Runner* Rendezvous came to town. I remember thinking that the magazine's editor, Ken Hulick, had the best job in the world. Little did I know it would soon be mine.

By then I had spent two seasons guiding rafting and sea kayaking trips in Alaska, another on Colorado's Arkansas River, and had even helped organize a private trip down the Grand Canyon. Paddling, and whitewater kayaking in particular, was firmly in my blood. While working as a business reporter two years later in Denver I received a call from Mr. Hulick saying he was looking for a journalist and safety kayaker to join an expedition on Ecuador's Quijos River. I jumped at the chance, and three months later, having burned through my limited vacation time, and unable to relate my stories to co-workers around the water cooler, I quit to join another expedition to Peru's Tambopata River.

By now I had convinced Mr. Hulick to let me have a column. After freelancing, and working the media side of an international skiing tour, I found myself interviewing for the editor's position of *Paddler* magazine. An entrepreneur had bought up four titles, including *River Runner*, and merged them into one serving canoeing, kayaking and rafting.

Even now, with kids and living just a block away from the Yampa that started it all—the last remaining free-flowing tributary of the Colorado River—some of these memories are as clear as the spring-fed creek at Jones Hole. And this reaffirms that even kissing a rock can shape your future.

EUGENE BUCHANAN of Steamboat Springs, Colorado, is the past long-time publisher and editor-in-chief of *Paddler* magazine and now holds these positions with *Paddling Life*. A business/economics graduate of Colorado College, where he captained his NCAA lacrosse team, the former ski patrol, kayak instructor and sea kayak and raft guide also enjoys a successful freelance career. He is the author of *Brothers on the Bashkaus* and has had articles published in the *New York Times, Men's Journal, Sports Afield, Outside, National Geographic Adventure, Adventure Journal, Ski, Powder, Bike* and other national publications.

Eugene is an avid adventurer with several first descents to his credit, including Colombia's Rio Negro. His passion for travelling, writing and paddling has taken him to more than 30 countries on six continents. He lives with his wife, Denise, and two daughters, Brooke and Casey. Although he enjoys white water, he also regularly embarks on multi-day rafting trips with his family on the tranquil waters of the Southwest.

RICHARD FISHER

Searching the Bungle Bungle sandstone canyonlands of the Kimberly Plateau, Western Australia. Richard Fisher

Canyoneer

For many years, the Yarlung Zangbo in eastern Tibet was known to be among the deepest valleys in the world. Its inaccessibility meant that its depth could not be directly measured—until 1993, when, after 10 years of trying, explorer Richard Fisher obtained the permits he needed to visit the area. British botanist Francis Kingdon Ward explored the Yarlung Zangbo at the beginning of the century, but no other Westerners were able to do so until Fisher led his expedition there.—Guinness Book of World Records, 1996

I was born in Washington, D.C., in 1952 and brought up in Indiana, Texas and California, but mostly in the canyon state of Arizona. From my earliest years, I was inspired by legends of a young man from the hills of Judea who bounced rocks off lions stalking his goats and, as he grew older, hunted giants with his slingshot. In later years, my inspiration came from the biography of Crazy Horse, the great Sioux chief who invested his efforts protecting his people and their way of life.

*"To be an explorer: one must imagine,
conceptualize, recognize, document, publish, defend
and ultimately survive the challenges of your critics."*

One day as a boy of 16 I discovered that if I could find water in the hidden canyons, I could enjoy and learn from nature year round. In a revelation in the late 1970s, I realized many of the most fantastic canyonlands in Arizona and Utah had never been professionally photographed. And in the 1980s and 1990s, that was true of canyons worldwide, opening up a career of incredible cultural, geographical, and historical discoveries.

I found my vocation during my college years when I discovered the Tarahumara Indians in the nearby Copper Canyon of Mexico's Sierra Madre. They still ran races of more than 100 miles, outlaw cowboys riding tough mules who made their living by growing hemp, and woman who still made their daily bread by hand. This was the life for me. I eventually experienced this lifestyle in canyonlands worldwide and brought the stories home to be shared.

My publishing career began in September, 1982, when the editor of *Arizona Highways* magazine contacted me on an urgent matter concerning my photography of West Clear Creek. The U.S. Congress was considering designating this canyon as a national wilderness, but no one had any photographs at all. Following my article, the canyon was subsequently designated a National Wilderness Area. My career has followed this path on a national and international basis since. My objective since 1990 has been to document photographically the earth's deepest canyons and record ancient tribal knowledge before these landscapes are lost to development and the native peoples absorbed.

Beginning in the American Southwest, I expanded into the extensive canyonlands of Mexico, Bolivia, China, USA , Tibet, Greece, Ethiopia, Australia, Spain, France, Namibia, South Africa, Venezuela, Bosnia, Monte Negro and Corsica. While doing so, I have guided over 1,000 special people on five continents—deaf, blind, juvenile delinquents, Native American youth and educational groups. Guiding, combined with photography, led to the publication of seven books, including *Copper Canyon Mexico*, and more than 100 articles in five languages in such magazines as *National Geographic, Outside, Readers Digest* and *Smithsonian* since 1985.

I have been very fortunate to be the first American to explore the earth's deepest canyon, in Tibet; assist the canyons of the Mogollon Rim, like West Clear Creek, to acquire National Wilderness Area designation; discover and sponsor the only championship ultra-long-distance Tarahumara Indian racing team (and deliver over 150 tons of famine relief since 1992); to be the only American to photographically document the largest crystals ever discovered, in Chihuahua, Mexico; to reconnect the ancient knowledge of the Hohokam and the Anasazi of the Chaco Canyon to the scientific world of archaeology; and to complete the first comprehensive documentary of all of Earth's great canyons. I feel honored and blessed to have been "chosen" to make these six significant discoveries and/or additions to human knowledge.

RICHARD FISHER is a name synonymous with canyons. He has a B.S. in Education from the University of Arizona. As a freelance photographer, climber, river runner and wilderness guide he's stacked up many first descents. He has dedicated his life to the preservation and sharing of canyons around the world.

Rick has a daughter, Mariah Sierra Williams Fisher, and lives in Tucson, Arizona.

MIKAEL STRANDBERG

-50°F along Russia's Kolyma River and loving it. Mikael and Titti Strandberg

"The true explorer is unselfish, curious and ready to sacrifice his life in the quest of discovering unknown areas and human limits. An explorer's life is a mission to make this earth of ours a better one to live in."

Bone Marrow and Fried Reindeer Brain

The day in April 2005 I arrived at the small Siberian settlement of Kolymskaya was the happiest of my exploring life. It was the end of the most demanding part of my expedition along the Kolyma River, one of the coldest inhabited places on earth. I had, together with my assistant Johan Ivarsson, spent most of the past five months hauling 660 pounds of necessities, mainly in utter darkness, experiencing terrifying cold with average temperatures around -50°F day and night. The cold made sleep almost impossible, gave us frostbite and ruined most metal parts of our equipment, like our ski bindings, and we therefore arrived walking, not skiing.

It seemed like every inhabitant greeted us with customary warmth and joy, most dressed in colourful traditional dress. We saw Chukchis, Even, Yakuts, Yugahirs and Russians. After the traditional welcoming offerings to the spirits, we were led into the local museum, where more cheerful and hugging villagers awaited around a table topped with delicacies. After having survived mainly on moose and raw, frozen fish most of the winter, we nearly cried when we spotted big plates of fried reindeer brain and cooked bone marrow. I suddenly realized, after 20 years of exploring extreme parts of our world and trying to understand the meaning of life, that from now on I'll stop thinking about the big worrisome issues and simply concentrate on the uncomplicated ones. Like the thought of more cooked bone marrow ....

I was brought up in a working-class environment in Dala-Järna, Sweden, 60 degrees latitude, population 1,000, where the basic values were hard physical work, loyalty to your employer, never forget where you came from and stick to your own kind. For this reason, we only had two books at home—*The Sea Wolf* and *White Fang,* by Jack London. My bricklaying father had them on loan indefinitely from the local library, to show our neighbours that our family had ambitions beyond the village limit. I wouldn't have touched them if I hadn't caught the measles and, as a bored ten-year-old, started reading them. But once started, I couldn't stop! In them I discovered that an unknown, exciting and important world existed beyond the narrow-minded limits of my village and I yearned to understand other people and to build bridges between them. As well, I then and there determined to live in the wilds of Nature. Those discoveries, combined with a mother who loved me above all else, gave me self-confidence and a sense of uniqueness.

As quick as I turned 16 in 1978, after avoiding the utterly boring knowledge taught in school, I set off for India to spend a year studying Mahayana Buddhism. But those studies only gave me diarrhea and gut pains. Instead, I ended up hiking, reading and travelling. When my money ran out, I returned home with a wish to build bridges of understanding by writing, lecturing, filming and through photography. I met a total lack of interest.

At that moment I realized that I had to do something that nobody else had done before. So over the next 7.5 years I cycled from Chile to Alaska, Norway to South Africa, and from New Zealand to Cairo. I pedalled 90,000 kilometres, passing through terrain as difficult and diverse as the Sahara Desert and the Darien Gap. Since then, I've been privileged to live my dream.

MIKAEL STRANDBERG was born in 1962 in Sweden and is a lecturer, filmmaker and writer. He has written six books and numerous articles, filmed several documentaries and is frequently consulted by broadcasters doing travel and adventure programs. In Sweden, Mikael has become a household name, and *National Geographic* has made a documentary about his life. For his Siberian adventure, King Carl XVI Gustaf awarded him the prestigious Travellers Club Silver Medal.

Mikael has cycled through 95 countries. In 1997 he, together with then-wife Titti, explored 3,000 kilometres of Patagonia by horse. In 2000, they walked through East Africa, exploring all the clans of the Masai people. In 2005 he returned from 10 months exploring the full 3,500-kilometre length of the Kolyma River in northern Siberia by canoe and skis.

Mikael is a Fellow of the Royal Geographical Society, The Explorers Club, Travellers Club and the Long Riders Guild. He lives in one of the coldest spots in Scandinavia, Sörberget, Sweden. There Mikael spends most of his time hunting and fishing.

STEVE VAN BEEK

"Exploration is letting your curiosity lead you wherever it wants to go. Being the first is unimportant; the only important thing is that it be a first for you."

The scent of water in any form is the Lorelei lure that draws Steve outdoors. Alaska's Lynn Canal. STEVE VAN BEEK

Inspired by a Liar

I suppose like all the firsts in one's life, my greatest exploration achievement was in 1988 examining my first river in a small teak boat—Thailand's Chao Phya. From its source in northern Thailand's hills, the kingdom's longest river at 700 miles flows through ancient dead cities and the very much alive Bangkok. I had no idea what to expect, or how to prepare, so everything was a surprise. Despite having lived in Thailand since 1969, I learned more about rural life in those 58 days than I had in the previous 20 years.

Where did my interest in exploring rivers have its headwaters? Every boy has an older neighbor kid who seems imbued with knowledge of exotic realms beyond the younger boy's ken. This older boy becomes a god, a fount of information on tricky questions like sex and the world at large. Of late, however, my mentor's wisdom had become suspect in my nine-year-old burgeoning grasp of the world. Tall tales, pulling my leg, are terms that come to mind now but at that time I was only dimly aware that perhaps I wasn't getting the full story.

In one of the best decisions my father made, we had moved from Portland, Oregon, to the rural town of Gresham. At eight, I found myself freed from the thrall of cheek-by-jowl city houses, living on a six-acre farm where I could run free.

And run I did. At the foot of the property was a railway line that ran to the town of Boring, the subject of endless jokes. Crossing the rail tracks and dropping down a horsetailed embankment brought me to the edge of meandering Johnson Creek, filled with crawdads and overhung with leafy boughs. Most rain-free days found me trudging through it, clear water splashing off my rubber boots. Spring floods compelled me to wander among the frog spawn and budding willows, heedless of safety amidst the rush of water, feeling the power of its press against my legs, exultant just to be immersed in nature at her finest.

One day, as I stood knee-deep in its surge, I mused aloud about the source of all the water. "Canada," the wise one intoned confidently. Maps were hieroglyphics to me in those days but somehow "Canada" just didn't seem right. Of course, one doesn't admit ignorance to a more sophisticated cohort. Instead, one nods in agreement and bides one's time.

The question and his reply plagued me all summer. When leaves were beginning to turn and the creek level was beginning to fall, I decided to find out for myself. One Saturday morning, lunch in my pack, I began splashing upstream, tingling with the anticipation of entering Canada. Hours later, weary and wet, I was far from the source. But from the way it narrowed, I knew that it didn't originate in Canada. I'd also learned that if I really wanted to know something, I couldn't trust others to tell me; I had to find out for myself. I've been walking upstream ever since.

This explains, in part, why I moved to far-off Thailand and became a writer; the former satisfied my curiosity about Asia and the latter was the only job in which I was paid to learn. It also explains why, after living for 11 years in a stilt house over Thailand's principal river and wondering, once again, where all the water came from, I began exploring in earnest. That whetted my appetite. In the years since, rivers have taken me into some of the world's oddest corners and the discoveries have enriched my life. And I owe it all to a liar.

A month out of the University of Oregon, STEVE VAN BEEK flew to Asia in 1966 and subsequently neglected to return home. Since he'd gone that far, he kept going. After three years in a small Nepalese village as a Peace Corps Volunteer working as an Agriculture Extension Agent (because he had a degree in Greek and Latin history), he moved to Bangkok. Exploring Thailand's River of Kings merely whetted his appetite and he has since explored numerous other rivers, including four first descents of the Mekong River as part of a Sino-American team.

Born in 1944, Steve is the author of 23 books (*Slithering South* recreates the Chao Phya adventure) and 42 documentaries, mostly for Asian consumption, but including the National Geographic channel. He was the scriptwriter for *Sir Peter Ustinov in Thailand*. Steve has spent more than a year paddling rivers and expects to spend a lot more in the future.

He's married to Piyawee Ruenjinda. They live on land in Bangkok where they design and lead educational trips through Southeast Asia emphasizing experiential learning, including cultural kayak tours of Laos' beautiful rivers.

13 The Survivormen

The difference between adventure
and disaster is often sheer luck.

—BIC PARKER

Matches? Who needs matches? Cooking gourmet over a fire started in the manner of our Neolithic ancestors. LES STROUD

Survivorman

I stood in the middle of the Amazon jungle learning how to hunt monkeys with a blowgun from a Waorani guide, a member of the most violent people in world history. Just forty years ago, the death rate was 60 percent homicide—by spear. Shortly after, that same guide dropped me off to survive alone in the middle of the jungle for one week. My goal: to best my greatest exploration moment every year I live.

My sense for adventure, passion for exploring, and intense aversion to the cup of mediocrity, did not come from strong parental guidance or a school system that fostered dream achievement. I was not a natural … anything. Never made a school team and barely passed high school.

Growing up in the seventies I devoured Tarzan movies and Jacques Cousteau specials. I remember one special Saturday when I was eight, watching *Tarzan* on our old black-and-white TV. The character started off as a James Bond-like man who was slick and savvy in the high finance world of New York. But when there was 'trouble in the jungle' he took off with nothing more than a knife and a loincloth.

> *"I think all great explorers are simply going after what they want in life; attending to their inside burning desires; scoffing at skepticism, accepting and coming up with answers to challenges. **Never** giving up."*

I thought that was the coolest thing I had ever seen. Such a fantastic juxtaposition! And with it, the seed of my adult life was sown.

Until I discovered rock and roll in grade eight, I wanted to be a *National Geographic* photographer. I wanted adventure. But a lower-middle-class kid from a dysfunctional family living in a boring white subdivision eating white bread and peanut butter and listening to Supertramp can't become a *Nat Geo* photographer. Can he?

Lack of guidance or mentorship can be as equally as debilitating for middle-class bored teenagers as for those who come from a 'rough background' that we usually hear about.

Ten years wasted by as I focused on becoming a rock star. I worked a hundred different blue-collar jobs, drank and smoked my way through the usual entrapments of the rock-and-roll lifestyle. Hovering by the edge of success in music without the smallest amount of guidance. But … something burned inside. There has to be more.

One rainy day in 1985 I stared out onto an alley from my office in the television headquarters of *MuchMusic* in Toronto … and I made up my mind. A change was needed. I quit my job as a producer and musical endeavours completely and left behind the drugs and alcohol. But now what? Adventure! That's all I really ever wanted. But I had no clue what to do or how. I learned quickly. The next ten years were spent training and guiding in all manner of outdoor adventure.

In 1994 my wife Sue and I decided to spend a year living alone in the wilderness. We lived as if it were five hundred years ago: no metal, matches or nylon … nothing to separate us from the wilderness … not even a tent. To this day it remains the greatest year of our lives and impossible to nullify the profound spiritual and psychological effects a year of living in the wilderness can have upon you. It's about going after what makes you happy in life. If you are not following your heart, then exactly what *are* you doing? That year cemented my philosophy. But another turning point was yet to come.

I had filmed the entire year for a documentary. But it had been a long time since I had been in television. It took the next five years, much perseverance and determination and two children later, to finish *Snowshoes and Solitude* and … to discover something: the *joy of completion!*

Great adventures and great explorations start out as great ideas. Mine was to combine my love for adventure and exploration with my filmmaking and so … Survivorman was born. Whether filming wildlife or making documentaries, this *joy of completion* is being experienced over and over again in my life.

Dreams are wisps of nothing unless turned into goals and acted upon. Goals must follow dreams. Choosing to work in a factory supporting a family is exploring a life of devotion. Climbing a mountain, kayaking a wild river, searching jungles, oceans, forests and polar landscapes, producing a TV show that takes you (me) to the ends of the earth, becoming a skilled doctor, accountant, computer technician. It's all exploring *IF* in the process you are going after makes you happy. I believe that Peary, Franklin, Hearne et al. were mostly about going after their dream, equals idea, equals goal … equals what made them happy. Again: if you're not going after what makes you happy in life, then exactly what are you doing?

LES STROUD was born in 1961 and brought up in Mimico, Ontario, Canada, where his father managed a beer store. He is the producer/host of Survivorman, televised on the Outdoor Life Network (Canada), The Science Channel (U.S.), Discovery (U.S.) and Discovery (International). It is the highest-rated show in the history of OLN and the Science Channel and has become hugely popular worldwide. Each episode strands Les completely alone without food, water, matches, shelter or camera crew in some of the most remote regions of the world carrying not much more than a knife!

Les has been an outdoor adventurer and instructor for over twenty years in whitewater and sea kayaking, hiking, dog sledding, winter travel and of course … survival. He has produced and hosted numerous television specials, including *I Shouldn't Be Alive— the Science of Survival, Expedition Everest* and *Off the Grid with Les Stroud.* His most recent production in development with Discovery and OLN is *Stroud's Legends,* which has him following in the footsteps of the world's greatest explorers. He is in production on a book series on survival, and has released a music CD with the Canadian band The Northern Pikes.

Les, wife Sue and kids Raylan and Logan live completely off the power grid in northern Ontario.

KEN KAMLER

"The greatest discovery an explorer can make is to find those unexpected strengths that we all have within ourselves."

Sorting through yak loads of medical supplies, Everest Base Camp, 1992.
FormAsia

Doctor in the Extreme

Riding up a precipitous pass in Peru in the back of an open truck with my climbing team in 1980, I watched in disbelief as another truck similar to ours, coming down the road, teetered over the edge of an embankment and tumbled into a ravine, spilling produce, animals and villagers. I had never before applied a Band-Aid in the wilderness—and now my first test would be facing a full-blown disaster. I was nervous enough at the prospect of testing my as yet unproven climbing skills and wasn't looking for additional challenges, but fate had intervened before I even got to the mountain. About a dozen injured people were strewn along a hillside. Many of the injuries were serious, but none were life threatening. I stayed calm by realizing that, although the setting was new for me, the injuries were not. I stabilized everyone, and our team loaded them into our truck. We drove to a place on the map marked "clinica." It turned out to be a cinder block house with empty shelves and a doctor who mostly just handed out birth control pills. He asked me not to leave until we could evacuate the injured to Lima. I stayed overnight until ambulances came, then returned to the mountains, climbing Yanapacha, a 19,000-foot peak. The climb was satisfying, but I realized that, for me, treating the injured people on the mountain had been the higher summit. It had brought out qualities in me that I never knew I had.

I've since summited peaks in North and South America, Europe, Asia and Antarctica—but I went on my first climb when I was eight years old. It was up my father's bookshelf to pull down a book called *Annapurna*. I had been intrigued by the funny title, but the story intrigued me far more—the ascent of what was, at that time, the highest mountain ever climbed. The book opened a world of exploration that I never knew existed. I lived in a housing project in the Bronx, New York. I didn't know anyone who climbed or even talked about climbing. I couldn't imagine anyone around me even imagining it.

It was much easier for me to explore through a microscope. That led me to study biology and then medicine, because I felt the human body contained more unexplored places than anywhere else on earth. I became a doctor, but I never lost my desire to seek out those faraway places I had read about. A patient had given me the phone number of a climbing school in New Hampshire and I kept it in my drawer for two years. As I felt myself being pulled along the prescribed route of a doctor's career, I decided I didn't want to regret not living the other half of my dream. I was 33 when I dialed that number and bridged two worlds more easily than I would have thought possible. The barrier between them had been largely in my mind.

KENNETH KAMLER is a microsurgeon in New York who also practises extreme medicine in some of the most remote regions on earth. He has treated bear bite in the Arctic and frostbite in the Antarctic. He has set fractures in the Andes and cared for out-of-breath scuba divers in the Galapagos. He has performed surgery deep in the Amazon rain forest and in an undersea mock space capsule. He has been on six expeditions to Mt. Everest as expedition doctor and climber. Four were with the National Geographic Society deploying laser telescopes and global positioning satellite receivers to measure the exact height and tectonic motion. On two, he served as Chief High Altitude Physician for NASA-sponsored research on physiological responses to extreme altitude.

Ken has climbed to within 900 feet of Everest's summit and was the only doctor on the mountain during the infamous 1996 storm that claimed twelve lives. His treatment of survivors, including ultimate survivor Beck Weathers, was portrayed in Jon Krakauer's book *Into Thin Air,* in the IMAX film *Everest* and in his own book *Doctor on Everest.*

He is a consultant for *National Geographic* and for NASA, and is a commentator for Outdoor Life Network. *New York Magazine* recognized him as one of the best doctors in New York. He is the subject of a chapter in *Biography Today: Medical Leaders* and has been profiled in numerous publications, from *The New York Times* to *Reader's Digest.* Besides writing a column for *National Geographic Adventure Magazine,* he has authored a second book, *Surviving The Extremes.*

Ken has two children, Jonathan and Jennifer.

WARREN MacDONALD

Exploration is a sense of discovery of self, brought about by venturing into the uncomfortable unknown. It is in these outer reaches, when we are forced to tap into resources rarely used, that we tap into who we really are. It's where we get to explore far more than geographical points; it is where we get to explore the very limits of our potential as human beings.

The picture of determination:
Warren MacDonald climbing
Mt. Kilimanjaro, 2003.
JEREMY SMITH

Can't Kick

Picking my way over the final few metres to the summit of Tasmania's Federation Peak, the undisputed icon of Australian wildness, I tried to keep a lid on my welling feelings. Each step in my custom-made prosthetics was an exercise in precision, accompanied by the tossing forward of my modified crutches to free up my hands. The moment arrives as in slow motion, as if I am watching from afar, as if time itself has stood still. It's only when I hear Ian Matthews approaching, having stood back as I reached the cairn, that I'm bought back to the moment. As he wraps his arms around me from behind I feel a wave wash over and literally through me. My heart lodged firmly in my throat, I struggle to contain my emotion—a Herculean effort considering the circumstances—and it's not until later when left alone on the summit that the tears come. With the help of an incredible group of friends, I have not just recovered a sense of self, long defined by the outdoors, but have surpassed the limits of my own comfort zone. Less than two years after the accident that claimed my legs, I haven't just reclaimed my life, but moved forward; an explorer of the very limits of human potential. And in that moment, stunned into silence by the sheer beauty surrounding me, I feel more alive than at any point in my 34 years.

My life seems segmented into separate, distinctly different "lives," with one experience post-accident standing out. Having had both legs amputated at mid-thigh five months prior, I'd felt the familiar urge to escape Melbourne, and set out with my brother-in-law Per Thomsen for The Grampians National Park. Over two days, we took short hikes before finding ourselves at the end of a trail that involved some serious four-wheel wheelchairing. I had to negotiate some of the bigger obstacles on my backside. The trail ended at a pool, and seeing it was a hot day I eagerly hopped out of the chair onto a large flat stone at the water's edge. Instinctively, without thinking of the enormous changes that had taken place, I disrobed and lowered myself into the water, the familiar bracing effect bringing a smile to my face. It spread further as it dawned on me; I'm swimming in a river again! I'd only just begun swimming indoors, and hadn't even considered swimming again outside.

Cooled, I shuffled back onto the rock and stretched out on my back. Per was beside me, unable to resist the water's calling himself. Together we must have made quite a sight. Feeling the sun's warmth wash over me, droplets of water on my skin, I once again experienced that feeling of utter aliveness. "If I can do this already, imagine what I will be able to do over time," I thought. Possibilities raced through my mind, the kind of thoughts dared dreamt by those with nothing to lose but everything to gain. "I bet I could climb again," the thought bringing a smile to my face. Like a flash came a vision of a mountain in Tasmania. "I'm going to climb Cradle Mountain. I can do it; I know I can …." Four months later, just ten after my accident, I did just that.

In 1997, at age 31, **WARREN MACDONALD** spent two days alone pinned under a one-ton boulder after a freak rock fall in Queensland. He survived, only to lose both legs. *A Test of Will: One Man's Extraordinary Story of Survival* is an Australian bestseller and his documentary, *The Second Step,* has won seven international awards. It aired on National Geographic. In 2003, this former contract painter, fledgling guide, adventure-traveller and conservationist became the first double above-knee amputee (AKA) to reach the summit of Mt. Kilimanjaro, and, in a spectacular effort requiring more than 2,800 pull-ups, created history once again in an ascent of El Capitan. He is also the only AKA to climb Alberta's 600-foot frozen waterfall, the Weeping Wall. The Australian Geographic Society honoured him with their Spirit of Adventure award.

Brought up in Melbourne, Australia, he fell in love early with hiking and conservation. He lives in Vancouver, British Columbia, with Canadian alpinist Margo Talbot.

14 Zoo's Who

Whatever you can do or
dream you can, begin it.
Boldness has genius,
power and magic in it.

—GOETHE

Happiness is a warm camel: John crossing the Sahara. John Hare

Crossing the Desert's Dusty Face

In 1999 I "discovered" two unmapped valleys that were lost among the crags of China's Kunlun mountains. It was like walking into the Garden of Eden, because they contained three endangered species: the wild Bactrian camel, the Argali sheep and the Tibetan wild ass. They had never encountered man and were consequently curious and unafraid. It seemed incredible to me that at the end of the 20th century there were still places left in the world that were unexplored and undiscovered!

"Something lost behind the Ranges. Lost and waiting for you. Go!" I was 10 in 1947 when I first came across those words from Rudyard Kipling's poem *The*

> *"Successful exploration is original discovery in, for example, a geographical, scientific or archaeological context."*

Explorer as a chapter heading in my favourite book, *Exploration Fawcett*. It was an account by Colonel Percy Fawcett's son of the disappearance of his father when he set out in Brazil to look for a fabulous, remote "lost" city in the 1920s. I loved that book and still retain the battered and much-read copy to this day. Three years later when my father, who had spent his life as a tea planter in Ceylon, now Sri Lanka, asked me what I wanted to do with my life, I unhesitatingly replied, "I want to be an explorer." I dreamed of exploring the remotest places on earth, of discovering what remained to be discovered.

My father was further taken aback when I later applied to go into the Colonial Service at a time when most of Britain's colonies were rapidly being prefixed as "ex." I slipped into the Service through the back door and had a glorious seven years in some of the remotest parts of West Africa. I worked in northern Nigeria with the British and Nigerian governments and lived for four years on the entirely roadless 550-square-mile Mambilla Plateau straddling the border between Nigeria and Cameroon.

A profound admiration of the camel and a great love of deserts came about when I had to make numerous sorties into the desert near Lake Chad. This led much later to expeditions into the Gobi—especially the Gobi in China—mounted on the two-humped Bactrian as I searched out the remotest corners of the planet.

For one six-month period in Africa I did not see another white face and travelled entirely by horseback or on foot. This experience equipped me for later life when in 1995 I found myself setting off into the former Chinese nuclear test area to survey the critically endangered wild Bactrian camel. I was the first foreigner into the area in 50 years and that was my introduction to China.

Three expeditions later, I was able to propose to the Chinese authorities that they set up the 155-square-kilometre Lop Nur Wild Camel Reserve. The project was approved in 2001 and money was obtained from the Global Environment Facility in Washington. Money for checkpoints, vehicles and radios was obtained from the private sector through the Wild Camel Protection Foundation, a U.K.-based charity I established in 1997.

Kipling is still one of my favourite authors and when I set out on a hazardous camel trip in Lop Nur or the Gashun Gobi, *Kim* is always tucked in my saddlebag. The call of the wild has always been in me; when it comes I have to answer. The skeptics inevitably comment, "Won't he ever grow up?" I sincerely hope not!

But never did Kipling's words echo louder than when I found those two hidden valleys in China. Something had indeed been "lost behind the Ranges" and we found them!

JOHN HARE of Benenden, Kent, U.K., has established in Mongolia the only captive breeding program for wild camels in the world. Fifteen captured wild camels form part of a carefully monitored breeding program that, it is hoped, will ensure the preservation of their unique genetic make-up.

National Geographic followed John as he crossed the Sahara desert on a 1,462-mile, three-and-a-half-month expedition by camel from Lake Chad to Tripoli in 2001–2002. In 1996 he led the first expedition in recorded history to reach the ancient city of Lou Lan in Lop Nur, China, from the east on foot.

He has been awarded the Ness Award by the Royal Geographical Society for "raising awareness worldwide for the critically endangered wild Bactrian camel" and the Lawrence of Arabia Memorial Award by the Royal Society of Asian Affairs in 2004 for "exploration under extremely hazardous circumstances." He has published *The Lost Camels of Tartary* and *Shadows across the Sahara*.

Amazingly, John is married and the father of three girls.

WILLIAM BURNHAM

"Conservation is at the heart of exploration, for without the former there cannot be the latter."

Bill with the other love of his life: a raptor. KURT K. BURNHAM

Boots, Rope and Falcons

My greatest achievement is not really mine—but rather the global conservation and research accomplished by others resulting from the opportunities I've been able to provide through the development of a world-class organization, The Peregrine Fund.

As a boy growing up in Colorado, I enjoyed fishing or frog and salamander hunting when younger and hunting ducks and doves once old enough to safely manage a single-shot .410. Trout fishing many times required being perched on my father's shoulders handling the rod while he waded down the center of the stream so I would not tangle the line in the trees and bushes on the bank. Fishing usually ended with me trying to trap a chipmunk to take home alive. A visit to a relative's farm resulted in me climbing around in the barn searching out pigeon nests. When I went to the city park with my grandmother, she brought a string and stew meat so I could catch crayfish. I dropped them into a bushel basket before counting and dumping them back into the lake.

I liked the out-of-doors and all forms of animals, but not plants unless a tree existed to climb for bird nests. Everything wild was an adventure. You never quite knew what critter might be caught or appear, what event might happen, or what discovery there was around the corner.

As I neared adolescence, my interest in washtubs with captured frogs and sala-manders and caged chipmunks waned. Also, you could only look into so many bird nests without a purpose or at least a larger variety of birds. Something was missing. I disliked school; nothing being taught seemed to have any connection to my interests and life.

While failing sophomore biology, the teacher requested that Pat Wood, a girl who sat near my desk and was an outstanding student, tutor me. At the same time he offered me a newly hatched, orphaned great horned owl to raise. While the success of the tutoring was debatable (I received only a D rather than an F), the teacher did introduce me to my companion and co-worker of nearly 40 years—Pat. From that point on, I knew raptors and the girl were two things integral to my future life.

Having done poorly scholastically, I went from a student to a construction laborer. Nearing the end of an electrical apprenticeship I found the job had too many limitations. When not working, I practiced falconry and fantasized about having a peregrine to fly. By then their populations had plummeted throughout much of North America, although I did not believe it. I thought they had simply moved to more remote breeding locations, probably because biologists kept bothering them.

Pat arrived home one evening from student teaching to find me with a new climbing rope and pair of boots, neither of which we could afford. I declared peregrines were still around and the others searching were just not looking hard enough. Two springs later I found my first peregrine eyrie with young. It *was* true, they *were* almost gone. Something had to be done.

Luckily, I came in contact with a scientist/falconer, Jim Enderson. Amazingly enough, he was actually making a living doing exactly what I wanted to do, but it seemed college degrees were a requirement. The vision now clear, the course could be set. With a supportive wife and determination, todays turned into yesterdays while looking forward to tomorrow. Nowadays, I pursue my dreams as a conser-vationist and scientist.

During the past 40 years WILLIAM A. BURNHAM of Boise, Idaho, has done research and conservation on birds of prey all over the world, from Arctic Greenland to the temperate mountains, plains and forests of North America; to the tropical forests of Latin America and the Asia/Pacific.

His nearly 100 publications (including books) reflect not only geographic regions of work, but areas of interest ranging from raptor ecology to captive propagation and endangered species restoration. After joining The Peregrine Fund in 1974 to develop the peregrine falcon restoration program in the western U.S., he was elected the President and Chief Executive in 1986. He still holds both positions today. He advises and works with governments and organizations on issues and programs, and serves on various boards nationally and internationally.

He received his Ph.D. from Colorado State University. He and Pat have one son, Kurt, who is completing a doctorate at Oxford. Recreational interests include falconry, fly-fishing, hunting, diving and writing.

Dances with orca. BRAD TATE

> *"Exploration is expanding your mind*
> *and seeking answers to questions either by*
> *physically getting into the field and travelling*
> *or mentally reading theories, postulating your*
> *own and writing your results."*

Orca Encounters

I have discovered that New Zealand orca, or killer whales, are willing to take an extra step towards interacting with people. They are unique and we need to give them credit for that—they have an intellect we are only just beginning to realize and a culture we have only just discovered.

As a little girl I collected animal pictures from magazines, like some kids collect baseball cards. One day I was asked by one of the kids if I wanted to swap. She managed to get a pile of my animal magazines for just one dolphin picture. But I was happy, and still have it today.

I remember my first close encounter with orca—my lifetime fascination. When I was 25, I had a call that there were orca off the beach nearby. I ran as fast as I could, grabbing my snorkelling gear on the way. There were already a number of people there. Some were clapping their hands and barking like seals, imitating the action shown on a recent documentary where orca were playing with seals they had seized, tossing them in the air like beach balls.

This didn't deter me, and I leaped into the water and swam out a bit. I couldn't see any, and wondered if it was a joke. The visibility wasn't good. I dived to the bottom and grabbed rocks and weeds to stay down.

When I came up for a breath, I just about had a heart attack: between the surface and me was an orca! I was entranced, but already on my way up, and I popped through the surface like a cork right next to her. She came up for a breath at the same time. She swam past me, then in a curve around me. I turned with her, then dove again. She had something in her mouth, but I wasn't sure what it was—a sack? She turned and swam off. I thought my experience with them was over, so I dove to hear their calls.

As I came up for another breath, there she was again. But this time she had a calf with her! It was thrilling, to be trusted enough by this female that she had brought her baby over for a look. And this time it was the calf that had the 'sack' in its mouth—which I saw now was a stingray. It was the first indication New Zealand orca ate them. The calf swam fast in the direction I was surfacing and suddenly it was a game for us, with the female watching on, just to make sure I didn't make a silly move. The calf swam around and around me, just below the surface, while I was in the centre, spinning as fast as I could and laughing hard. It was difficult to believe that this was happening. After a lifetime (a few minutes?), I was so dizzy I broke eye contact with the calf and it was as I feared: it was all over.

As I staggered up the beach, the reaction of the onlookers was now one of stunned disbelief. They stared at me like I was on some serious drugs—and I *was* spinning out, so excited and buzzing and jabbering away about the calf and the ray and the ....

Not long before, I had read some American Indians believe wherever they are, it is the centre of the universe. For that moment I fully understood what they meant.

INGRID "ORCA" VISSER has lived and breathed orca for as long as she can remember, since she was born in 1966 in Wellington, New Zealand. She received her Ph.D. in Environmental and Marine Science from Auckland University, and has published numerous scientific and popular articles describing their unique foraging behaviour.

Ingrid's photographs have been published in National Geographic and BBC's Wildlife. Discovery Channel produced a documentary for Animal Planet about her work with the New Zealand orca. She has written two children's books, and an autobiography Swimming with Orca: My Life with New Zealand Killer Whales about her work. She follows orca all over the world, and founded the Orca Research Trust to study them in the South Pacific, and the Adopt an Orca Program for Australasia.

"Orca" lives on the North Island at Tutukaka.

15 Wanted: Dead or Alive

Curiosity is one of the permanent and certain characteristics of a vigorous mind.

—SAMUEL JOHNSON

LARRY AGENBROAD

Just a grown up kid still playing in the dirt: Larry uncovering a pygmy mammoth, Santa Rosa Island, California. CHANNEL ISLANDS NATIONAL PARK

Mammoth Moments

It's difficult to identify my single greatest discovery, because I've been blessed with several! The Jarkov mammoth I helped excavate out of the Siberian tundra—featured in *Raising the Mammoth* on the Discovery Channel—is certainly up there, but so are the development of the Mammoth Site research facility in Hot Springs, South Dakota, where visitors can tour an active paleontological dig; the recovery of a pygmy mammoth skeleton on Santa Rosa Island; and the "Hope Diamond of Mammoth Dung" from Bechan Cave in Utah; not to mention the Hudson-Meng Alberta Culture bison kill in Nebraska!

Having been raised in Idaho, on land homesteaded by my father, I always had a "feel" for the outdoors. Discovering a circa 5,000-year-old obsidian spear point in one of our fields at the age of 14 kindled an interest in prehistory. That spear

"Exploration consists of the sensation of discovery and adding new information to a field of interest."

point was unlike any arrowhead I had previously seen. I couldn't help but wonder … How long since it was last held in a human hand? Who was the craftsman that fashioned it? What, or whom, was it intended for? Was it a miss that was never recovered? Or did it find its mark? These questions, and more, prompted my search for answers from prehistory. I love the sensation of *discovery,* adding new information to a field of interest, and exploring new places.

After the military, I obtained a couple of degrees in engineering and geology. I worked as a mining geologist and then as an exploration geophysicist in 1983 where I was exposed to a myriad of canyons and cliff dwellings in Utah that were inaccessible to normal motor traffic. These caves and alcoves were just waiting to be explored—including the one we named "Bechan," which contained the first intact mammoth dung boli in the hemisphere.

Returning to graduate school, I became involved in the geophysics, geology and hydrology of underground nuclear tests. Following my Ph.D. in geology, in 1970 I was invited to be the assistant director of several early man/mammoth-kill excavations in the Upper San Pedro Valley of southeastern Arizona. We found multiple mammoths and associated fauna that had been hunted, killed and consumed by early hunters (Clovis Culture) at circa 11,300 radiocarbon years ago. It was exciting and rewarding to find kill and butcher sites and to be able to link them to campsites and activity areas. We could often perfectly fit impact flakes lost in the bone bed to the discarded spear point bases from the camp and activity areas, even after 11,300 years!

I constantly raised a question during these excavations: "Why don't we recover the mammoth bones?" The usual response was, "They take too much storage space." One excellent specimen remains a vivid image in my mind, just left behind because it was in strata that couldn't have the possibility of human contact. That single experience led me to research of mammoths, associated fauna and early human hunters.

In 1974 I received a note stating that there were mammoth remains in Hot Springs. Initial testing indicated we had multiple mammoths in the fill deposits of an ancient sinkhole. I decided to leave the remains in situ. As of July, 2005, we have 55 mammoths plus 40 species of associated fauna preserved in The Mammoth Site of Hot Springs. They date to 26,000 years ago and there is still about 40 percent yet to excavate!

In 1994 I received a call from Channel Islands National Park, California. On Santa Rosa Island we recovered the most complete skeleton of a California pygmy mammoth yet recovered.

In 1999 I joined a French-Russian-Dutch expedition to the Taimyr Peninsula of Siberia. There we extracted a 23-ton block of permafrost containing the remains of a woolly mammoth, and airlifted it to an ice tunnel in Khatanga.

Mammoth moments are still occurring, but I relate them all back to that one skeleton that was left in the field in southern Arizona. I abandoned the hunt for the hunters, and focused on the hunted. It has been a fabulous experience ... and it is not over yet!

LARRY AGENBROAD was born in 1933. He taught at Chadron State College and Northern Arizona University, and has been actively involved in Quaternary studies since 1966, conducting fieldwork in America, Mexico and Siberia. For several years, he served as assistant director of both the Murray Springs Mammoth Kill Site, and the Lehner Ranch Mammoth Kill Site in the San Pedro River Valley. From 1970 to 1976, he was the principal investigator of the Hudson-Meng Site, an Alberta Culture bison kill in northwestern Nebraska, dating to 9,820 years ago. From 1974 to the present, he has served as the principal investigator of the Mammoth Site of Hot Springs. Commencing in 1986, he was the principal investigator of a series of bison jumps in Owyhee County, Idaho. Since 1994 he has been principal investigator of pygmy mammoths on California's Channel Islands.

Larry has published numerous papers in geology, hydrology, archaeology and palaeontology. He has also authored or co-authored three books, including, with Lisa Nelson, *Mammoths: Ice-Age Giants*.

He and his wife Wanda have sons Brett and Finn, and live in Hot Springs, South Dakota.

JEROME HAMLIN

At the controls of the steam launch
Wendigo *on a remote section of the*
Big East River, Ontario. DIANA DYJAK

"Exploration is self-justifying. It's an expression of our genome and does not require a scientific or commercial rationalization—although those are often needed for funding. Exploration is a natural high. And if you get a focus, you yourself become a force of nature."

Dinofish

I'm asleep, but I hear a gentle tapping at my door. "Monsieur! Monsieur!" The voice is soft but excited, the accent French Comoran, the speaker of African/Arab descent, and a hotel employee. I wake from a forgotten dream to the mission at hand. "Un coelacanthe!" he goes on. I'm morphing quickly into emergency mode. "Un coelacanthe vivant!" Check watch: 7:00 a.m. I'm at the door. Is it possible? A living coelacanthe, the 400,000,000-year-old living fossil, at my doorstep? The odds against seeing one alive are astronomical. Yes, two fishermen have caught one, and towed the living creature to the lava shore just in front of my bungalow! I climb into their canoe. Its eyes glow with ancient fire in the bright morning sun. I float a plastic Hefty bag over it as a shield. Don't let it touch the boat. My hand slides down the slimy flanks....

That was 1986. The next hours began the first of the close encounters—three alive and 10 dead—unfolding over the next 20 years and the Coelacanth Research Center being built on those very same lava shores.

Many years before, as a 12-year-old, I sat on the sofa on a cold winter's night in Buffalo, NY, watching my favorite TV show: Science Fiction Theatre. The host had a block of ice in front of him, and in it was a fish. He explained that some fish could survive being frozen in ice, and would resume normal life when the ice thawed. I was transfixed by a variation of this idea.

As the years went by, when my normal urges for travel were fulfilled, I settled into the quest for a fish frozen not in ice but in time. In that fish—the coelacanth (see-la-kanth)—I saw the key to evolutionary puzzles, but also something more universal. If you pick one good starting point, the world expands from it and the universe unfolds—such is the nature of exploration.

In my childhood during the 1950s, a serial called Tim Tyler's Luck ran on television and as a comic strip that spurred me on. A prototype for Indiana Jones, Tim's adventures in Africa left me with an insatiable desire to get over there! Jim Fowler's exploits on Wild Kingdom only added to the frenzy. These dreams became a reality when I made a schoolboy visit at 17 to the "dark continent" in the company of the famous Quentin Keynes, great-grandson of Charles Darwin. I encountered Tim Tyler's gorillas in Rwanda! I started recording on film and later tape. From that point there was no turning back.

In 1965 I produced a conservation film for the African Wildlife Leadership Foundation. From 1974 to 1984, however, I was diverted by filmmaking and my robotics business. I designed and built the world's first computer-controlled domestic robot that was sold by Neiman Marcus in 1981.

Collecting hot volcanic samples in Ecuador for Columbia University's Lamont-Dougherty Earth Observatory in 1985 led to the pursuit of another exotic—the coelacanth as an obscure object of desire that lives in the Indian Ocean off Africa. While my expeditions were successful in returning frozen specimens for scientific research, the very frustration of quickly acquiring a live specimen deepened my involvement until the journey became the destination—perhaps the ultimate form of exploration! With so many visits to the sanctums of this creature, the people, the animal, the places and the events merged with me until we had a common heartbeat. From 1985 on, the Coelacanth Project was added to my filmmaking and inventing activities.

JEROME F. HAMLIN was born in 1943 in Buffalo. His father was (literally) a rocket scientist working on propulsion systems for such projects as the X-15, Atlas and Saturn V. Jerome graduated from Yale in 1966 with a B.A. in Philosophy. In 1964 he attempted crossings of Australia, and, in 1966, India, but an encounter with a holy cow required a hospital stay.In 1967 he invented a type of inline roller skate. Expeditions include traveling the length of the Amazon from Iquitos to Belem; to Lake Turkana, Kenya, to film a solar eclipse; to the erupting Sangay volcano, Ecuador; and several coelacanth projects. Among his films is Fish out of Time.

Jerome and Diana Dyjak Montes de Oca live in New York and Poland. She has a grown son, Tawa.

16 Picking the Lock to Davy Jones' Locker

*From birth, man carries the weight
of gravity on his shoulders. He is
bolted to earth. But man only
has to sink below the
surface and he is free.*

—JACQUES COUSTEAU

ROBERT BALLARD

Capt. Nemo commanding the R/V Connecticut *in Thunder Bay, Lake Huron.* GASPAR TRINGALE

Twenty Thousand Leagues under the Sea

When people hear my name, if they recognize it, they immediately think of the 1985 *Titanic* discovery. When scientists look at my discoveries, they point out my greatest contribution was, as Co-Chief Scientist of the 1977 Galapagos Rift Expedition, when we discovered hydrothermal vents and their exotic life forms. During this period I also discovered that the entire ocean recycles over time through the Earth's crust, explaining for the first time its mineral content.

Yet neither of these historic discoveries was dancing in my head while growing up in San Diego. When I was 12 in 1954, I was so riveted by the movie based on Jules Verne's prescient book starring Kirk Douglas and James Mason that when I floated out of that theater my dream floated with me to be Captain Nemo! I too wanted to be an undersea explorer and go where no one had gone before!

> *"An explorer is a person who never stops*
> *asking the question that first enters their mind*
> *as a child when they open their eyes and*
> *ask, "Where am I?"*

I read the adventures of Jason and Odysseus, the voyages of Captain James Cook. But unlike these explorers, I was never interested in the top of the ocean or the magical islands they encountered. Like Nemo, I was interested in what lay beneath. In its unexplored mountain ranges, its great chasms and lost relics.

Once my quest to explore began, it was like riding a giant wave of enthusiasm and inquiry. There were many crossroads and turning points, many tests of head and heart, many failures that I had to endure. I fell in love with the process, driven by Joseph Campbell's words "that life is the act of becoming, that you never arrive at a final destination." The tools of exploration I was forced to build opened the doors of the deep.

By the time I was 17, in 1959 I had been dreaming for years, had spent years beachcombing whatever Neptune had sent ashore. But that only scratched the surface. I needed to go even deeper, to enter Davy Jones' locker.

I wrote a letter to the Scripps Institution for Oceanography in La Jolla—the world's largest. Through a miracle of the Gods, a kind Dr. Norris Rakestraw helped secure me a summer scholarship on Scripps' research vessels. The first voyage sailed into a storm. The second ended when the ship was struck by a rogue wave that nearly sank her. I was too young to fear death and was hooked. What an adventure, but like Captain Cook, one with a purpose—the purpose of discovery, of advancing the frontiers of knowledge.

It propelled me into college and a hunger for knowledge. As the journey continued, the academic waves became more challenging. At times, the mental push-ups were fatiguing and I asked myself if I should go on. How strong was my dream?

My next opportunity came as a surprise. It was the early 1960s and our nation was in an unpopular war. I had been a Cub, Boy and Explorer Scout, and entering the military seemed natural. All healthy males were required to enroll in Reserve Officer Training Corps but all they had at the University of California at Santa Barbara was Army. After the mandatory two years, I signed up again, becoming a 2nd Lt. in Intelligence in 1965.

I headed to graduate school in Hawaii, expecting Vietnam to enter my life eventually. But a chance visit to the Naval Recruiting Center led a year later to a knock on my door in Belmont Shores, California. A naval officer said, "You have six days to report for active duty as an ensign."

Recovering from that shock, I found I was assigned to the deep submersible *Alvin* at the Woods Hole Oceanographic Institution—and the keys to Captain Nemo's new *Nautilus* were placed in my hands!

Discoveries followed. Following our 1977 Rift find, we returned in 1979 with biologists. I took Dr. Holger Jannasch on that first dive. I concentrated on testing a new digital television camera mounted on *Alvin* until I felt Holger's breath on my neck. "What are you doing?" I asked. "Looking at the monitor," he replied, "I can see better than from the viewport."

A light bulb came on. Why not build a robot that can carry our minds, eyes and hands to the deep! I went on to build many that, yes, discovered the *Titanic* and the *Bismarck* and now I have one named *Hercules* and the greatest discovery I will ever make is about to happen ....

ROBERT D. BALLARD, PH.D., of Lyme, Connecticut, is a National Geographic Society Explorer-in-Residence with over 100 deep-sea expeditions to his credit. He was born in 1942 and is best known for his discovery of the *Titanic* as well as the *Bismarck, Lusitania, Yorktown, Britannic* and *PT-109*. He has also discovered 14 warships in Iron Bottom Sound from the Battle for Guadalcanal; the first ancient shipwreck in the deep sea, which happened to be in the Central Mediterranean; and the first perfectly preserved ancient shipwreck in the Black Sea. Robert is also one of the world's foremost oceanographers, using submersibles to explore the deep ocean.

He's the author of several books and has hosted National Geographic television's *Explorer* program, as well as acted as a special adviser on Steven Spielberg's *Sea Quest*. Each year, he takes thousands of schoolchildren on an interactive expedition through his innovative Jason program. He is also the president of the Sea Research Foundation's Institute for Exploration in Mystic, Connecticut, and a Professor of Oceanography at the University of Rhode Island Graduate School of Oceanography, where he is Director of its new Institute for Archaeological Oceanography. Robert is an Honorary Director of The Explorers Club and a recipient of both its Citation of Merit and its Explorers Medal, among a host of other awards and honors.

Robert is married to Barbara,and they have three kids, Douglas, Benjamin and Emily Rose.

PAUL BERKMAN

"Exploration is a process of discovery driven by curiosity, challenges of the unknown and a deep understanding that life is too short."

All dressed up and nowhere to go. PAUL BERKMAN COLLECTION

From Warm Times to Cold Climes

I remember my first expedition to Antarctica at 22 in 1981—a year-long experience that will bubble insights for as long as I live. I had just graduated from UC Santa Barbara with a bachelor's degree in aquatic biology when I joined a Scripps expedition. I have made nearly 200 scuba dives but none as daunting as those under the Ross Ice Shelf, with thousands of cubic kilometers of glacial ice overhead—less than 1,500 kilometers from the Pole. These dives were down a metre-wide hole that had been melted through 20 meters of ice—the deepest dives ever made through ice, as well as dives made farthest south during the austral winter. At the underside of the ice hole we discovered stones that had been buoyed off the bottom by anchor ice, which grows in super-cooled bodies of water.

During winter, it was like diving through air with nearly 200 meters of visibility except when we turned off our 1000-watt light to sense the deep darkness at the end of a tether under the sea ice far from home. Along the way, we encountered meter-tall glass sponges, standing like large Greek amphorae, covered with undulating feather stars; armadas of brittle stars; and ice fish that circulated antifreeze through their blood. One of my favorite discoveries established that the Antarctic scallop (*Adamussium colbecki*) can live in excess of a century—the longest known lifespan of any Antarctic species—in contrast to temperate or tropical scallops, which generally live only a few years!

My interest in oceanography emerged from growing up along the coast of southern California within walking distance of the beaches in Pacific Palisades. There were always were small treasures in the sand, within the twisted clumps of kelp and in the rock piles that appeared after the surf was up. I still can see the small swell shark that I played with for hours when I was nine or 10 in a tide pool surrounded by sea anemone and barnacled rocks until the returning waves washed it home. This creature was my first fascination with the sea and by 12 I knew that my career was in oceanography.

From the opportunities that followed—I've been back to Antarctica eight seasons over 25 years—I have learned that it is the passion that matters most in making childhood dreams come true. Centered with the support of family, I have had the good fortune to explore the world we live in with an eye toward contributing to the sustainable development of humanity into the distant future.

PAUL BERKMAN of Columbus, Ohio, integrates science, policy and information technology as a Research Professor at the Bren School of Environmental Science and Management at the University of California Santa Barbara. Paul also is the CEO and co-founder of EvREsearch Ltd., which provides Digital Integration System (DIGIN®) applications around the world. His book *Science into Policy: Global Lessons from Antarctica* evolved from his winter-over expedition and the course that he began teaching in 1982 as a Visiting Professor at UCLA at the age of 24. After working in Washington, D.C., as a consultant on Antarctic affairs, he completed his M.S. and Ph.D. in Oceanography in 1986 and 1988, respectively, at the University of Rhode Island, where he was a National Science Foundation graduate fellow.

By age 30, Paul had traveled to all seven continents with subsequent fellowships from the Byrd Polar Research Center at Ohio State University; the Japanese Ministry of Science Education and Culture at the National Institute of Polar Research in Tokyo; the University of Canterbury in New Zealand; and NASA at the Jet Propulsion Laboratory. Paul carried Explorers Club Flag #28 on two of his Antarctic expeditions, and for the last sixteen years he has been exploring the world with his wife, Julie, and two daughters, Kathryn and Anna, who are kindred spirits.

Directing the Downwind Expedition,
1958. SIO ARCHIVES UCSD

"Exploration is adding to know-
ledge and then telling about it.
In my case, it's geographical. Ex-
ploration starts with a question:
'Why are things the way they are
and where can I go to find out
why they're that way? And how
can it be carried further?'"

Atlas at an Early Age

One might say I was one of the pioneers filling the reservoir behind the dam that burst to reveal plate tectonics.

Among those drops, perhaps, beginning in the 1930s: my father answered my queries thoughtfully; he took me into the Pasadena library and showed me its troves. Several early teachers recognized and nurtured my widening interests—geographic and scientific—although those hard times overall precluded educational travel except to nearby Mexico or the contiguous West. I read widely, each day the genteel *Pasadena Star-News*, but also all of the prolific Rafael Sabatini, much of the prescient Jules Verne, and the timely *National Geographic* accounts of Roy Chapman Andrews, William Beebe and the Johnsons, Martin and Osa. My father and I collected British Colonial stamps, those magical bits of paper that had been everywhere!

Through junior high I discovered and read all of Richard Halliburton, a charismatic model for today's "made-for-TV adventurer"; in my innocence I never puzzled who was invariably present to photograph his intrepid actions at Angkor, or "swimming" the Panama Canal, or riding an elephant over the Alps "like Hannibal." Halliburton's 1939 legacy to me was a wanderlust, a romantic curiosity for first-person observation that has permeated my scientific life. On reflection, all these factors contributed to my becoming an expedition leader/academic scientist with several true "firsts" in deep-sea geological exploration devoted to examining how the earth works, and ultimately becoming an invitee to The Explorers Club.

After 70 years, one simple clue stands out as indicative; it provides an ironic foreshadow of four decades of my life's explorations. Accustomed to flat world projections, e.g., Mercator, my grade-school instructors loosely spoke of "China through the earth." Early on I had a 12-inch globe at home. One day I decided to find out exactly what lay opposite—that is, the farthest anyone could go. One index finger firmly on Southern California, I felt around with the other. Land nearest that second point seemed to be tiny Mauritius, once home to John Tenniel's unique dodo. I told my parents (and my classmates at "Oral Reports") that I would get there some day; I even did some reading about the remote region. From library sources Madagascar and East Africa seemed much more interesting and knowable.

The irony is that those latter locales I have known in good part, but Mauritius has arguably become my second home. My next visit will be my fourteenth. To me it is the most beautiful, and intellectually the most stimulating (historically and culturally) of the scores of islands I have explored—or touched upon—in nearly 60 years of traveling worldwide.

So, indeed the twig was bent, and apparently that early. It's been a wonderful adventure!

ROBERT LLOYD FISHER, born in 1925 in Alhambra, California, lived near Pasadena until naval service in 1944–1946. He returned to complete his B.S. in Geology from Caltech in 1949, attended Northwestern University and then moved west to receive a Ph.D. in Marine Geology from Scripps Institution of Oceanography (UCSD—La Jolla) in 1957, and remained at SIO throughout his academic career.

Commencing while a graduate student in 1952, Bob organized and led several Scripps geological-geophysical investigations of the Middle America Trench lying offshore from Banderas Bay, Mexico, to Panama. In 1954 his two-ship expedition there, CHBASCO, established the first crustal structure trench model (from seismic refraction measurements) demonstrating the process later called "subduction"—one key element of plate tectonics. From 1952 to 1960 Bob led shipboard exploration to determine definitively the locale and greatest depth of 12 of the score of deepest trenches. Notably these included (in 1952) Horizon Deep, 10,800±10 km in Tonga Trench, deepest in the Southern Hemisphere and (in August 1959) the deepest in the oceans, 10,915±10 m in Challenger Deep southwest of Guam. That world maximum depth was confirmed five months later by manometer on bathyscaphe *Trieste*'s classic descent piloted by Don Walsh and engineer-inventor Jacques Piccard.

Following 1959's two-ship SIO exploration of the Gulf of California (and its resulting portrayal of still-current seafloor topography), Bob found his enduring object for field study, the Indian Ocean. From 1960 he led six multi-faceted SIO expeditions within the U.S. share of geological-geophysical investigation of the Indian Ocean. An elaborate collaboration, dubbed the International Indian Ocean Expedition 1959–1965 (with follow-up explorations in key areas to 1984), involved 20 countries and more than two-score research ships. By 1969–1972, Scripps fieldwork by Bob had found and recovered first "ground-truth," i.e., fresh specimens, from the oceans' lowermost igneous crust and its upper mantle, both almost uniquely exposed at the faulted Southwest Indian Ridge. As a final bow, 40 years of collaborative bathymetric interpretation has recently (2003) been published as a seafloor topographic-tectonic portrayal of the entire Indian Ocean and environs, nearly one-fourth of the Earth's surface area.

Bob was married to the late Sallie Coburn and he has a son, Carlos Andrew. Bob lives in La Jolla overlooking the Pacific Ocean.

VICE ADMIRAL JOHN "NICK" NICHOLSON

"I learned that significant exploration can be accomplished in conjunction with the development of military capabilities."

Congratulating the Sargo *crew after surfacing through at the North Pole, Feb. 9, 1960* "Believed taken by U.S. Navy"

Twice Under the Pole

As Commanding Officer of the *USS Sargo* in 1960, the nuclear submarine and I were cited for exceptionally meritorious conduct. *Nautilus*, the world's first nuclear submarine, and *Skate* had previously conducted under-ice operations in the deep portions of the Arctic Ocean in 1958 and 1959, but it was believed that a winter patrol to the Arctic Basin through 900 miles of shallow water when it would be covered by massive ice ridges extending almost to the bottom was vital to demonstrate that the submarine could control the ocean despite conditions. *Sargo* successfully conducted the patrol, discovered a previously unknown ridge, surfaced through three feet of ice at the North Pole—and finally fulfilled my dream. We also gathered extensive oceanographic data and finally cleared the ice pack after 31 days, 20 surfacings and 6,000 miles under ice.

Perhaps because of circumstances during the Depression, I don't recall early dreams. My dad's construction firm was wiped out and we moved to Nevada. We were quite poor, though Dad finally got back into business and I studied engineering upon entering the University of Nevada and enlisting in the Navy V-5 program. There, something changed my life. A fraternity brother returned from an interview at the U.S. Naval Academy. He didn't make it, but asked if I was interested. I knew nothing about it except a movie (1937's *Navy Blue and Gold*, I believe). I said I'd be thrilled but didn't see how it could happen. Unbelievably, he arranged a meeting with Senator McCarran's secretary. It still didn't look like it would work out, but four months later I received a telegram offering me an appointment! *Then* was born my first dream—of exciting opportunities instead of the contracting business. Annapolis?! Me?

Two years after graduation in 1946 I was on an APD (small ship with landing craft) in New Guinea feeling no one knew who I was or cared. But a sudden notice for submarine volunteers seemed to be the opportunity I needed to prove myself although I had never seen one. It worked and I was selected in 1950 as one of Captain Rickover's first two choices as a junior officer aboard the *Nautilus*. One night at dinner after extensive exercises had proven the increased capability of the nuclear submarine, the commanding officer said the next goal was, "Under the Pack to the Pole and Back!" Those words struck an exciting chord within me. Another dream was born—to surface at the North Pole!

From *Nautilus* I was ordered as executive officer of *Skate*, the Navy's third nuclear submarine. *Skate* was scheduled for an under-ice patrol to the Pole. In 1958 we approached, expecting to be the first to reach it. I was also navigator and was shooting sun sights through the periscope when we heard via BBC that *Nautilus* had beat us. Although we were terribly disappointed we decided to prove that a submarine could operate throughout the Arctic. We reached the Pole the next day, then completed an under-ice patrol of 11 days, nine surfacings and more than 652,000 recorded soundings, and were cited for "outstanding performance during under-ice operations in the Arctic Ocean." However, we were unable to surface at the Pole due to lack of polynyas (lakes). My dream was yet to be fulfilled.

Vice Admiral JOHN HARRIS "NICK" NICHOLSON of La Jolla, California, was born in 1924. Following graduation from Annapolis he served aboard two surface ships and, upon completion of submarine school, the *Tiru*. After duty on *Nautilus* and *Skate* he commanded *Pickerel* and *Sargo*, where he was cited for exceptionally meritorious conduct during "the most extensive under-ice exploration of the Arctic Ocean yet attempted by a submarine."

After a tour in the Office of the Chief of Naval Operations, Nick commanded in succession: *Stonewall Jackson*; US Navy Nuclear Power Training Unit, Idaho Falls, Idaho; and *Merrick*, where he was cited for meritorious service during combat operations in Vietnam. Following instruction at Industrial College of the Armed Forces he commanded Submarine Squadron Fifteen in Guam until 1972, when he was selected for Flag rank. His Rear Admiral tours included duty as Deputy Commander, Naval Ship Systems Command; Director of Strategic Submarine Division and Trident Program Coordinator; Commander Submarine Group Eight; Commander Submarines Mediterranean, Nato; and Deputy Assistant Chief of Staff, Plans and Policy, Supreme Headquarters Allied Powers Europe. In 1979 he was promoted to Vice Admiral and served as Vice Director of Strategic Target Planning until retirement in 1980.

His decorations include the Defense Distinguished Service Medal, Navy Distinguished Service Medal, Defense Superior Service Medal, Legion of Merit with Gold Star, Bronze Star with Combat "V", Navy Commendation Medal and Navy Unit Commendation Medal with one star.

Nick is married to Pat Addison. Their daughter Laurie has a daughter, Kristen.

ED SOBEY

Blackbeard marauding from Yokosuka, Japan, to Seattle aboard his 54-foot ketch, Enterprise. BARBARA SOBEY

"The thrill of discovery and seeing things for the first time still arouses my passions and I continue to travel and explore. That's my image of exploration: conducting basic research in remote areas under cruel conditions."

An Ocean of Adventure

My team pioneered techniques of remote working and living in Antarctica while conducting oceanographic research in winter. We demonstrated that we could work independently to collect data on the formation of bottom water.

The pages of *National Geographic* spawned my interest in exploring, and in doing what others had not done. So early was my dream born that I can't really remember the exact moment—but the earliest picture of me shows my grandfather reading from an issue of the *Geographic* to my sister and me! It was the stories of Jacques Cousteau, the Conshelf Divers and Don Walsh that launched me in a quest to join them as ocean explorers.

I looked for more accounts of the exploits of underwater scientists. When I was 12 years old, I found a copy of *The Silent World* in my uncle's den. I set up his movie projector and watched in amazement. We were at his house to attend a party, but engrossed in the film, I was oblivious to the festivities on the other side of the den door.

The Silent World was the documentary that won Cousteau the top award at the 1956 Cannes Film Festival and propelled him into international eco-stardom. The film showed Cousteau's buddies using skin-diving gear Émile Gagnan and Cousteau invented in 1943. For the first time humans could really be part of the underwater environment.

The film took me underwater with Cousteau and his aquatic band of adventurers while they ventured into aquatic caves, encountered marine animals and faced unknown physiological challenges. When the film ended, I knew what I was going to do with my life. They were heroes in the best possible way: brave, adventurous, and dedicated to exploring the mysteries of the watery world.

A summer job in Florida allowed me to learn scuba diving. With bachelor's degrees in physics and math, I headed to Oregon State University to study oceanography in graduate school. In those days, graduate students had to spend at least 10 days a year at sea. I would have opted for many more!

That first marine expedition was dramatic. We worked at night during a storm to retrieve expensive current meters that been lost. Dragging the bottom with a grapple, we found the ground line and pulled it up. The night was pitch black and the seas were running with eight to ten foot waves. Success nearly in hand—the cable parted, smashing a light and sending sparks everywhere! With tons of weight on the other end of the cable, it shot down from the A-frame crane, nearly killing one of the crew.

Following three years as a naval officer, I continued towards my master's degree. It was then that a life-changing opportunity presented itself. My major professor had a research grant for exploration in Antarctica. I was rewarded with a position. We spent half a winter and early spring near McMurdo Base. What an experience! Back home I discovered that I was now an explorer doing what explorers do—conducting basic research or observations in remote areas under cruel conditions.

I continued work on my Ph.D. and worked as a polar oceanographer for four years. A major change in career direction was joining the South Florida Science Museum as Director. The job entailed different kinds of exploring. To find exhibitions, I traveled to Peru (Incan gold and conquistador's armor), Egypt (the tools of the ancient Egyptians), Kenya (casts of early humanoids), China (artifacts from the Great Wall), and England (armor). I also participated in several scuba expeditions to collect specimens for our museum aquarium.

I have directed five museums, published 16 books and dove in many of the best sites in the world. Another of my greatest accomplishments has been, and continues to be, getting young people learning actively about the world in general and science in particular.

ED SOBEY, PH.D., is a global evangelist for creativity-based learning. He leads the Northwest Invention Center in Redmond, Washington, that creates traveling exhibits for museums in the U.S., Europe, and Asia and gives workshops on "inventing to learn" science around the world. Ed is an avid runner, scuba diver and ocean kayaker, and participates in a variety of other outdoor activities. He has hosted two television shows on science and inventing. Ed has participated in dozens of expeditions, sailed across the Pacific, sea kayaked to Alaska, been attacked by sea lions and sharks, hit by a whale and lost on seven continents.

He and Barbara live in Redmond. Woody and Andrew are their boys.

"*Exploration is curiosity acted upon. We are born with the exploration gene; most of us sublimate it by early adulthood. A fortunate few don't and this is the raw material from which explorers are made.*"

After diving in the Russian MIR submersible behind him to the Bismarck, *2001.* DON WALSH

Running Away to Sea

I was selected by the U.S. Navy as the Bathyscaph *Trieste*'s first commander in 1959. A year later Jacques Piccard, son of the Swiss designer Auguste, and I climbed down into the spherical steel cabin the size, and temperature, of a large refrigerator and in five hours dove nearly seven miles into the deepest place in the world's oceans, the Mariana Trench. To our surprise, we spotted fish on the bottom, proving that life can survive those cold, remote depths.

My interest in the sea began during my childhood, in the mid-1930s. We lived in a house in the Berkeley Hills that had a magnificent view west across San Francisco Bay and beyond the Golden Gate. From my perch at the big front window I watched the two bridges being built and the bustle of shipping traffic. Ferryboats, cargo ships and warships all were part of that ever-changing seascape. West, beyond that bay, was the far horizon of the Pacific that excited a small boy's curiosity. What was out there, over that horizon and would I even go there? I was "imprinted" with a lifelong love of the sea. I knew that someday I would be a sailor.

After high school I had hoped to go into the merchant marine. However, this was in the early post-World War II years; there were too many qualified mariners and not enough ships. No chance. So I joined the Naval Air Reserve and found myself flying over the Bay and the Pacific as a crewman in torpedo bombers. I added being a naval aviator to my sailor dream.

Still that far horizon beckoned—I had to go there.

My seagoing life began when I entered Annapolis in 1950. A year later I was crossing the Atlantic on a battleship on my first midshipman cruise. After graduation my first duty was as an officer on a cargo ship. Then in 1956 I joined the Submarine Force instead of Naval Aviation. Now I was not only on the sea but under it as well.

That old curiosity flared up again; what's under there? My opportunity to answer that question came when I volunteered for the *Trieste* program. We conducted a variety of scientific diving operations in the Pacific and achieved many engineering "firsts" with cameras, lights, instrumentation and sampling devices. Today, the early *Trieste* team has its fingerprints all over the current underwater technologies. Eventually over 200 manned submersibles were built and put into service from the early 1960s onwards.

Sadly, no one has returned to the deepest place in the ocean. After 1977, when the last French bathyscaphe was retired, there was no manned vehicle in the world that could dive deeper than 20,000 feet. Today there are only four that can reach that depth. Hundreds of people have summited Mt. Everest and rocketed into space but only two have reached the deepest depths of the sea. However, it is not about making records; it is about exploring the far depths, adding to our knowledge about the ocean.

Today I continue to dive, most recently to the *Titanic* and the *Bismarck*. I spend about four months a year on diving expeditions and seagoing trips to the Polar regions. I first went to the Arctic in 1955 and the Antarctic in 1971, making over 50 Polar expeditions. I have sailed all seven seas, plumbed the greatest depths and crossed through ice-covered polar oceans. What more could a sailor ask for? Perhaps a seaplane, but that's another story....

For the *Trieste* achievement, DON WALSH received a medal from President Eisenhower at the White House. Born in 1931, he has been involved in diving operations with 16 different manned submersibles, piloting six. He has also worked at sea with remotely operated vehicles and with NASA determining how spacecraft could be used to study the oceans. He has a Ph.D. in Oceanography from Texas A&M, 1968. His contributions to polar exploration were recognized when The Walsh Spur, a mountain ridge in the Antarctic, was named for him. Don is the author of over 200 publications, has given over 1,500 lectures and appeared on TV and radio programs in 64 countries. His travels have taken him to about 112 nations.

The *Trieste* is on exhibit at the Navy Museum in Washington, D.C.

Don and wife Joan live on a ranch with a salmon river running through it in southwest Oregon in the Coast Range Mountains. Kelly and Liz are their children.

17 Six Fathoms Under

Exploration is really the essence
of the human spirit.

—FRANK BORMAN

Genie with Jaws. DAVID DOUBILET

Early Determination of a Dream

After my first few dives with sharks in the South Pacific, I had a chance to study lemon sharks at the Cape Haze Marine Laboratory in 1955. We trained them to push a target to get food. Then we gave them two different targets and they learned to choose the correct one. When we took them away—for as long as two months—they immediately chose the correct target when we tested them again. It was thrilling to know that they had the ability to learn, be conditioned and had a memory.

Another thrilling moment was the discovery that a small sea bass, *Serranus subligarius*, can change its sex in ten seconds. It can mate as either a male or a female with another fish, change its color pattern and mate again in as little as ten seconds as the opposite sex.

*"In my case exploration would be looking
for something that hasn't been found before;
a new fish or animal. Then there is the
responsibility and satisfaction of
publishing this new finding."*

The lead article in my August 2005 issue of *Ichthyological Research* from Japan starts with a 1938 quote from William Beebe on the "mating" of a male ceratioid anglerfish:

> To be driven by impelling order headlong upon a mate so gigantic, in such immense and forbidding darkness, and willfully to eat a hole in her soft side, to feel the gradually increasing transfusion of her blood through one's veins, to lose everything that marked one as other than a worm, to become a brainless, senseless thing that was a fish—this is sheer fiction, beyond all belief unless we have seen the proof of it.

This is one of many hundreds of Beebe's magical descriptions of fish phenomena. In the 1920s and early 1930s I was greatly impressed with his comments on all kinds of animals in his books *Edge of the Jungle, Jungle Days, Galapagos: World's End,* and *Arcturus Adventure* and his articles in *National Geographic.*

I remember a single incident in my youth when I was determined to be an explorer of the sea. I seriously declared to my family I wanted to study fish for the rest of my life. They were amused, but concerned. "Maybe you can take up typing and become a secretary to someone like William Beebe." I said I didn't want to be anybody's secretary! I wanted to be an explorer *like* William Beebe!

My Japanese mother, eager to encourage me, searched bookstores for all of his books when she couldn't be with me during her long working hours. We lived in Woodside, Queens, but she worked at the cigar and magazine stand in the lobby of the New York Athletic Club in downtown Manhattan near the wonderful Battery Park Aquarium, where she took me for the first time when I was nine.

I was mesmerized by the beautiful fish, from the little neon gobies to the big sharks, and felt I wanted to spend the rest of my life studying these wonderful creatures. I had learned to swim when I was two and loved water. It was the huge aquarium with murky water where I saw my first living shark. It looked like a mysterious and wonderful place. I leaned forward as close as I could get to the glass and pretended I was on the bottom of the sea with it.

The turning point in my life came in high school when the accumulated thrills of reading Beebe and visiting the aquarium launched my improbable but irreversible dream to follow in his footsteps.

In the 1950s I heard Beebe lecture at The Explorers Club. He ended with a dramatic flair by telling his rapt audience that he was about to study jungle life to further observe "sights you can't see, sounds you can't hear and phenomena you can't imagine" as he rushed out of the lecture hall without a thank you or a bow to thunderous applause. He launched many a career, including mine.

Now at 83, I know I made the right decision. I cannot imagine a more wonderful life than I have had.

EUGENIE "GENIE" CLARK, born in 1922, is a world-renowned ichthyologist and authority on sharks popularly known as The Shark Lady. She received her Ph.D. in 1950 from New York University and is Professor Emerita in the Department of Biology at the University of Maryland. She was a research assistant at Scripps Institution of Oceanography, at the New York Zoological Society and at the American Museum of Natural History in New York. Genie also was the founding director of the Cape Haze Marine Laboratory in Sarasota, Florida, now a leading center for shark research called the Mote Marine Laboratory.

Genie is the recipient of innumerable accolades, including three honorary D.Sc. degrees and awards from the National Geographic Society, The Explorers Club, the Underwater Society of America, the American Littoral Society, the Gold Medal Award of the Society of Women Geographers and the recipient of the President's Medal of the University of Maryland. She's authored three books, including *Lady With A Spear*, over 170 scientific and popular articles, as well as 12 articles for *National Geographic*. She has conducted 71 deep submersible dives and over 200 expeditions.

Her children are Hera, Aya, Tak and Niki Konstantinou. She lives in Sarasota.

"Exploration is a lifelong process of feeding curiosity whether planting tomatoes in your own backyard or diving on reefs off Madagascar."

Anne, never far from water, her second home. STANFORD SHANE

Deep Blue

My greatest exploration discovery is a personal one: in thirty years of exploring the Earth's oceans, I have witnessed a complex combination of overpopulation, pollution, over-fishing and global warming. Our planet's future is critically dependent on the interaction of people and nature. Programs of conservation and sustainability urgently need development. Life on teeming city streets and coral reefs are now intricately linked.

I grew up in the summers at Magnolia, Massachusetts, on the shores of the North Atlantic Ocean. I had an idyllic and privileged childhood during my first 12 years. Wrapped in imagination and freedom, I roamed the beach seeking pirate treasure buried in the sand from the time school let out until it resumed. I dove under the foamy waves pretending to be a mermaid playing with sibling seahorses and horseshoe crabs. I collected seaweed and shells and stones and built elaborate sandcastle estates. I turned blue from the water temperature and have no recollections of the cold. Now I can scarcely dip my adult toe in the North Atlantic without shivering.

During the autumn of my twelfth year in the early 1960s I was struck with an uncommon childhood illness, St. Vitus's Dance, which paralyzed me for a year.

Frustrated with the inability to move, I rolled out of bed and inched toward the windows to see the blowing winter snowdrifts and then the spring songbirds. During one of those journeys on the floor I vowed that if and when I recovered I would swim underwater to see and explore all the fascinating places in my childhood imagination.

At about 19, I was the only girl in the scuba certification course in Beverly, Massachusetts. The army drill sergeant instructor barked orders and I doubted my ability to pass muster. But I survived and on my first open-water dive off Andros Island in the Bahamas I opened my eyes into the deep blue Caribbean Ocean. Feeling like Alice entering Wonderland, I swam along the upper reaches of a continental shelf bordering on the Tongue of the Ocean. The top of this shelf, "The Wall," starts in about 90–100 feet of water and then drops, precipitously in some places and gradually in others, to 6,000 feet. Swimming out over the edge of The Wall looking down into the eternal blue changed my life forever. All my childhood images swirled into history as reality surpassed fantasy.

After going "Over the Wall," the ledge at 185 feet was bathed in ethereal blue light. A touch of nitrogen narcosis or "rapture of the depths" added to the disorientation. Only by tracing my exhale bubbles with my hand did I definitively know which way was up. And only the firm, reassuring grasp of my excellent dive buddy, Margo Birch, kept me from spinning down into the beckoning depths. I was amazed at the amount of light filtering into such depths—a wonderful difference from the dark grey North Atlantic. Swimming around on this submerged sandy shelf that used to be a beach before the last ice age filled me with awe.

Thousands of dives later, this awe is ever-present. Going underwater is always like visiting another planet without leaving Earth. Recently, I returned to Andros to dive Over the Wall to the ledge with my daughter, Emily. Coincidentally, she was the same age as I was on that first trip to an enchanted realm.

ANNE L. DOUBILET of Manhattan has dived in almost all of the world's oceans as a freelance member of an underwater team for the National Geographic Society. She has worked on over 30 stories worldwide for *National Geographic* as well as various books and advertising projects for the Society.

One of the first females to dive in a shark-cage off Australia to observe Great Whites, Anne is a recipient of the Scuba Schools International Platinum Pro 5000 card for having done over 5,000 dives.

She founded and managed a stock photography business of marine-life images with international sales and has co-curated photography exhibitions.

Anne is the author of, and contributing photographer to, the award-winning children's book *Under the Sea from A to Z*. As an editor for children and adult books, she is experienced with varied subjects including fiction, history, sociology and wildlife. Presently, Anne is the founder of ALD Consulting and works on several writing projects.

She serves on the Advisory Board of Wings Women of Discovery Awards given by Wings WorldQuest, an organization of women explorers, and has judged the Wildlife and Conservation category of The Explorers Club Documentary Film Festival since its inception in 2002.

ANN McGOVERN

"To me, exploration is solving deep mysteries, testing courage, expanding horizons, imparting knowledge ... all of which I first learned in imagination on that wonderful, life-saving, childhood bed."

Soaking up life like a sponge. MARTIN SCHEINER.

A Magic Horse-Drawn Carriage

In 1985, I carried The Explorers Club Flag to the underwater coral reefs of China's Hainan Island, where Eugenie Clark and I mapped these coral reefs for the first time. Ours was the first American team to scuba dive in China.

I was six in the 1930s when my dreams of exploring began. My father had just died and my mother was sunk in misery and had no time for me. I often felt very alone and sad. The only way I could escape an unhappy childhood was at night, when I transformed my four-poster bed into a carriage pulled by four white horses. I traveled through deep forests and golden cities of exotic countries, and I ended my nightly adventures by swimming with incredible sea creatures, even sharks, in turquoise waters off islands ringed with palms. My horse-drawn carriage held plenty of books, chocolates, maps and journals.

I stuttered a lot and never spoke in class. Of course I had feelings I wished to express but since I couldn't talk about them, I began writing poems and keeping diaries. No one knew. From the time I was eight years old, I always felt better about myself after writing.

I didn't see the countryside or a cow until I was ten years old, but I loved growing up in New York City. I climbed a special tree in Central Park until I got to my favorite branch where I would sit and read for hours. I would visit the library every day after school. Whenever she saw me, the librarian would say, "You again!" She was very kind and helped me find my favorite books of fairy tales and travel adventures. I was in the library more than I was home, I think.

I went out west to the University of New Mexico and married my English teacher. I had a son when I was just 20 years old. When he was just 18 months old, my marriage was over and I returned to New York. I remember the hard times, living in a fifth-floor walk-up tenement, with the bathtub in the hall and only cold water. But in times of sorrow or longing, I could always will myself back to my dreams. I worked as a waitress, as a model, in publishing companies. Working at one in the 1960s inspired me to try writing a children's book. They accepted it!

When I married my late husband in 1970, I learned to scuba dive and sail. We explored the seven continents, on land and beneath the sea. Airplanes and dive boats became the "carriages" of my childhood dreams. In many ways, I never traveled far from that childhood bed because I began to incorporate my travels and adventurous explorations into my books and later my poetry and collage art.

Many of **ANN McGOVERN'S** 55 books for children reflect her interests in the underwater world and exploration. Some of her award-winners are: *Down Under, Down Under: Diving Adventures on the Great Barrier Reef; Night Dive; Shark Lady: True Adventures of Eugenie Clark; Playing with Penguins and Other Adventures in Antarctica; Swimming with Sea Lions and Other Adventures in the Galapagos Islands.* More than 20 million copies of her books are in print.

Ann lectures to schools, conferences and writing groups and is a tireless promoter of literacy around the world. The Ann McGovern Reading Room at the New York Public Library's Muhlenberg Library provides an important resource for the Chelsea neighborhood. She's on the Board of Goddard-Riverside Community Center and a strong supporter of peace and justice around the world. She was awarded the 2002 Laura Parsons Pratt Award for her efforts to improve the status of women and children. Her poetry workshop conducted for inmates of Bedford Hills prison resulted in the publication of *Voices from Within.*

Her poetry has appeared in many literary journals, including *Confrontation, Georgetown Review* and *South Carolina Review. Bribing the Fortune Teller* is her first poetry collection for adults, illustrated with her collage art.

Ann lives in Manhattan and has four children, Peter, Charlie, Annie and Jim, and three grandchildren.

JUDITH W. SCHRAFFT

The ultimate thrill for a diver: riding a whale shark. WILLIAM PRAHL

"The privilege of discovery, of being the first footprint on the beach, the first eyes to see something long lost or unknown to the world, all epitomize exploration. It is a test of endurance beyond experience, of ingenuity under adversity, of overcoming obstacles through tenacity and untested ability."

Underwater Ultimate

The closest to nirvana for any scuba diver—amateur or professional, no matter how blasé—is an encounter with a whale shark. Divers scour the world for a glimpse of these behemoths. For me that special moment was only a half-hour boat ride from home in Palm Beach, Florida. On a garden-variety dive to our favorite "Rock Pile" at 100 feet, a polka-dotted presence slowly angled down, an unmistakable and irresistible vision. In an instant I had attached myself to the left fin of this 35-foot specimen, while a friend held its huge dorsal fin. As our eyes met in wonder over its back, I was reminded of our local mantra: "There's no such thing as a bad dive."

Horseshoe crabs on New Jersey beaches may not seem properly inspirational for a lifetime focus on all matters pertaining to the sea, but just one small nudge is enough to propel a 10-year-old budding marine biologist into a fanatic, one who probes tide pools and high-tide wrack lines for all manner of unappetizing debris, dead and alive. These collections ripened in the summer sun and were regularly replaced with yet more accumulations.

But it wasn't until I adopted the beaches of Florida in my mid-twenties in 1965 that I realized the marine world offered pickings far more colorful, and led to scuba diving—which consumes me. My active outdoor life began with my first checkout dive. For a Manhattan-born-and-bred urbanite who had cut her teeth on snorkelling around home base and in the nearby Bahamas, the indelible thrill of circumnavigating the wreck of the *Mizpah* at 80 feet in the clear blue Gulf Stream was an epiphany. The experience changed the direction of my life and made available to me parts of the world that no one without this focus would attempt to visit.

That episode was further affirmed by a trip a few years later to Cocos Island, a two-day sail from the Costa Rica coast, where the lure was the yearly migration of hammerhead sharks. There on the shores of Wafer Bay were boulders with the names of passing whalers and private yachts chiselled into the rocks, including my old pal the *Mizpah* and the date of 1927.

Diving expeditions included algae-collecting on the Great Barrier Reef, conducting the first-ever underwater survey of the reefs between Bali and Ambon, sailing through the steamy Seychelle Islands on a converted Norwegian whaler with no ventilation, toughing out a cyclone in New Guinea and being stranded overnight on a flea-infested Palauan islet. But as any true adventurer knows, discomforts and misery are all part of the game. For me, the advantage of my passion is that my expeditions take me to warm, sunny, tropical locales. Shortly after my first scuba dive, my snow skis went to a thrift shop.

As Palm Beach is close enough to the Everglades to be considered a part of the overall system, research is constantly being done there with an emphasis on inland water discharges into the ocean and its effect on beach restoration, offshore reef systems and the health and productivity of local fish stocks and species.

Science and scientists are a constant in my life, and add another level of interest. I joined a paleontological dig in the Gobi Desert headed by Philip Currie and in 2005 was on John Loret's 50th anniversary trip to Easter Island to celebrate his work there, begun with Thor Heyerdahl in the 1950s.

JUDY SCHRAFFT is Chairman of the Coral Reef Society, which monitors the local marine environment, participates in beach and reef cleanups and is involved in other matters pertaining to the well being of the Atlantic Ocean close to Palm Beach. The Indian Ocean has become a favorite diving locale, as well as the Pacific. She has authored two books, *Places* and *Other Places*. She has also made overland treks through Mali to Timbuktu and from Alexandria along the Mediterranean coast to Tripoli.

18 The Sea Hunters

Ship me somewhere east of Suez,
where the best is like
the worst,
Where there aren't no
Ten Commandments
an' a man
can raise a thirst.

—ON THE ROAD
TO MANDALAY,
RUDYARD KIPLING

GEORGE BASS

"Exploration is seeking to discover and understand the unknown, whether on Earth, in outer space, or within, say, the human brain."

Happy soon to be climbing into the MIR *submersible to dive on the* Titanic, *2003.*
DAVID CONCANNON

A Convergence of Interests

I was first to excavate an ancient shipwreck on the seabed, revealing an unsuspected Semitic presence in the Bronze Age Aegean, thereby rewriting accepted history. I'm also pleased to have turned nautical archaeology into an accepted academic discipline.

Sometimes dreams are subtle. As a child, I never actually dreamed of becoming an archaeologist or diver, although it seems I was fated for both. The earliest drawings I recall making, in the 1930s when I was five or six, were of divers. What was easier than a circle for the helmet, a smaller circle (with cross bars) for the faceplate and little circles for bubbles? But I also had a dashing archaeologist uncle, Robert Wauchope, a Harvard doctoral student, who regaled me with tales of tipping his canoe in a crocodile-infested Guatemalan river and cutting a boa constrictor off with a machete!

Dad joined the faculty at Annapolis. Bob's favorite book was Jules Verne's *Twenty Thousand Leagues Under the Sea* and we tried in vain to get the Naval Academy to obtain the 1916 silent film, marveling at the 1936 autobiography of its photographer, The Explorers Club's John Ernest Williamson. About then we made our own diving helmet, cutting a rectangular opening in a square oil can in which we mounted a faceplate of window glass, held in place with putty and cut arched openings, padded with tape, for our shoulders. Thankfully we never actually tested it in nearby Weems Creek!

In early 1943, when I was ten, I left my sickbed to attend a movie I *had* to see, soon writing to my grandparents: "'Reap the Wild Wind' had a good octopus fight in which one of the heroes was eaten."

This special fascination with the underwater world was only part of my curiosity about the universe. High school friends tell me I was destined to become an explorer. I mounted a reflecting telescope on my roof, kept a scrapbook of rocketry and devoured books by those who climbed mountains, uncovered dinosaur eggs or descended in a bathysphere. Richard Halliburton's books held a special fascination. One of my dad's colleagues had known Halliburton, so I listened in awe to his every word about that consummate adventurer.

My first visit to Turkey was in 1953, when I spent six days traveling from London to Ankara by third-class train, sleeping in luggage racks and on park benches, visiting Halliburton's haunts. I returned to Turkey in 1957 to assist in the Gordion excavations. I'd already gained excavation experience at Bronze Age Lerna, in Greece while I was a student at the American School of Classical Studies at Athens 1955–1957. At Lerna, I snorkeled in the adjacent bay, naively looking for preclassical pots—and am told that I often said the future of archaeology lay in the sea. Indeed, in Athens I had more books about diving than archaeology. But, ironically, I never dreamed of learning to dive.

Then, in 1959, my early interests all came together—diving, archaeology, the Bronze Age and Turkey—when Peter Throckmorton wrote to the University of Pennsylvania, where I was studying, to say that he had found a Bronze Age shipwreck off Turkey. He thought it would be possible to excavate under water. Knowing of my love for the Bronze Age, my professor asked if I'd learn to dive to be archaeologist on a University of Pennsylvania Museum expedition. Without hesitation I took the course that enabled me, the following summer, to became the first person to excavate an ancient shipwreck in its entirety on the seabed. The rest is history!

GEORGE F. BASS, PH.D., is founder of the Institute of Nautical Archaeology, now based at Texas A&M University, where he is Distinguished Professor Emeritus. He has been called the "father of underwater archaeology" by *National Geographic,* and an "underwater Indiana Jones" by *Time.* He has been awarded an Explorers Club Lowell Thomas Award, the Archaeological Institute of America's Gold Medal for Distinguished Archaeological Achievement, a National Geographic Society La Gorce Gold Medal and Centennial Award, the J.C. Harrington Medal from The Society for Historical Archaeology, and honorary doctorates by Boğaziçi University in Istanbul and the University of Liverpool. In 2002 President George W. Bush presented him with the National Medal of Science. George has described his internationally televised work in eight books and half a dozen *National Geographic* articles.

He and his wife, Ann, divide their time between homes in College Station, Texas, and Bodrum, Turkey. They have two grown sons.

Creature from the Black Baltic *climbs aboard the R/V* Mare *after a 50-metre dive to the Russian ironclad monitor* Russalka, *2005.* MARC PIKE, OPEN ROAD PRODUCTIONS/ECO-NOVA MEDIA GROUP

The Sea Hunter

I was standing, knee-deep in blue-black, stinking mud, hose in hand, washing away the thick mass to reveal the charred but intact remains of a shopkeeper's inventory, perfectly preserved by its muddy burial. As the water gently melted the mud and silt, jars of olives, kegs of butter, a barrel of salted pork, a crate of whiskey

"My favorite form of exploration is scientific inquiry, probing the planet, the oceans, the heavens, the human body, the mind and the structure of the universe for knowledge."

appeared. It was a "Pompeii" moment, a long-forgotten fire forever frozen in time. The store's floor, weakened by the flames, had collapsed into San Francisco Bay on May 4, 1851—a day when the entire Gold Rush city was destroyed—and now I was standing on it, the smell of charred wood mixing with the mud's odour.

How did it all begin? It was in the fifth grade in San Jose, California, which had yet to bloom and become Silicon Valley. Back then it was known for orchards and fields of hay. Teachers and librarians fired my soul with a passion for history and archaeology, encouraged my extracurricular studies, and provided books that took my 10-year-old mind to faraway places and ancient times. One afternoon after school, after intently scanning the pages of a school library book and staring for what felt like hours at a photo of Tollund Man, seemingly asleep after 2,000 years in a bog, a Maya pyramid at Tikal and Tutankhamen's golden mask, I decided to visit the local museum and take in a tour of their full-scale model of an Egyptian rock tomb. At the base of the stairs, in the faint light, we turned a corner and stepped into the tomb chamber to find the sarcophagus, its lid broken by tomb raiders. That was all it took; I knew then what I would do in life. I didn't want to be a raider. I wanted to be the archaeologist who got there first.

I went on my first dig at age 14, learned to dive at 20, and have never regretted becoming an archaeologist. The turning points have been many, aided by mentors, friends and incredible opportunities. My favorites are the projects that do not deal with the famous, but the everyday, learning about lost and forgotten people who in their anonymity speak volumes about the human experience. Learning to dig and dive was the first step. Learning to share the finds—in exhibitions, books and presentations—was another. It means nothing to find something, to make an important discovery or to learn a lesson if you do not share it. My passion for the past is matched by my desire to make history accessible to all.

Life is a journey of exploration if we choose to seek and to learn, to challenge ourselves. But that doesn't mean I don't thrill to the simple physical achievement of a quest, to facing a challenge of nature or one's own limits to go farther, faster, or to be the first. In all these ways, we celebrate life and chafe at the boundaries, and it is through challenging boundaries that we advance as a species.

JAMES DELGADO, born in 1958, has led or participated in shipwreck expeditions around the world. His explorations include a deep-sea submersible dive to RMS *Titanic*, the discoveries of *Carpathia*, the ship that rescued *Titanic*'s survivors and the notorious "ghost ship" *Mary Celeste*. As well, he has surveyed the USS *Arizona* at Pearl Harbor, the sunken fleet of atomic-bombed warships at Bikini Atoll, the lost fleet of Mongol emperor Kublai Khan off Japan, the polar exploration ship *Maud* wrecked in the Arctic and the 1846 wreck of the United States naval brig *Somers*, whose tragic story inspired Herman Melville's *Billy Budd*.

He led the crew that restored the *Ben Franklin*, the oceanographic deep-sea research submersible built in Switzerland for famed undersea explorer and scientist Jacques Piccard and famously employed on a historic 30-day "drift mission" along the eastern seaboard of the United States in 1969. It is now on display at the Maritime Museum in Vancouver, British Columbia.

Jim is past Executive Director of the museum and now is Executive Director of the Institute of Nautical Archaeology founded by George Bass. Previous to both, he was the head of the U.S. government's maritime preservation program and was the maritime historian for the U.S. National Park Service. He also hosts the National Geographic International television series *The Sea Hunters,* featuring best-selling author Clive Cussler.

Jim is the author or editor of nearly 30 books and numerous articles, including *Adventures of a Sea Hunter: True Adventures in Search of Famous Shipwrecks*.

Jim has two children, John and Beth, and he and wife Ann Goodhart live in Steveston, B.C., a historic fishing community on the Fraser River.

EDWARD VON DER PORTEN

Hang ten: Ed surfing for Spanish shipwrecks. Eric Von Der Porten

"Effective archaeology brings together a wide range of sometimes contentious scholars to tease out knowledge and understanding from the often intractable shreds of physical objects and traces in the soil which we are privileged to bring to light. Ultimately we reconstruct and explain human lives and experiences."

Diving to a Dream

The little patch of coarse sand where I sat was surrounded by powder-fine dunes stretching for miles to north, east and south. To the west lay the gentle surf of the Pacific Ocean. I was brushing sand off a large block of amber-hued beeswax from the wreck of the galleon *San Felipe*. My fingers probed tunnels in the wax: teredo tunnels! Instantly, those tunnels revealed the ship's tragic fate.

On our three expeditions from 1999 through 2003, I had investigated the scattered porcelain and stoneware fragments, the lead hull-sheathing studded with rusted iron tacks, the wax blocks and a unique cloisonné plate rim. The porcelains and documents had dated and identified the ship, but the teredo tunnels told me the story of her loss. How? Teredo larvae could only have reached the wax after the hull had flooded, and the size of their tunnels showed how long the ship had lain offshore.

The *San Felipe* had been a ghost galleon, her crew dead or dying, sailing out of control through the coastal haze of Baja California after a half-year voyage from Manila in 1576. A few hundred yards off shore, she had struck the shoals and come to a shuddering halt. The desert or the sea had killed any survivors. Then the derelict had lain canted in the shallows for a year or more, her flooded hull and cargo tunnelled by teredos. Eventually a rare storm had shattered her timbers and driven the wreckage onto seven miles of turbulent beach.

The route to the galleon in the Baja California desert had started 60 years earlier, in 1942, when I was eight. My family was sailing upriver aboard a Hudson River Dayliner with a huge walking-beam steam engine ponderously driving her side paddlewheels. Passing along the Manhattan piers, we came to the French liner *Normandie* lying on her side, the victim of fire and flooding. To this day, I need no photograph to revisit that scene of desolation.

Nautical experiences were all around us in World War II Brooklyn, from the beaches covered with oil from sunken tankers, to the Navy Yard where we walked the hangar deck of the *USS Franklin* and looked up at the sky through the flight deck, shattered by Japanese bombs, ammunition explosions and gasoline fires. With war's end, we climbed to the decks of the *USS Missouri* and visited the Japanese surrender site. These indelible impressions, added to a good public library with its copies of Charles Nordhoff, and James Hall's *Bounty Trilogy*, set my course toward a career in nautical history. But the route into archaeological exploration would come a few years later.

Visiting an archaeological dig at Drakes Bay, north of San Francisco, in 1956, I watched a fragment of Chinese blue-on-white porcelain float to the top of the blackened sand and broken shells in a rocker screen. I reached down and touched history in a very direct way. The sherd came from a plate, either abandoned by Francis Drake in 1579 during his voyage around the world or lost in the wreck of the Manila galleon *San Agustin* in 1595.

Six years later, I began leading Santa Rosa Junior College crews in digs at Drakes Bay. Twenty years later we definitively separated the Drake from the galleon porcelains, using art-historical and sherd-wear techniques. When the Baja California galleon came to my attention in 1997, my colleagues and I were ready to probe its secrets. One result of the work, the traveling exhibit "Treasures of the Manila Galleons," will eventually become a permanent exhibit in Baja.

From that first dig at Drakes Bay, through the discovery of how the gunport was invented, while working on Henry VIII's warship *Mary Rose*, and feeling the surge-and-coast rhythm as 18 of us paddled the early Iron Age Hjortspring boat replica in Denmark, to that moment brushing off the wax block in the Baja desert, I repeatedly re-evaluated my definition of archaeological exploration.

EDWARD VON DER PORTEN of San Francisco, California, is a nautical historian and archaeologist, maritime museum director (retired), writer and educator. His research has delved into early European shipbuilding, the Hanseatic League, explorers, naval cannon, Chinese trade porcelains, the World War II German Navy and the inventions of Johann Gutenberg. Born in 1933, he graduated from Stuyvesant High School, then moved to California and received bachelor's and master's degrees in history from San Francisco State College.

He and his wife Saryl celebrated their fiftieth anniversary in 2004 with their sons Michael and Eric, daughters-in-law Elaine and Cathy, and four grandchildren.

Holding a mustard condiment bottle recovered from the U.S.S. Monitor. Robert E. Zaworski, M.D., Collection

"As far as the Monitor was concerned my definition of exploration was the act of investigating and examining this historic shipwreck, trying to learn what it was, how it was made, how it worked. With this information I was able to better understand and appreciate the men who fought and died in this most horrendous Civil War."

Diving to a Dream

My greatest adventure was diving to America's first ironclad warship, the *U.S.S. Monitor*, and bringing up the first diver-retrieved artifacts. After her historic duel with the *Merrimack* in Virginia in March, 1862, the *Monitor* was visited several times by President Lincoln, who examined and felt the nine dents in the turret produced by Confederate cannon balls. During the stormy New Year's night of December 31, 1862, while under tow, she went down with four officers and 12 men. America's first ironclad warship was lost for over a century.

I was born in 1947 and raised in Lorain, Ohio, on the north coast of Ohio and Lake Erie. At 11, after watching Mike Nelson in *Sea Hunt* and reading *The Living Sea* by Jacques Cousteau, I developed a deep interest in underwater exploration. With my Voit 50-fathom regulator and tanks, I began to explore the fresh water wrecks of Lake Erie.

College and medical school interfered with further underwater exploration, but the call of the deep, or the exploration of the unknown, was always there. While progressing through medical school and residency, I became enamored of the challenge and lure of the mountains and started on the course that many mountaineers embark upon: attempting to summit the highest peaks of the seven continents (I've done five to date). My climb of Elbrus in the Soviet Caucasus convinced me that a member of our team, Beck Weathers, was one of the strongest mountaineers I ever had the honor to climb with. If I had continued mountaineering, I'm sure I would probably have been with Beck in 1996 and been a footnote in Jon Krakauer's *Into Thin Air* as the doctor who died trying to summit Everest. Instead, an opportunity presented itself that brought me back to my early days of underwater exploration.

For 111 years, the *Monitor* had kept her secrets. Then, in 1973, Duke University's research vessel, *Eastwind*, discovered the long-hidden wreck. The first remote-controlled photographic study was published in the January 1975 issue of *National Geographic*. That same month, The National Oceanographic and Atmospheric Administration (N.O.A.A.) designated the wreck site as a national marine sanctuary in order to protect this historically significant shipwreck. It wasn't until 1990 that the first dive expedition was awarded a federal permit to visit the site.

Being a scuba diver for 30 years with deep-water training, and a Civil War historian for almost that long, the opportunity to visit this time capsule was a dream come true. With the assistance of Ed Bearss, a friend and Chief Historian of the National Park Service, I became a member of the 1992 and 1993 expeditions to the *Monitor* wreck site. The ironclad rests 20 miles off Cape Hatteras, North Carolina—where I brought up five condiment bottles, which now rest in the Mariner's Museum in Newport News, Virginia. The dives to 246 feet, done with compressed air, certainly "pushed the envelope" but luckily occurred without incident. Present on the turret were the dents from the Confederate cannon balls—large enough to put your hand into—just as Abraham Lincoln did so long ago. The travel, preparation, equipment and research that were required to make such an exploration only made the moment when I was able to actually touch the dents in the turret, or swim into the engine room, more extraordinary.

My tent mate on Mt. McKinley is still on the mountain and my dive buddy on the *Monitor* drowned the next year, but I still carry the desire for exploration and will forever carry the flag of their memory.

ROBERT E. ZAWORSKI, M.D., is a plastic and reconstructive surgeon who has been in private practice for 25 years. He was elected to membership in the American Alpine Club in 1984 and The Explorers Club in 1986. His outside interest in American history, especially the American Civil War, has resulted in his being elected a member of the Sons of Union Veterans, as well as an honorary member of the Sons of Confederate Veterans. He is a member of the Society of Civil War Historians and has published *Headstones of Heroes: The Restoration and History of Confederate Graves in Atlanta's Oakland Cemetery*.
   Rob and his wife Linda live in Atlanta, Georgia

19 The Bone Hunters

Go confidently in the direction of your dreams. Live the life you've always imagined.

—HENRY DAVID THOREAU

Sue with her electrifying discovery— the T. rex *Sue in situ.* PETER LARSON BHIGR

A *T. rex* Named Sue

On Aug 12, 1990, I was on a dinosaur dig in the Black Hills with Peter Larson. That morning our Suburban had a flat and most of the crew left to get it repaired and escape the heat. I stayed and hiked seven hours to some insignificant sandstone bluffs. It sounds crazy, but it was like this *T. rex* was calling me—like she had mystically slashed that tire so we couldn't leave. I spotted crumpled bones on the ground. Looking up the cliff eight feet, I spotted more! I clambered up and saw three huge articulated vertebra, parts of a rib, femur and pubis. It was a *T. rex*! The thrill defies description—it's chemical, physical, emotional—a full-body experience!

The *T. rex* was the largest and most complete of the only 11 found to that date—with 300 bones, over 80 percent of the skeleton was there! My namesake had teeth a foot long, was 67 million years old and took three weeks to remove. After protracted court battles over ownership, it was acquired by Chicago's Field Museum for almost $8.4 million. What did I get? Well, legal costs of over $100,000. I never expected to be paid anything looking for fossils anyway.

I grew up in Munster, near Chicago. As a child I was painfully shy, so shy that I always looked down while walking … that serendipitously got me interested in looking for stuff! Sometimes I'd follow ditches. When I was five, I'd poke in garbage burners. One day, I'll never forget it, I spotted a shiny piece of metal glinting in the dusty blackness. I reached down and pulled out a small brass perfume bottle. It was beautiful—smooth and bright and with a tiny white heart! That was the real start of my treasure hunting. I still have that bottle today. That same year while visiting relatives in Fort Lauderdale, I found a conch shell, which launched my interest in marine archaeology.

When I was a kid and couldn't sleep, I'd imagine myself on a deserted island,

> *"I'm driven to explore, yes, to add to the world's knowledge by following my curiosity, but I really do it because I love it. I'd die of sadness if I didn't."*

picturing what I'd do to survive. I guess even then I just wanted to be alone to figure things out.

I hated my hometown and school … so I dropped out. My boyfriend liked to dive and I loved water so we bought a sailboat and painted boats in Sausalito for a living. After we split up, I dived commercially for tropical fish, later lobster, and then for conch shells and started buying their pearls. In 1973 I was invited to join a salvage operation in Key West, and the following year, an archaeological dive in the Dominican Republic. There I searched out amber mines, which launched my interest in paleontology. In 1985 while searching for whale fossils in Peru, Swiss paleontologist Kirby Siber introduced me to fossil hunter Pete Larson of the Black Hills Institute

I've always loved the thrill of finding things. I'm addicted, like a junkie, to looking for them. My friends rolled on the floor laughing when I was chosen one of *Glamour* magazine's "10 Women of the Year for 2000." I live in boats and tents, often have dirty fingernails, have been known to cut my hair with a Swiss Army knife and have gone months using a toaster as my only mirror. Glamorous? Me? I'm just a kid who didn't grow up. I do all the things you wanted to do when you were young—digging for dinosaurs and diving for shipwrecks!

SUE HENDRICKSON was born in 1949. Her exploration interests are as broad and deep as her legendary generosity. (Many of her best ambers and pearls have been donated to museums; when Hurricane Mitch hit Honduras, she had 150 islanders take refuge in her home, then bought 30 acres and donated it to build homes.) Besides fame as a fossil hunter, she's a highly respected marine archaeologist and entomologist expert on insects found in amber. Sue has explored Napoleon's ship *L'Orient*, which Admiral Nelson sank in the Battle of the Nile; Cleopatra's palace underwater in Alexandria; the sunken city of Herakleion; and the 400-year-old sunken Manila Galleon *San Diego* off the Philippines.

This (straight A) dropout received an honorary degree from the University of Illinois; is the recipient of a Medal of Honor from Columbia University; a Member of the President's Panel on Ocean Exploration; a Wings Women of Discovery Award for Ocean given by Wings WorldQuest; and is a Sagamore of the Wabash. She's been the subject of several documentaries for both *National Geographic* magazine and channel, Discovery, and NHK in Japan, and numerous articles and books. Her autobiography is *Hunt for the Past: My Life as an Explorer.*

Sue lives on Guanaja Island, Honduras, with her numerous cats, pet deer, horses and 13 dogs.

Hamlet contemplating Yorick's skull in the form of a T. rex *toe.* CELESTE HORNER

The Bone Hunter

My research team's greatest discovery is the area in western Montana we named Egg Mountain. In 1978, we found the nesting grounds of at least three different dinosaurs, including the duck-bill we christened *Maiasaura* ("good mother reptile"), the little meat eater *Troodon* and a primitive little plant eater we named *Orodromeus*. It was this area that produced hundreds of eggs and dozens of embryos of *Troodon*, and nests full of babies representing *Maiasaura*. We

> *"Exploration is not a definable thing.*
> *It is a habit, a way of life. Exploration*
> *is curiosity in motion."*

discovered both *Maiasaura* and *Troodon* nested in colonies, and they carefully constructed mud-rimmed nests. *Maiasaura* babies were nest-bound for some period, while *Troodon* babies were precocial and left the nest after hatching.

When I was a young boy growing up in Shelby, Montana, starting around five or six, I had a passion for discovery. Everywhere I walked, I searched the ground for stuff, like rocks, sticks, even old bones that dogs had probably chewed on. I also loved digging holes, especially in my parents' yard, or the vacant lot next door. It didn't really matter what I found, either on the ground or in a hole, because everything was a treasure, and in my imagination everything was part of a story. Stories made up from my discoveries were very important when I was young, and have become even more important as I have grown older and become a paleontologist. Two paleontological adventures, and two very important realizations, provided the foundation for me becoming a dinosaur palaeontologist.

The first story of adventure came at the age of eight when my father, having realized that I had an interest in fossils, took me to a place that had once been his ranch. He and I took the trip in his Willys Jeep, and we drove more than 50 miles on gravel and dirt roads to a location near the Rocky Mountains. Then we got out and hiked into the foothills, and eventually came to a place where my father remembered seeing large bones weathering from the edge of a rocky cliff. We crawled around for nearly an hour before my eye caught sight of a bone. It wasn't a large bone, but it was fossilized—heavy and brown—much heavier than the bones I'd found in the vacant lot next to our house in Shelby. When I returned home I put my new discovery in my growing collection of rocks and fossils, and numbered it 104A. It was my first dinosaur bone, and even though I'm unsure as to what kind of bone it is, or the identification of the dinosaur, it is a treasure that resides on my desk to this day.

At the age of eight, in the third grade, after having found that first dinosaur bone, I decided that I wanted to become a dinosaur palaeontologist. I asked my parents to take me to more places to look for bones, and my mother did so because she liked to travel around. We often drove into Alberta, where I was able to find many bones and teeth. But, it was this time in my life, nearing the age of 10, that I had my first realization that becoming a palaeontologist might not be possible. At nine, I still couldn't read! I loved books, and I was very good at looking at pictures, but reading was the most difficult thing that I had ever encountered. Collecting fossils and making a collection was much easier.

My second adventure occurred shortly after I struggled through college, not getting a degree. I began driving truck, hauling liquid fertilizer around Montana. I soon began to realize that many of the places where I drove had badlands with the potential of yielding dinosaur skeletons. One day in 1974 I stopped my 18-wheeler next to the highway, unhooked the trailer and drove the tractor part of the truck into the badlands. After about ten miles I pulled over, got out and walked through the badlands searching for bones. In less than half an hour I found a partial skeleton of a duck-billed dinosaur. My friend Bob Makela and I later collected the specimen for the University of Montana. It impressed me enough that I decided to study duck-bills.

A year later I landed a job as a preparator and assistant curator at Princeton University. My job was to find dinosaurs, prepare them, and write scientific papers ("stories") about them. Even though reading is still the hardest thing I do and writing isn't much easier—dyslexia wasn't understood when I was a kid and it came as an enormous relief years later to discover that I wasn't just plain dumb!—I have followed my dream. I am what I'd always wanted to be.

JOHN "JACK" HORNER is Regent's Professor of Paleontology and Curator of Paleontology at the Museum of the Rockies, Montana State University in Bozeman, Montana. Born in 1946, this university dropout was awarded an honorary doctorate of science from the University of Montana in 1986 and the same year was awarded a McArthur fellowship (referred to by the press as the "Genius Grant"). In 2005, The International Dyslexia Association honored him with its Special Achievement Award for his outstanding accomplishments in paleontology and for serving as a role model for individuals with dyslexia.

Jack studies duck-billed dinosaurs as well as dinosaur evolution, ecology and behaviour, and has done digs throughout the world. He was the model for the scientist Alan Grant in *Jurassic Park* and served as technical advisor for the Steven Spielberg trilogy. Despite his dyslexia, he has written six books, including *Dinosaurs: Under the Big Sky,* and more than 100 scientific papers; his work has also been published in *National Geographic* magazine and broadcast on their channel as well as the Discovery channel. Jack teaches paleontology, evolution and literature at Montana State and lectures worldwide on dinosaurs and following your dreams.

He has a son, Jason, and lives in Bozeman, Montana.

DON JOHANSON

At Hadar, the site of Don's stunning Lucy find, with elephant bones. ENRICO FERORELLI

> *"Exploration is a combination of passion, dedication, preparation and opportunity combined with deep self-belief and a thirst for adventure."*

Lucy in the Sky with Diamonds

On November 24, 1974, I was 31 and co-directing an expedition to the remote desert region of Ethiopia known as the Afar Triangle. It was a warm, clear Sunday morning when one of my students and I went out to map a fossil locality. After our work was finished we headed back to our Land Rover under blistering heat. I spotted part of an arm bone that I immediately recognized as coming from a hominid ancestor. Looking up the slope to my left I saw other parts of a skeleton! After several weeks of excavation at the site we recovered much of a 3.2-million-year-old skeleton that was ultimately named after the Beatles' song *Lucy in the Sky with Diamonds*, and ever since has been known as Lucy.

I remember vividly the moment when I decided to become a paleoanthropologist. Growing up without a father in Hartford, Connecticut, I was fortunate to know a professor of anthropology who had a remarkable library. When I was about 13 I selected a book from his shelves entitled *Man's Place in Nature* by Thomas Henry Huxley. After reading this slim volume I became fascinated with the origins of humankind and decided I wanted to travel to Africa and discover my own fossils.

When I was an undergraduate at the University of Illinois I initially began my studies in chemistry but my true passion was for anthropology and geology. I switched majors to anthropology and devoured courses in bones and stones, learning details of how humankind had evolved. I had a series of professors who believed in my dream and supported my goals with sage advice and remarkable enthusiasm. It was becoming ever more clear that Africa was waiting.

In 1967 I recall having a conversation with a fellow student just after I had entered graduate school. While archaeology rewarded my immediate desire for exploration and excavation, my heart simply was not in mid-western archaeology. I told my fellow student I wanted to work in Africa, but as he pointed out no one at the U of I was working there.

After thinking deeply about this dilemma I called the University of Chicago and asked for the office of Professor F. Clark Howell, a scholar working in southern Ethiopia. Much to my surprise he answered the phone and I made an appointment to see him. I was fortunate to have been taken under his guidance at Chicago and in 1970, he invited me to participate in his expedition in the Omo region of Ethiopia. On that expedition I met several French colleagues, including a geologist who was working in the Afar Triangle, where he had spotted large areas rich in fossils. He invited me to work with him and after seeing the astonishing fossil fields, I decided this was where I wanted to work. It was here that I would make my big discovery—at a site called Hadar.

In today's scientific community few men have created the kind of excitement and controversy that **DONALD JOHANSON** of Scottsdale, Arizona, has brought to the field of paleoanthropology. His 1974 discovery of the world's best-known fossil—Lucy—brought him the kind of attention usually reserved for rock stars. His name became synonymous with a new understanding of human origins.

His career, now spanning some 35 years since he received his Ph.D. from the University of Chicago, has led him to undertake field explorations in Ethiopia and elsewhere. He believes that "understanding who we are is not just a matter of idle curiosity. It is a matter of survival for our own species as well as for the millions of other species with whom we share Earth. For without a clearer understanding of who we are, we will fall far short of the kind of future we would want for ourselves and for our children."

Currently Don is director of the Institute of Human Origins at Arizona State, a human-evolution think tank he founded in 1981. IHO fosters the pursuit of integrated solutions to the most important questions regarding the course, cause and timing of events in human evolution.

He has published in *National Geographic* and in innumerable scientific journals, and co-authored six books. Don's *Lucy: The Beginnings of Humankind,* (co-written with Maitland Edey), won the 1981 American Book Award in Science, and intimately chronicles his discovery of the remarkable skeleton. He hosted and narrated an Emmy-nominated PBS/Nova series entitled *In Search of Human Origins*. He is an honorary board member of The Explorers Club and a Fellow of the Royal Geographical Society, as well as being a member of many other professional organizations, and has received several international prizes and awards.

Don is unmarried but has an adopted 21-year-old son from Ethiopia named Tesfaye Meles Johanson.

20 Exploring In and Out of Africa

*Curiosity killed the cat
but satisfaction brought
him back.*

—EUGENE O'NEILL

On the 1980 Congo expedition with a security guard cum spy. James Powell Collection

Epiphany, Aftershocks and Vindication

The climax was the 1980 expedition to Congo. Its object was to determine what—if any—reality lay behind the legends of the mokele-mbembe said to inhabit the 55,000 unexplored square miles of the Likouala swamp. For sheer physical hardship, our slog through these jungles dwarfed anything I had experienced. We never found mokele-mbembe, nor did we claim it was a dinosaur. But the media did. In a dinosaur-obsessed world, two adventurers searching for the last dinosaur in the last unexplored jungles of Africa struck a nerve and we awoke to find ourselves minor celebrities. Discovery channel still occasionally runs it.

But to start at the beginning. February 1, 1943—one day shy of my tenth birthday—I saw that great classic of the Spanish Main, *The Black Swan*. When I walked out of that theatre I was certain of one thing: I wanted to be some sort of adventurer. But what sort? Buccaneering was out of fashion.

"The goal of exploration is knowledge. The explorer has been defined as a traveler in search of geographical or scientific discovery. It is this union of adventure of the body and adventure of the mind that makes exploration unique."

The turning point came in the fifth grade in Plainview, Texas. I was chosen to portray Coronado in a pageant. As I recreated his exploits on stage, a realization became suddenly transparent: explorers were *important*. They were not just colorful swashbucklers. They even got into grade school history books!

I now knew what sort of adventurer I wanted to be. And there remained worlds to conquer. My geography book stated that large areas of South America and Africa were still unexplored!

In the seventh grade we were required to compose our career ambitions. Busily writing, I encountered an obstacle: how many *a*'s were there in "Africa"? Was it "Africa" or "Afarica"? I raised my hand. "Teacher, how do you spell "Africa"?

My teacher exploded. "James, don't be ridiculous! This is important. It will become part of your school record. So don't write something silly! For *once* be serious."

Of course, I *was* serious. For the rest of the period my teacher ridiculed me, to my classmates' escalating derision. That incident did more to harden my resolve than any amount of encouragement.

My first adventure came at 15 in 1948. I had heard rumors that Pancho Villa's widow was still alive, somewhere in Chihuahua, and set out to find her. And succeeded! She had turned her large house into a refuge for the poor. In the courtyard was the bullet-riddled car Pancho had died in. She made me very welcome, even showing me their wedding album. Many years later, Villa's death car was officially "discovered" by the Mexican government, with much fanfare. I smiled. I had been there before. I still have the faded photograph of the car.

I started climbing in 1951 but didn't get my first big chance for adventure until 1964 when, alone and on foot, I twice crossed the Gran Desierto of northwestern Sonora, described then as "a huge, largely unexplored area of sand," discovering four archaeological sites. From 1965 to 1975 I surveyed crocodiles in Mexico,

Central America, the Florida Everglades, Africa and the southwest Pacific with the International Union for Conservation of Nature and Natural Resources

I first learned about The Explorers Club as a college freshman and watched spellbound as *Kon-Tiki* unfolded on screen. Yet, impressed as I was by Thor Heyerdahl's epic achievement, I think I was even more impressed that The Explorers Club flag flew atop the mast!

On the morning of Saturday, November 2, 1968, I opened my mailbox as usual. Only that morning it wasn't as usual. Inside was formal notice from The Explorers Club that I had been elected to membership! Eight years later, I was awarded the first of four flags to carry on expeditions to Gabon, Cameroon, Congo and Kenya. I subsequently did 18 expeditions, everything from paddling dugout canoes up South American jungle rivers in search of tree frogs, to recovering artifacts from a wrecked Spanish galleon off Yucatan.

For an "hour of infamy" in the seventh grade I felt vindicated. Also, I now knew how to spell "Africa"!

JAMES POWELL, of Plainview, Texas, was born in 1933. He is a member of the American Alpine Club, the Adventurers Club of Chicago and the American Oriental Society. He holds a B.A. from Columbia and a masters from Texas Tech University. He worked in the family hardware business. He's climbed 56 peaks and written some 30 articles. His explorations have been written about in 10 books.

MAGNUS ANDERSSON

"To widen one's knowledge, to learn and to understand—not to conquer; to bring home facts—not to leave traces; to make friends—not to dominate. That's what exploration means to me."

Greeting an old Dani friend in the Baliem Valley, Western New Guinea. ANDERS RYMAN

La Fleur that Bloomed

Following in the steps of Swedish explorer Sven Hedin, I led a Swedish TV team into western China in 1989. We were the first foreign TV team allowed in after the Tiananmen Massacre. The highlight of our two months' filming was the camel ride into the Taklamakan Desert in search of the lost city of Kaladun that Hedin had discovered at the end of the 19th century. The last possible day of our journey, when water was almost finished and we had to live from watermelons, we found the ruins. Not really a city, Kaladun was an important caravanserai until about the seventh century. Now Kaladun has become something of a tourist destination.

My mother, Ann Marie, was French and my father, Algot, was a Swedish glove-making craftsman. They met when my father ended his eight-year European apprenticeship with a one-year stay in Grenoble, France. After an intense love affair and subsequent wedding, they settled in Helsingborg, Sweden, and managed a small, well-reputed glove-making factory with a couple of outlets.

I was born during the dark years when Europe was paralyzed by World War II. Cross-border travel was impossible and direct contact with relatives in other countries unthinkable. It was not until 1947 that my mother, after many long years, could again return for a visit to her native France. She brought me along.

At four, I can of course not recall much of this, my first foreign trip, but one memory is still vividly alive. Holding my mother's hand firmly, I got off the local bus that had brought us from the railway station in Grenoble to the little alpine village of Vaulnaveys le Haut. It was just a few hundred metres walking distance to the countryside house where my aunt's family lived. My mother rushed as soon as she caught sight of her sister and they embraced. Only the cruel separation by a long war could cause such intense hugs and so many tears of happiness. They had at that moment no time for their two children!

My same-aged cousin Marie-Thérèse and I were therefore sent out into the garden to play even if we could not understand each other's languages. After less than thirty minutes, we abruptly opened the front door and rushed into the building to see our mothers. Each holding a flower in our hands, my cousin shouted *blomma* and I shouted *fleur*! Swedish and French for flower. I had by the most natural way learned my first word in a foreign language.

It was at exactly this moment that my eyes opened to the importance of knowing foreign languages, to be able to communicate with and understand peoples in other parts of the world. I had found the key that opened up the whole world! Nobody at that moment ever thought that this little episode was so important that it would form my whole life.

After ending school, my sight was set for more distant travel. First, two months of travel by Greyhound buses around most of the United States, then long journeys into the deepest parts of Africa, then Asia ....

For 32 years, more than half of my life, I have been taking groups of 12–15 persons on expeditions to some of the most distant parts of the world to encounter peoples living their traditional and untouched lives. To get to know them, to appreciate their culture and to learn from them is what interests me the most.

It started with the little word of *flower* and today, almost sixty years later, I know thanks to the knowledge of languages that we have much more in common than what separates us!

MAGNUS ANDERSSON of Helsingborg, Sweden, left the army as a captain (engineering) in 1973 and worked for Danish explorer Jorgen Bitsch as an expedition leader. In 1980 he was a field delegate for the League of Red Cross Societies, and the United Nations High Commissioner for Refugees in Somalia and Chad. Magnus Andersson Expeditions takes Scandinavian, German and American participants to remote areas. He had also been the production manager of Swedish TV documentaries.

Magnus is a Founder and member of the Scandinavian Geographic Society 1988. He is fluent in Swedish, English, French and German and semi-fluent in Indonesian.

"Exploration is the poetry of life and explorers are the poets of action."

Racing towards the Silver Medal at the American Ironman competition in Virginia Beach, Va., 2005. ALLEN LESTER FOR TRI DUO STUDIOS

A Life Well Lived

In 1987, I was first to explore the Upper Yangtze River in China by kayak through the Great Bend Gorge. There were 17 of us—topographers, geologists and professional river-runners. The story was told in Richard Bangs' and Christian Kallen's *Riding the Dragon's Back: The Race to Raft the Upper Yangtze* and in a documentary about me, *Challenging China's Yangtze*.

My desire to explore first hit in two places, at school and work. I was about 10, listening to the teacher drone on, pointing to a map. Outside, a typical nor'easter blew off Atlantic City. Casinos hadn't arrived yet. It was 1954.

"Pay attention, Mr. Fogel," the authoritative figure yelped, slapping his pointer against the blackboard. "If you ever want to learn anything, you must stop daydreaming!"

The rain pounded against the window, but I was off, mentally traveling down some dark jungle river that the map showed only as a green, curving line. That day taught me that we must *first* dream in order to live our dreams. My teacher was wrong. The dream would someday lead me to a reality that I could never have imagined.

Two years later, I was in my father's office. He manufactured commercial refrigerators in Philadelphia. On the weekend, I would travel to the factory to be "exposed to the family business." On top of his desk sat a catalogue of dealers and salesmen. The bright fluorescents glared down on face after anonymous face. Suddenly I was lost in a maze of men in grey flannel suits. Something clicked … I was determined at that moment that I only wanted one thing: to live an interesting life.

The sea was my first turning point. My grandfather, a commercial fisherman, took me on his boat, *The Bluefish*, for days on end. I was only five or six. I used to get really sick, and complain that I wanted to go home. "The sea *is* your home," grizzled old Captain Joe Broome would chuckle. "She's your Home and your Mother … so learn to love Her and stop squallin'."

In school, I would dream. Sweeping the floor in my father's factory, I would dream more. Later, when I was about 16, I became a lifeguard on the Margate City Beach Patrol. That was great … saving people and being admired by pretty girls. That job nearly spoiled me for life.

At the University of Hawaii, where I studied marine zoology and worked as an assistant curator at the Sea Life Park on Oahu, I met Mr. Jacques Cousteau while working on his Conshelf project. I was assigned to him as a "runner"—running for gas, food and coffee for him and his Navy divers. Captain Cousteau taught me a lot. He gave me a deep respect for Mother Ocean and all that She does for us. "Remember," he said, "the Ocean has given us everything! We are from Her."

In 1970, with his encouragement, I paddled a kayak from New York to Florida to film and report on water pollution. This was the beginning of WaterWatch International, a non-profit worldwide water-monitoring group that I founded to educate the public about the need for clean water. And it led to Lowell Thomas sponsoring me into The Explorers Club.

Throughout, I fought dyslexia, Crohn's disease and later chronic fatigue syndrome. Illness and handicaps can bring out a "rebel" streak in some: they see the distress as a challenge. I'm a sea captain who gets violently seasick and is allergic to salt water; a pilot afraid of heights; a master diver who is claustrophobic; an actor who has appeared in 15 motion pictures, including *Rocky V* and *Dead Poets Society*, and hundreds of commercials, who can't read the teleprompter; and an American Ironman National Champion, surfboat champion and 100-meter freestyle Senior Olympian who has four herniated disks, two blown knee caps, a torn hip socket and a torn rotator cuff. You deal with the fear and pain, then gradually find ways to overcome it to accomplish your dreams. Rehabilitation is my motto. Patience is my mantra.

CAPTAIN JOEL FOGEL, a 100-ton Coast Guard captain, was born in 1944 and has led nearly two dozen major expeditions, everything from living with an Ethiopian stone age tribe, to exploring underwater caves in Puerto Rico, to documenting, in *Twilight of the Primitive*, an Amazon tribe, to studying Volga mussels. He was VP of International Marketing for the Fogel/Jordan Commercial Refrigerator Co. for nearly 40 years … but eschewed grey flannel. A holder of the Audubon Society's Golden Osprey Award for environmental awareness, he's kayaked the Grand Canyon, the Mississippi and the lengths of both U.S. coasts reporting on water quality. After saving a woman whose car went off a bridge into icy water, he was awarded a commendation from President Reagan and was nominated for the Carnegie Hero Award.

Joel and Coty have children Sandy, William, Ellen, Anna and Jolina. They split their year between homes in Somers Point, New Jersey, and Manzanillo, Mexico.

Three moai *on Easter Island. The*
one without the stone face is Brian.
CONSTANCE DIFEDE

*"Exploration means
going into the field with a
scientific purpose, discovering or
researching something entirely
new regarding your destination,
and then bringing that new
information back and sharing
it openly with others. Because
the explorer is frequently going
into unknown or uncharted
territory, there is typically an
element of risk associated
with exploration."*

In the Footsteps of Thor Heyerdahl

Spending the Easter of 2004 and 2005 exploring Easter Island with fellow Explorers Club members has been among my most memorable experiences during 22 years in the field. Working alongside Dr. John Loret, a colleague of the late Dr. Thor Heyerdahl, was a special honor. We carried two Explorers Club flags to the island of Rapa Nui. The first was in search of the ships' anchors lost by Dutch Admiral Jacob Roggeveen during his fleet's chance discovery of Easter Island on Easter Sunday of 1722. The second was granted for our dig at a previously untouched *ahu*, or ceremonial site. Alas, we did not find either of Roggeveen's lost anchors—but instead an immense forest of unexplored and unusually large coral heads at 22 fathoms, the depth at which the anchors were ripped loose during a storm, according to the admiral's log.

Our dive team determined that the missing anchors most probably formed the nucleus of two of these huge coral formations and that their discovery on a future expedition would require the use of a magnetometer or other metal-detection device. Regarding the *ahu* uncovered, we were amazed to discover that the heads of the two fallen *moai* (the towering stone figures) were facing skyward. Typically, the enemy clans who desecrated one another's ceremonial sites pushed the *moai* face down. We retrieved soil samples from beneath one of the *moai* to help us determine when this desecration took place.

My dream of exploring the world came quite by chance at age 12 in 1954. My eyes were opened to the thrill of exploration and field research while reading Thor Heyerdahl's classic *Kon-Tiki*, a book I picked out at random in a library near the Pentagon, where my father was assigned during the early 1950s. A few years later I was intrigued by his treatise on Easter Island, *Aku-Aku*. Thor Heyerdahl became a special hero to me and I relish the memories of meeting and speaking with this great explorer on two occasions, first on the dais of an Explorers Club Annual Dinner at the Waldorf-Astoria, and second in his hometown of Oslo, Norway. I have long been both fascinated and inspired by the coincidence of Dr. Heyerdahl becoming a member of The Explorers Club in 1942 and my being born that very same year.

Growing up an Air Force "brat," I was provided an early opportunity to start exploring the world. Six months after I was born my dad became Base Commander of Laredo Air Force Base. I was "on the move" with my family for the next 18 years! Shortly after reading *Kon-Tiki*, I found myself poking around Taipei, Taiwan, and Bangkok, Thailand, during my father's remote tours of duty.

I was introduced to The Explorers Club by Max Gallimore, M.Ed. 1982, fraternity brother at the University of Texas and the Sweeney Medalist for 2005. We also served together as officers in the Air Force and used this opportunity to explore remote areas of the world together. Prior to joining The Club, I participated in two Explorers Club flag expeditions organized by Max. The first involved a hydrology and wild game study in the Okavango Delta of Botswana, and the second, a coral reef study off the coast of Belize. I was hooked on both the mission and mystique of The Explorers Club. Max sponsored me into The Club in 1984.

BRIAN P. HANSON was born on Goodfellow Air Force Base, San Angelo, Texas, and graduated from the University of Texas in 1965 with a B.S. in Chemical Engineering. He also earned an M.S. in Systems Management from the University of Southern California and an M.B.A. from Texas A&M University at Kingsville. Brian worked as a chemical engineer, manager and director with Hoechst Celanese Corporation for 33 years. He also served in the Air Force for five years, attaining the rank of Regular Captain. He received the Air Force Commendation Medal and the Bronze Star Medal for Meritorious Service in Vietnam. He has served on The Explorers Club Board of Directors, numerous committees, and as Vice President for Chapters and is currently Ombudsman. Brian has led or participated in 14 Explorers Club flag expeditions. He was awarded the Citation of Merit in 1994 and the Sweeney Medal in 2003.

Brian lives in Austin, Texas.

"Exploration is the "process" that we go through in life where we choose to open doors or leave them closed. Why one individual can do this and not others leads me to believe there's an element of genetic inheritance at work as well."

With elders working on the Maasai Oral Histories Project, 2005. ARTHUR PHIPP

Follow Your Dreams

Everyone told me I was crazy when I decided to leave the good life in America with my wife and two children to live in Italy because I wanted to write a book and explore the Mediterranean for shipwrecks. That 1969 trip was, in fact, the beginning of my self-discovery, the catalyst for a lifetime of exploration—and in retrospect, perhaps my greatest discovery was that very moment when I turned my dreams into reality.

The first door that opened when I was a child was actually a window—television. Living in a small town in 1947 when I was eight, with two hardworking parents running a restaurant, television was my window to the world. I discovered the seductive appeal of Hollywood's concept of exploration—movies like *The Big Sky, Roger's Rangers, The Last of the Mohicans*—and, of course, the Tarzan films. Later on, the documentaries of Jacques Cousteau, Marlin Perkins and Jim Fowler inspired my fantasy career goals.

While I was still in high school, my father opened a concession at Lost Village, Birthplace of the American Pioneer, in Pawling, New York. It remained "lost" as far as tourists were concerned, but it gave me time to read, to discover the books that were the sources for Hollywood screenwriters—Isak Dinesen's *Out of Africa*, Thor Heyerdahl's *Kon-Tiki* and Richard Meinertzhagen's *Kenya Diary*. The epiphany was, hey, this stuff was real ... they weren't making it up! As I walked the wooded pathways of "Lost Village" every day it was easy to imagine myself in Africa one moment and surrounded by Indians the next. My "aha moment" lasted the entire summer! Books about exploration became my escape from life in a small town. By seventeen my brain was hard-wired for travel, adventure and exploration.

The only door open to me at the time, however, was creative, and my first job was as a medical illustrator. A few years later I was in New York City directing and producing a short film for *Life* magazine. This opened other doors, including an assignment for *2001: A Space Odyssey*, when I met Stanley Kubrick. By now I was beginning to feel confident enough to put the "venture" part of adventure into action. I was still in my twenties when I decided to pack it in and move to Italy to go scuba diving. It changed my life forever.

Life in Italy was full of synchronicities. My neighbors were Luigi Fusco, an Italian coral diver that I teamed up with to co-discover a Greek shipwreck in the Aeolian Archipelago dated circa 175 BC, and Thane Riney, Chief of Wildlife and Forestry in Africa for the United Nations. Two years later I moved back to New York City and started learning to speak Maa in preparation for my first trip to Africa in 1973. In 1974, shortly after starting an advertising agency, I was introduced to Jacques Cousteau and produced all the material for the Cousteau Society on a pro bono basis for the next five years.

What next? In 1978, while looking for an apartment on the Upper East Side, I noticed a small brass plaque on a building that said ... The Explorers Club. Curious, I entered.

Then the adventure really began.

ROBERT PEARLMAN was born in 1939 and lives on Martha's Vineyard. In 1984, he received a Lindbergh Foundation grant for a project titled Learning How the Maasai See. Filmed by British television for inclusion in a 13-part series titled Village Earth, the Maasai segment was later aired on the Discovery Channel. From 1989 to 1991, Bob worked as a USAID consultant for the Botswana government and from 1984 to 1989, he was a member of Yale University's Council Committee for the Peabody Museum of Natural History. He also led a youth initiative called Planetfest that brought together 25 school-age essay winners and Carl Sagan to watch the Voyager encounter with Saturn at the Jet Propulsion Laboratories in California. Bob was also a member of a Whale Rescue Expedition to Baja where they tested equipment for marine mammal strandings. From 1999 to 2003, he organized and led a series of expeditions to document Flaccid Trunk Syndrome, a mysterious disease that causes paralysis in African elephants. In 2004–2005, he organized and led the Maasai Oral Histories Project, now known as "The Maasai Cultural Conservation Project: Preserving the Past, Preparing for the Future."

Bob's kids are Scott (deceased), Ilana, Ashley and Alex and he's married to Karol, whose sons are Michael and Richard.

21 The Partners

*The greatest adventure you can take
is to live the life of your dreams.*

—OPRAH WINFREY

Making a living by playing in the dirt too: Meave and Louise excavating a hominid cranium, 2005. Josephine Dandrieux, © Koobi Fora Research Project.

African Origins of Humankind—Three Generations of a Kenyan Family

Meave's discovery: It was 1970 and another hot, dusty, windy day by Lake Turkana in northern Kenya. This was my second season with Richard Leakey's field expedition. The crew had spread out over the rocky landscape, each concentrating on the many fragments of fossilized bone. I walked to a cliff face; everywhere were fossils. As the hours slipped by, the heat intensified, but my conviction remained: somewhere in this extraordinary landscape I would find evidence of our ancestors. Then I saw it: a bluish-grey fossil that I immediately recognized as a beautifully preserved human mandible with a set of extremely worn teeth. The thrill was intense! As I held the precious fossil in my hand I felt a direct link with this elderly individual who had eked out a living and eventually died here 1.5 million years earlier. How different were our lives and yet we were related. This was the first human ancestor that I discovered, and although subsequently I found others, and led expeditions that found new species of our predecessors, that first discovery was unforgettable.

Louise's discovery: Exploration for fossil remains of species that lived in Kenya's arid north between four and one million years ago is not a one-person job.

Meave: *"Exploration is the quest to discover and to understand the unknown, and is driven by our insatiable curiosity, an ancient human attribute that may well have led to our ancestors' first dispersal out of Africa, 1.8 million years ago."*

Louise: *"True exploration is covering new ground in search of the unknown, motivated by an intense passion for the subject (whatever it may be) and a desire to share the difficulties and the triumphs with others."*

It involves a large team—the "hominid gang"—of skilled explorers, each with an extraordinary eye and a competitive spirit. The pioneering exploration, led by my grandparents, Louis and Mary, and subsequently my parents, Richard and Meave, resulted in numerous important discoveries that put Africa firmly on the map as the place from where we evolved. My mother and I continue to explore at Lake Turkana with the continued support of the National Geographic Society.

One of the more recent discoveries was a new fossil hominid we named *Kenyanthropus platyops*—or flat-faced man. Barely exposed in the cracked brown clay was part of a brow ridge, spotted by Justus Edung. This find demonstrated that at least two distinct species coexisted 3.5 million years ago in East Africa, shattering conventional thinking which pictured a single species from which all later hominids radiated. When the find was announced in 2001, it created international headlines and sent a shockwave through the scientific community.

Meave's dream: As a child growing up in tiny Bredgar, Kent, England, I loved finding rocks and fossils, anything related to natural history, and I had a small collection of my favourite objects. But my first ambition was to be a marine biologist; I was fascinated by the sea. However, after my studies I found it difficult to find work because of my gender. I decided there were other places to explore and when a small advertisement in the London *Times* was brought to my attention I applied. An interview with Louis Leakey led me to Kenya to take up a position in a primate research center he had developed. It was 1965 and I was 23. The day after I arrived I flew with him to the spectacular Olduvai Gorge. As I looked from the window of the small plane at the brown, barren landscape I was overwhelmed by the enormity of Louis's and Mary's search and struck by their commitment. Whenever time and circumstances permitted, between 1931 and 1959 they were searching for proof that, prior to dispersing around the globe, humans lived exclusively in Africa. In spite of opposition and ridicule, Louis and Mary continued until finally being rewarded in 1959 with the discovery of a skull of a hominid species 1.8 million years old. That day at Olduvai with Louis changed my life. Not only was his enthusiasm infectious, but his passion for investigating and understanding the unknown was irresistible. By the end of the day I decided to do anything to follow his and Mary's example. I changed course and studied modern monkey skeletons for my Ph.D. in zoology.

After my doctorate, Richard invited me to join his expedition to Lake Turkana. He was excited by the area's potential, and predicted that great discoveries were waiting to be made and that 1969 would see some of them. That field season exceeded my wildest dreams and paleontology became a passion. I quickly came to understand the compulsion that drove Richard and his parents and I determined to make my own discoveries.

As we rode camels over the otherwise inaccessible landscape, *Apollo 11* was speeding towards the moon. We followed its progress each evening by radio, and spent our days searching. Then Richard made a discovery that sealed my commitment. As we wandered down a stream channel, Richard let out a cry. Just ahead, lying on the sand facing us, was a complete skull! It was one of those moments when the events are so thrilling and so improbable that one feels it has to be a dream. This 1.6-million-year-old primitive, small-brained creature was testimony to the long path we had taken to reach the moon.

In 1989, when Richard took over management of Kenya's National Parks, I began to lead expeditions. Because I was particularly curious about the early stages of human evolution I focused on a time period prior to that which we had been working on. This led to the discovery of a new 4.1-million-year-old species of australopithecine: the earliest known, *Australopithecus anamensis*, and the earliest secure evidence of an upright-walking ancestor.

Louise's dream: I grew up with the excitement of this work, and the enthusiasm of my family and their colleagues at each discovery. My earliest memories are of feeling very hot and quite unenthused, following my parents around while they collected fossils. We used to have a jerry can of cold water poured on us mid-morning to cool down. But I also remember the excitement of the large crocodile teeth that my mother brought back to me in camp after their morning sorties. I remember also the 3D jigsaw puzzles we worked on in the shade, sticking together broken fossil pig teeth with glue, paintbrush and sand. At six, tired, I flopped down in the dust and picked up a shiny sliver—which turned out to be an 18-million-year-old hominid tooth! I was also fortunate to be with my grandmother when they opened up the Laetoli hominid footprints; they provided overwhelming evidence that human ancestors were bipedal over three million years ago.

But I think the moment when my family's enthusiasm really hit was when I was 12 during the Nariokotome Boy find of 1984. The pieces of this perfectly preserved *Homo erectus* skull were coming in daily and were just clicking into place as we watched. Each excavated fragment was exciting. We were doing a big jigsaw puzzle. It was very satisfying to see it fill out although missing pieces could be incredibly frustrating.

At 12 I learned to drive a beaten-up Land Rover down dry sand riverbeds from which we collected our drinking water. Learning to fly at 18 was another important step. Apart from the intense pleasure I gained flying over the beautiful, stark deserts, it also greatly facilitated operations. A letter to me from the late Robert Savage, a renowned paleontologist, made me decide to enroll for a Ph.D. at London University.

In 1993, shortly after my 21st birthday, my mother Meave was leading the annual expedition. During its first week a tragic event led to my joining the "family business." My father, Richard, crash-landed his Cessna 206. At the time, I was writing university exams in Bristol and I rushed back to Nairobi, where, at the hospital, Meave asked me to take over the expedition, as she would travel to England with my father for critical medical attention. As the youngest member, leading a large, very adult, very male, gang of highly motivated treasure hunters was a challenge, compounded by worries about my father, but soon a sense of intense excitement set in. From the moment I realized that even I could rise to the challenge and drive a talented and motivated group, everything changed.

Our story: Together, we explore the fossil exposures of north Kenya and the Turkana Basin for evidence of our past, with a field crew of experienced, keen and enthusiastic young Kenyans. However, fieldwork requires considerable talent in leadership and logistics: planning where to be and how to best explore the vast area of fossil exposures. Our individual talents and experience are complementary and we divide the tasks to minimize duplication and maximize efficiency.

The mother-daughter team of MEAVE and LOUISE LEAKEY are National Geographic Society Explorers-in-Residence.

Meave was born in 1942 in London, England, and obtained her Ph.D. from the University of North Wales. She is also an Adjunct Professor at Stony Brook University New York and a Research Associate of the National Museums of Kenya. She worked in the museum's Paleontology Department from 1969 to 2001. She and Richard have daughters Louise and Samira.

Daughter Louise is a fourth-generation Kenyan. Her other exploratory pursuits include developing a Pinot Noir in their family vineyard on the edge of the Rift Valley, one of the highest-altitude wineries in the world. With a passion for aviation, she flew with her husband from France to Kenya in a homebuilt plane powered by a converted Subaru Legacy car engine. She is also a Young Global Leader.

Louise and husband Emmanuel de Merode of Nairobi announced the heir to this remarkable bone-hunting dynasty August 31, 2004, with daughter Ina Seiyai Leakey de Merode.

PHILIP CURRIE AND EVA KOPPELHUS:

A dream come true: bone hunting at Roy Chapman Andrews' Flaming Cliffs, Mongolia PHOTO PROPERTY OF PHILIP CURRIE AND EVA KOPPELHUS

Snap, Crackle and Pop

Philip's discovery: I knew they were there because a sharp-eyed local girl, Wendy Sloboda, had found bits of fossilized eggshell, so I led a team to the Devil's Coulee region in southern Alberta in July, 1987. On the very last day of that three-week field expedition, when we were already feeling good about what we had found, an excited technician, Kevin Aulenback, shouted that he had discovered something. We ran after him to see eroded eggshell and baby bones cascading down a hill. We followed it up to a perfect circle of eggshell, recently exposed—and saw baby dinosaur bones inside. I picked up a lower jaw of one of these duckbill dinosaurs, and turned it over to see all these perfect, tiny *Hadrosaur* teeth. I couldn't help myself—I dropped it, and rubbed my eyes, and picked it up again! They were only the second *Hadrosaur* embryos ever discovered, and the first in Canada.

Eva's discovery: When I developed a special interest in paleobotany, I participated in a field trip to Eriksdal, Sweden, with one of our professors. This locality is well known in paleontology circles for its beautifully preserved, 150-million-year-old plant fossils. It was one of those beautiful autumn days when leaves had turned spectacular hues. We looked for plant fossils at the bottom of the clay pit, then used geological hammers to uncover rock not previously exposed. As we split the rocks along the bedding planes to reveal planar surfaces, we experienced one of those magic moments in paleontology! Ancient leaves of Ginkgo (the maidenhair tree) appeared. Because of their sudden exposure to the wind and dry air, the cuticles of the multi-million year old leaves quickly dried up, peeled off and blew

"To explore is to push beyond the boundaries of existing knowledge and abilities (physical and/or mental) to determine what lies beyond, to extend our knowledge, to push the limits of our physical capabilities. The best part about exploration is how interesting and fun it is."

away to mix with the recently fallen leaves. To this day, I recall the exhilaration of having seen something very special!

Philip's dream: I was six when I discovered my first dinosaur in 1955—in a box of Rice Krispies! It took me years to learn that *Dimetrodon*, whose plastic reconstruction I had recovered, was not a dinosaur at all. But it didn't matter, because I was hooked. Over the next few months I ate my way through box after box of cereal trying to find the ultimate prize—a plastic *Tyrannosaurus rex*! I collected the rest of the set, but only got to hold the "king of the tyrant lizards" when my best friend let me play with his prized toy!

In 1957, my parents bought me the first "Prehistoric Times Play Set" of plastic dinosaurs. It was the best Christmas present I got as a child, and it kept me occupied for years. Three years later, I wrote to the manufacturer and they sent me, gratis, an updated set!

I loved dinosaurs when I was a kid. However, I might never have become a paleontologist if I had not stepped on a nail. For the next few weeks, I had to spend recesses confined to my grade six classroom. A book—*All About Dinosaurs*—from the back of the classroom was impossible to close. It was written by Roy Chapman Andrews, and was not *just* about dinosaurs. In fact, it was mostly about the excitement of hunting them in an exotic corner of the world—the Flaming Cliffs of Mongolia.

Andrews was the leader of the American Museum of Natural History expeditions to the Gobi Desert in the 1920s. I never thought about collecting dinosaurs professionally before the day I read that book. But Andrews (president of The Explorer's Club 1931–1934) painted such a vivid and romantic picture of being a field scientist that the same day I announced to my parents that I was going to become a paleontologist!

My mother, an artist who had collected fossils in England as a child, was encouraging. My father was reserved, however. It was several years after I became a professional before he accepted the idea that one could really make a living as a paleontologist.

I was lucky to have been born close to a major display of dinosaur fossils at Toronto's Royal Ontario Museum. At an age when most children lost interest in dinosaurs, I sustained mine by looking at their magnificent skeletons. After noticing that the majority had been collected in Alberta, I set my sights on hunting dinosaurs in the West. My mother took me to meet Dr. William ("The Dinosaur Man") Swinton, who gave me sound advice about schooling and autographed one of his dinosaur books for me.

He was the first of many paleontologists to encourage me. In 1976, I was offered a job in Alberta hunting dinosaurs for the Provincial Museum of Alberta. Remembering the positive influence the Royal Ontario Museum had on me, I set out to build the best dinosaur exhibits in the West. We opened the doors of the Royal Tyrrell Museum of Paleontology on September 25, 1985. Within a month, an agreement was signed for a series of multinational, multidisciplinary expeditions to the Gobi Desert, an area that had been effectively closed to western scientists after the great expeditions led by Roy Chapman Andrews and Sven Hedin! I did not really believe this was happening until I woke up in the baking heat of the Gobi sun one day in 1986. I had not only followed a dream initiated by the writings of Roy Chapman Andrews, but I had even followed him into the desert, albeit 75 years later!

My greatest aspiration is to have the same positive influence on children, by appealing to their interest in dinosaurs and exploration, as Andrews had on me.

Eva's dream: I grew up in a small village in Denmark. My three siblings and I were encouraged by the example of our parents to study and learn. Most mornings, we would have breakfast together and my father would tell stories about what he had read the evening before. Through his retelling, I travelled the deserts of China and Mongolia with Sven Hedin long before I had a clear idea of where these places were. I remember specifically the stories of Henning Haslund-Christensen, a member of the Hedin expeditions—the fact that someone from our small country could experience such wonderful adventures really captured my imagination and lit the fire of adventure in me. They were stoked further when I also heard about the important expeditions to Greenland, the North Pole and Antarctica that were conducted by our Scandinavian explorers. Little did I know that later in life, I would explore these and other exotic places finding fossils!

My mother is very good with languages, and showed me how learning those of the regions you visit makes it so much easier to be accepted. Both my parents, now retired landscape architects, have a spontaneous interest in nature, and knew a lot about trees, bushes and shrubs. They would take my siblings and me for long hikes, and would teach us about plants in the forest and stones and fossils on the beach. One time when we were out—I was about eight or nine—I suddenly had a moment when I realized just how totally fascinated I was with nature, and started to study botany. Given my background, I soon moved ahead of my classmates, and became fascinated with naming and classifying everything.

My parents took me on many European tours. I became familiar with travelling and sleeping in unfamiliar places, eating different food, listening to people who looked different and spoke different languages. When I left to study biology at the University of Copenhagen, I never missed a chance to go on excursions or to do fieldwork. I became interested in the evolution of plants and a professor pointed me to micro-fossils, like pollen and spores, as the richest area of research. The more I studied them, the more fascinated I became.

In 1986, I landed my first job at the Geological Survey of Denmark. It was a dream come true when in 1993 I was sent to eastern Greenland to explore areas where the paleobotanist Dr. Tom Harris (Cambridge University) had been working at the beginning of the century. Whereas he had collected leaf fossils, I worked with fossil spores and pollen.

I consider myself a very lucky person. Not only have I lived a very exciting life, but I have also been able to study the ancient dust (spores and pollen) of many continents.

Our story: Living and working together in Drumheller, Alberta, has been a dream come true. *Dinosaur Provincial Park: A Spectacular Ancient Ecosystem Revealed* marks the culmination of our research at that important World Heritage Site. But we also work together in the *Albertosaurus* quarry in Dry Island Park and have also experienced together many dinosaur-hunting expeditions to the Gobi Desert of Mongolia and China, and to Patagonia. We have written several children's books.

PHILIP CURRIE and EVA KOPPELHUS, both Ph.D.s, are a husband and wife team. *Time* magazine in 2003 listed Philip as one of Canada's top five contemporary explorers. He is a leading proponent of the dinosaur-bird link, has led and participated in expeditions to the Arctic, Antarctica, Argentina, China, Mongolia and many other regions. Eva, born in 1953, is a palynologist. She has been an adjunct research scientist at the Royal Tyrrell Museum of Paleontology since 1996. Together they edited the landmark *Dinosaur Provincial Park: A Spectacular Ancient Ecosystem Revealed.*

Philip, as Curator of Dinosaurs and a research scientist at the Tyrrell and a professor at the University of Alberta, has published more than 80 scientific papers, 14 books and close to 100 popular articles. He has appeared in hundreds of articles and television interviews and has given more than 600 public lectures around the world.

Eva worked for more than a decade at the Geological Survey of Denmark and Greenland, where her research focused on flora of the Triassic, Jurassic and Cretaceous geological periods. At the Tyrrell, she has worked with material from the *Centrosaurus* bonebeds in Dinosaur Provincial Park to determine more about plants associated with this dinosaur.

After years in Drumheller, they moved to Edmonton in 2005. Phil still has that first plastic 'dinosaur' he found in that breakfast cereal and it holds a place of honour on his desk.

In the frigid field shooting their landmark Antarctica *photographic book.* GLEN KEOUGH

The Aesthetics of Exploration

A full-blown Antarctic blizzard, a colony of 4,000 snow-shrouded Emperor penguins, and we're lying prone on the frozen Weddell Sea with our cameras at the ready. Not content to document the scene and head back to the relative safety of our tent, we spend hours actively watching, while slowly stiffening, alert for the convergence of visual relationships that satisfies our artistic instincts. We are a husband-and-wife team of photographers and private press publishers. *Antarctica*, our 27-pound photographic tome ($3,500, or $20,000 a copy if annotated by 31 polar luminaries), occupied us for a decade. This handcrafted book, recipient of 21 prestigious awards for the world's best this and the world's best that, is considered among the finest art books created in modern times. Prince Charles hosted its unveiling at St. James's Palace during the launch of the Save the Albatross Campaign, which is the beneficiary of all net proceeds. The connection is that the stormy seas encircling Antarctica is the realm of the world's largest seabirds, the Royal and Wandering albatrosses.

The dream of becoming explorers began early. You might say we were *already* explorers of sorts while still children.

"For the two of us, exploration stimulates and satisfies a lifelong need for discovery, challenge and accomplishment. The explorer is one who is driven to search out the unknown. Some bring back dinosaur bones, knowledge of a lost culture, or a moon rock. Others bring back artistic impressions of our natural and human heritage."

Rosemarie's dream: Back in the early 1960s when society was relaxed about youngsters playing sans parental supervision, I would disappear with my friends into a world of nature and make-believe. Our home was on the outer fringes of London, Ontario, where our backyard abutted a derelict farm. At four, I was already leading expeditions through trackless meadow grasses. My romantic memory recalls the dense vegetation rising above our heads and being wary of imagined tigers. Our destination was a mature woodlot, set like an island in the midst of a grassy ocean. In the cool, shaded depths of these woods, rich with ferns, flowers, towering trees and tangles of hanging vines I became an explorer.

Fast forward to when I was 16 and studying in Europe. The transition from snapshot photographer to art photographer came that spring as I delighted in creating images of flower blossoms during a freak blizzard. To this day I enjoy exploring and photographing anywhere in the world, yet I find that it is in association with nature and wild places that my soul is nourished.

Pat's dream: I grew up with nature close at hand. Perhaps I was attracted to the outdoors because, being the eldest of eleven, our small family home was always crammed with demanding babies, mostly girls. Money was scarce and while we didn't have television, we had scads of *National Geographics*, old and new, which fuelled my dreams of exploring far-off places. That fabulous photograph of Thor Heyerdahl's *Kon-Tiki* (with The Explorers Club flag on the mast) riding a rough sea is burned into my memory, epitomizing adventure, daring and exploration of the fabled South Seas.

At age nine, a buddy and I "borrowed" an old pump handcar and ventured along a disused rail line far into the countryside. By 14, I had a great time working summers deep underground, mucking ore in the gold mines of northern Ontario. Still in my teens, I saved just enough money to fly one-way to Australia. There, in the remoteness of the Great Sandy Desert, I saw an Aborigine holding a spear, poised on one leg atop a blood-red sand dune. My Instamatic camera failed miserably to capture the moment—but that indelible image sparked my passion for photography. On the next trip to Perth, I bought my first 35mm camera. Later, on Norfolk Island, I helped friends build a trimaran and—with *Kon-Tiki* dreams of the South Seas—set sail. Having survived awesome storms in the Roaring Forties and Furious Fifties, we explored the South Pacific, living off the bounty of the sea and landing in places like the Marquesas, the Tuamotus, the Australs, Rapa Ita and many other remote islands. Not infrequently, we were the only Caucasians the islanders had seen in decades. Documenting this journey was my first serious photography.

Our story: The turning point in our lives happened in 1984 with our chance meeting on a whitewater canoeing expedition down Canada's legendary South Nahanni river. Paddling the same canoe for a month, we never once overturned in 540 kilometres of wild water, nor did we ever feel tempted to bat our partner with a paddle, which speaks volumes about respect and communication while under pressure. The chemistry was strong and we married four months later.

While honeymooning in the Periyar jungle of southern India, camped alone in an abandoned observation tower surrounded by a dry moat so wild elephants wouldn't knock it over, we photographed pachyderms and gaur by day; and, as the sun set, dreamed about how to continue this wonderful lifestyle together. Both of us, at that time, were managers in the corporate world with shared passions for photography and exploration. To realize the dream, we decided to produce books of our photographs—in spite of being totally naive regarding the challenging world of publishing!

For the next two years, Pat continued to manage operations in the gas industry, a career in which he started as a roughneck and then a toolpusher on oil rigs two decades before. Rosemarie, a former finance manager, marketed our images and wrote articles, while working towards self-publishing our first coffee-table photography book, which showcased the natural beauty of the Ottawa Valley, our home at that time. This book became a bestseller. Shortly thereafter we returned to the Nahanni, hiked 2,000 kilometres, and ran most of the rivers shooting photos for our second book, and also film for a television special.

Our subsequent photographic expeditions—from Sable Island, Nova Scotia, realm of wild horses, seals, and shipwrecks, to Antarctica, the Great White Continent—are the means to spending long periods of time in parts of the world that interest us. By virtue of being in the field, we are occasionally the first to record and report something of unusual interest, such as certain karst features in Canada's subarctic, or specific killer whale behaviour in the Ross Sea. While curious about all that we experience, we are dedicated to taking evocative photographs of the regions we explore. Our photos tend to portray the familiar in an unusual way, for example, splatters of penguin excrement rendered through our lenses as abstract art. We're good at what we do because we inspire one another constantly, and also because we love each other so much that we view the world through a veil of confidence and happiness. This beauty from within is transferred to all we create.

PAT and ROSEMARIE KEOUGH live on Salt Spring Island, British Columbia. They are Cherry Kearton Medallists of the Royal Geographical Society. They have published seven books, directed or appeared in several films, and are currently working on future volumes in their series of luxurious books. International publishing, graphic arts, printing and photography societies have bestowed ten international gold awards, one silver and a further 10 Canadian honours on the inaugural volume in the series, *Antarctica*. Further distinctions awarded the book include World's Best Photography Book 2003, International Nature Photographer for the Year, Outstanding Book of the Year, Best Book Arts Craftsmanship, Gold Ink Award Fine Edition Books and the Craft Art Science Award. Reviews and articles about *Antarctica* have appeared worldwide. The many institutional collectors of the book include Yale and Brown universities, the Japanese National Institute of Polar Research and the Chrysler Art and British Natural History museums.

Pat was born in 1945 in Vancouver and Rosemarie in 1959 in London, Ontario. Rebekka, their daughter, is in university and has cycled 8,000 kilometres across Canada. Their young son Glen accompanies his parents on most expeditions, including the Antarctic. Pat's 90-year-old father also carries the exploration gene. As Canada's eldest active pilot, he is in the air at the controls of his Citabria every fine day.

PAT AND BAIBA MORROW

Always happiest when exploring mountains: Lago Carrera, Carretera Austral, Chile.
<small>PAT MORROW'S LEFT HAND</small>

ƒ8... And Be There!

Pat's greatest exploration achievement: Some might say it was being the first person to summit the highest peaks on all seven continents, but for me it was co-founding with Baiba and friends, in 1984, Adventure Network International, the first and still the only commercial airline/expediter to give amateur explorers/ skiers/climbers access to Antarctica's interior. Also in 1984, I helped lay the groundwork with the Indonesian government for formalizing the permit process to reach Australasia's highest peak, Carstensz Pyramid.

Baiba's: Winning the People's Choice award for *The Magic Mountain* at the Banff Mountain Film Festival in 2005 was the plum. But it started with document- ing humanitarian Cynthia Hunt's work; knowing it was a story that went beyond the usual adventure fare and realizing that the eight months spent editing, after following her for months on a gruelling circuit of the remote villages she services with health education projects in Ladakh during winter, had made a difference.

Pat's dream: My first exposure to climbing was at 16, being drawn by the spectacle of two rock climbers glued to a 50-metre face near my hometown of

"We were lucky to have been born into an age when we can be anywhere on the planet in 48 hours and still find cultures and landscapes that have had minimum impact. Every minute, from here on, that window of possibility shrinks. That's exploration today."

Kimberley, British Columbia. The leader popped off, and fell nearly the whole height of the crag before being caught on the rope by his partner. At the end of their climb, they tossed down one end of the same rope and told me to tie in. As soon as I put my hand on the rock I was hooked!

As a teen, Lionel Terray's *Conquistadors of the Useless* inspired me. He was a world-class climber, yet he chose a title that downplayed his considerable contributions to the sport, maintaining that he pursued this high stakes game merely to satisfy his curiosity. It taught me to keep things in perspective while trying to nurture a professional career in adventure journalism.

In 1975 freelance photographer Art Twomey introduced me to slot canyons in Arizona and Utah. We'd emerge at dusk, from a whole day of exploration, latent images of fluted arches and finned formations from the flood-carved sandstone underworld feeding our imaginations. Lying on the desert at night, staring at the constellations, the music of Paul Horn's echoey *Inside* (the Taj Mahal) album fed our canyon spirits. Art gladly passed along his secret formula for survival as a freelancer: "Don't squander your money on a new car, a new house or have kids (his farsighted global conservation ethic). Instead, put all your savings into a bag of Kodachrome, a beater car that may or may not get you to your destination, and live life to the fullest." I'm still following his advice.

A couple of years before I launched into the seven summits project, I discussed its concept with my partner in a stormbound tent on Mt. Aconcagua, Argentina. There is one geographical sore spot in the project. Australia's highest point can't really be classified as a mountain (you can drive a golf cart to the top), so I would set my sights on Carstensz Pyramid, highest peak in Australasia, which I had read about in Heinrich Harrer's *I Come From the Stone Age*. Carstensz is the most exotic and technically difficult of the seven, thus "heightening" its desirability in the climbing world.

But first, I had to "knock" Everest off.

In 1982 I topped out on the "Big E" with the Canadian team, and while I have averaged one international high-altitude climb annually since, I get bigger rewards from sharing long treks and overland journeys with my wife, Baiba.

Baiba's dream: I come from a very traditional family, rooted in all things Latvian—language, friends and customs. I was trained as an occupational therapist at McGill University in Montreal, then moved to Calgary to work in a children's hospital. Becoming a freelance photographer, writer and now filmmaker was never originally in my dreams—but meeting Pat and finding a companion in love and life changed that! My mother has long since stopped asking when I'll get a real job.

I feel privileged to have climbed Vinson Massif in Antarctica in 1991 when Pat and I guided a couple of Americans. It was especially sweet, since I had hoped to be with Pat on his seven summits quest in 1985. After working so hard to get it all together, at the last moment, I had to give up my spot on the plane to a Chilean climber/observer.

Taking up pen and camera was a way to make a living and be out there where both of us thrive. After trekking in the Himalaya, up and down for weeks at a time, I feel at my best, my mind flushed clean. It's only then I realize I have not been thinking of anything, only being; keeping eyes wide open; not questioning and analyzing. Really, that's what it's all about for me.

Our story: We met, via mutual friends, at the Canmore Folk Festival in the late 1970s but didn't get together until a year before our marriage in 1984. We were on a photo shoot in the slot canyons of Arizona with Paul Horn and several other friends, including landscape photographer Janis Kraulis, and spontaneously decided to hire a justice of the peace and get hitched near the entrance to Antelope Canyon. Paul graciously played a tune on his flute, Janis snapped a wedding photo and we spent our honeymoon night at the Navajo Trails Motel in Page, Arizona.

Then, as now, we share all aspects of photography, filming, expedition planning, financing, execution and follow-up. Baiba is self-taught in writing, photography, directing, narrating and sound. She is particularly good at organizing the intricate travel details and keeps the shoot on track no matter where we are in the world. Although Pat has accumulated most of the images and footage in our collection, several of Baiba's photos are our top money-earners through stock photo sales.

We love mountains: climbing them, exploring them, sleeping beneath their majestic ramparts under a blanket of stars and living among the ancient tribes that have carved out a life in their harsh shadows. While our professional experiences reach far beyond the mountain world, we concentrate our efforts there. We circumnavigated the entire Himalayan range on a seven-month, 10,000-kilometre journey in 1987, making a checklist of cool places to return to and spend more time in. We also trekked 80 days along the spine of the Himalaya from Annapurna to Everest, made a 30-day, high-level traverse of the Japanese Alps, and circumhiked Mt. Kangchenjunga, the third-highest peak in the world. After a gruelling 30-day trek through the Kunlun Range with the Wildlife Conservation Society's chief naturalist/zoologist, George Schaller, we located the Tibetan antelope's birthing grounds, but were unable to stay to photograph the actual birthing since our pack animals were starving.

PAT MORROW was born in Invermere, B.C., in 1952 and Baiba, 1955, in Montreal, Quebec. They are best known for documenting mountain cultures and adventures worldwide. Their books include *Beyond Everest: Quest for the Seven Summits* and *Himalayan Passage*, a collaboration with Jeremy Schmidt. They have won eight national magazine awards in Canada. Pat received the Order of Canada and, at the Banff Festival of Mountain Films, the Summit of Excellence award for documenting and being first to climb the seven peaks. In 2002, in recognition of the International Year of Mountains, Canada Post created a handsome postage stamp set based on Pat's photos of the Seven Summits. He's also done publicity stills for such movies as *K2* and *Seven Years in Tibet* and worked as camera operator on over 40 films.

Pat and Baiba live in Canmore, Alberta, in the Canadian Rockies they love so much.

STEFAN HARZEN AND BARBARA BRUNNICK

"Exploration is an activity motivated by curiosity, sustained by tenacity and perseverance, and made possible by ability, good fortune and courage."

The beachcombers at Comporta, south of Lisbon. STEPHAN GRATWOHL

Flipper Redux

Our greatest discovery relates to the socialization of spotted dolphins. The fascinating thing is that male and female assume specific roles—not so different from some human societies. Genders follow separate paths early on: male alliances last a lifetime, while female relationships are more fluid, influenced by reproductive status.

Barbara's dream: Random acts of kindness are not limited to the human experience; they can cross the barrier between people and dolphins. I know because it happened to me. This discovery began on a warm sunny day in southern California when I was about six and treated to a boat trip. I remember little of the day except getting caught playing with an older boy's snorkeling gear and being pitched into the sea for my naughtiness. I can still see the boat as it sailed away, my mother waving frantically from the stern. Then it happened. A sleek grey body swam past me at great speed, I felt the water move as it glided by; a dolphin, agitated, was swimming fast in tight circles around me, blowing bubbles and whistling. I dove under water as far as I could and the dolphin stayed by my side, following me to the surface as I inevitably floated up from my dive. The experience was captivating; I never realized the trouble I was in. Occasionally, the dolphin stopped swimming and we made eye contact. In that instant two things became apparent: one, I was in love, the kind that lasts forever; and two, I was facing an intelligent creature who was intently trying to tell me something, a secret. I built my life and career developing that love and exploring that secret.

My mother was frantic to see a creature circling her youngest, but the dolphin made it easier for the captain to keep his eye on me and come to my rescue.

Those few minutes have been the foundation from which a true explorer was built. I embraced adventure, and whenever possible, traveled to find other dolphins, searching for the one who would expand on the secret I shared with the first. As a teen, I summered on Vancouver Island, where I could swim daily with orca and share breakfast with bald eagles. In the winter months I cruised the Pacific on private whale-watch excursions, long before this activity became an industry.

I sought out the highest authorities on marine mammals and studied at several universities, but ultimately found myself a favored student of Dr. Kenneth Norris, who arranged for me to get hands-on experience as a trainer and handler while developing my skills as a scientist. Well aware of my love of dolphins, Dr. Norris arranged for me to explore their underwater secrets in the Bahamas. My doctoral research on the social life of wild dolphins was a fitting reflection of that first encounter so many years before. On the eve of my very first field expedition there, I was introduced to a colleague who would ultimately change my own social life, and eventually become my partner, my best friend and my husband.

Stefan's dream: I arrived in Lisbon in 1986 to explore the lives of dolphins, leaving Germany with no idea what to expect. In just weeks, I found myself less than 10 meters from the animals that had captured my imagination as a child.

My journey was unlikely. My family has very little interest in nature, and I was 16 before I stood on an ocean beach. By then, however, the seeds of my passion for marine mammals had been planted by the great Jacques Cousteau. Many precious hours of my youth were spent pouring over the books, documentaries and papers from the *Calypso*, and the dolphin smile became my beacon. By the time I attended orientation for future biologists at the University of Bielefeld in 1980, I was already in full pursuit of my dream to become a cetacean scientist.

There were very few people in Germany who studied marine mammals and I had to search far and wide for others to help promote my career. Fortunately, a number of scientists from the U.S. were working at the university and one of them invited me to accompany her to an international symposium of the European Association for Aquatic Mammals. That opened my perceptions, and my future stretched out in front of me. I have met wonderful people, fellow explorers, scientists, trainers, photographers, filmmakers and entrepreneurs whose support and friendship have contributed more to my life than anyone could have expected. Meeting interesting people and forging friendships has been a central theme of my life and my career ever since.

In 1986, I found myself cruising across the Sado Estuary on the west coast of Portugal, testing my abilities as a field scientist and appreciating my good fortune as an explorer. I discovered how dolphins learn to live off the oceans and it became apparent that social contact is vital to these wonderful creatures. I came to know individual dolphins that showed me their behavior, foraging postures and acoustic markers.

I also came to know Mario and Odette Amaral, who took me in as family and introduced me to local customs, cuisine and the Portuguese language. These human friendships sustained me just as the estuary sustained the dolphins.

As I observed how humans polluted the estuary, I helped create an environmental conservation program, and my own studies expanded to include environmental and waste management.

After completing my doctoral research, my field exploration came to an end. Fortunately, I had participated in a two-week expedition to explore dolphins underwater in the Bahamas. After a successful tour, with almost daily dolphin encounters, the crew joined for a final dinner at a local bar in Juno Beach, Florida. It was there that I saw Barbara, my wife to be, for the first time.

Our story: Exploring together makes for a fantastic life-journey. Being able to experience every day with someone who shares a similar curiosity and fascination is a rare and special treat. We met in 1993, and although we hardly noticed each other that first night, it was enough. A few months later, at a marine mammal conference in Galveston, Texas, we found each other again and have been together ever since.

Our commitment to marine mammal science and exploration has taken us on many exciting adventures through Europe, the tropical Pacific and the Caribbean. And while we continued to work on projects we had initially pursued independently, we have also launched new ventures together.

We are focusing on the lives of bottlenose dolphins off Palm Beach County and produce a number of outreach activities, including a weekly two-hour radio program, a series of guest lecturers and school programs for our community. At the same time, we continue to promote cross-fertilization between the business and science community to improve the health and survival of all living things and our beautiful planet. Most of all, we are still exploring oceans, landscapes, cultures and relationships around the world.

STEFAN HARZEN and BARBARA BRUNNICK were both born in 1958 and live in Jupiter, Florida. They promote research on marine mammals and their environment, while consulting to research organizations, universities and businesses. They have published *The Bottlenose Dolphin of the Sado Estuary, Portugal* and numerous papers.

Stefan, born in Wuppertal, Germany, received his doctorate from the University of Bielefeld, Germany. He has one daughter, Jennifer Rhea, in Germany. He has delivered seminars and lectures on waste management, industrial ecology and ecosystem management to business and academia in Europe and North and South America. He has participated with developers on waste management and marine biology issues in the Turks and Caicos Islands, identifying investment opportunities for natives and locals living in protected areas. Stefan co-founded the Projecto Delfim Research Group in Portugal, the Portuguese Eco-Institute of the Essprit-Icarus Foundation and The Taras Oceanographic Foundation in South Florida. He is a Charter Member of the Society for Marine Mammalogy, a Fellow with the Florida Center for Environmental Studies in Palm Beach, a member of the Scientific Advisory Board of Arqueonautas Lda, Portugal, and an adjunct professor at Florida Atlantic and NOVA Universities.

Barbara was born in North Hollywood, California. She is an alumna of the University of California at Santa Cruz, received her doctorate from the Union Institute and University in Cincinnati, Ohio, and is an expert on dolphin social structure. She has been a naturalist on over 1,000 whale watch trips and has given countless presentations all over the United States.

Her research into the lives of dolphins continues in Palm Beach County, while she also works on large-scale conservation projects in the Bahamas. She is an adjunct professor at the University of Miami and research director of The Taras Oceanographic Foundation. She is a long-standing member of the American Cetacean Society, the Society for Marine Mammalogy and the Society for Conservation GIS.

Between hurricanes, rowing the Atlantic. KIRK ELLIOT

Magellan May Have Been First
But, Hey, He Did It the Easy Way!

In 2006 Colin completed the first human-powered circumnavigation of our planet—a 43,000-kilometre journey without sails or motors. Joining the adventure, Julie became the first woman to row across the Atlantic Ocean from mainland to mainland and the first Canadian woman to row across any ocean. By propelling ourselves using only oars, pedals and our feet, we hoped to promote the use of non-emission forms of transportation, such as cycling and walking, as a means to curb greenhouse gas emissions.

The circumnavigation began from Vancouver. We cycled 1,600 kilometres north to Hyder, Alaska, at which point Julie returned home to manage expedition logistics and her work as a molecular biologist, and Colin continued with another teammate, Tim Harvey. We travelled by bike to the Yukon River in Whitehorse, loaded our equipment into an aged canoe, and paddled to Fairbanks, Alaska. Exchanging the canoe for an ocean rowboat, we continued down the Yukon River to

"There is nothing left to explore, we are often told.
So what were we doing as kids when we used to
spend hours every day in the forest behind the school,
turning over logs, climbing trees and searching for
secret hiding spots? We called it exploring. This notion
has stayed with us into adulthood as we've had the
pleasure of exploring the nooks and crannies of planet
Earth. Sure, hundreds if not thousands of people
have always been there before, but for us the
feeling of wonder at seeing nature first-hand
is far from diminished knowing that others
have shared the same experience."

the Bering Sea and across 1,000 kilometres of treacherous waters to Provydenya, Siberia, becoming the first to row the North Pacific.

In Siberia, we skied, cycled and hiked 3,650 kilometres through roadless wilderness, a distance greater than the breadth of Antarctica, in temperatures colder than those faced by polar expeditions. From Siberia's most eastern road—the Road of Bones—Colin continued alone by bicycle 10,000 kilometres to Moscow, where Julie rejoined him. We pedalled 5,500 kilometres across Europe to Lisbon, Portugal, and then launched our rowboat on an epic ocean crossing and into the worst hurricane season in recorded history. After 145 days of rowing, punctuated by four tropical storms (including two hurricanes!) we crossed 10,000 kilometres of sea and reached the port town of Limón, Costa Rica. Once on land again, we cycled 8,300 kilometres through eight countries to complete a journey that returned us to the exact spot where we had started 720 days earlier. In doing so, we went through 4,000 chocolate bars, 250 kilograms of freeze-dried food, 31 dorados pulled from the ocean, two rowboats, four bikes and 80 kilograms of clothes.

Colin's moment: At the age of 12 I found a dusty book in the school library, *Dove*. This novel detailed the five-year solo sailing circumnavigation of the world by Robin Lee Graham in 1965. While the winter monsoon drummed down outside our home, I was completely captivated by tales of foreign lands, exotic peoples and dangerous storms. It was upon finishing that book, in our tidy suburban living room, that I decided that one day I too would get a sailboat and head off into the high seas for a life of adventure!

I was raised in the depressed working-class mill town of Port Alberni on the West (Wet) Coast of Vancouver Island. Opportunities to learn how to sail were limited. Instead I spent hours in the local library gleaning information from books and magazines. Mostly out of societal pressure, I started at the University of British Columbia, studying science, but it didn't take long for me to question my choice. I hated school. I remember sitting in one particular English class—the only one with windows—looking out at Vancouver's English Bay while the professor droned on monotonously. Battered but proud fishing boats churned by and sailboats scudded the harbour. I suddenly had another epiphany—one that reinforced my earlier one: sailing *was* the key to the life I wanted to live! From that day on I devoted all my efforts to sailing books and planning. When I left university everyone thought I was giving up a lot but I was giving up nothing. I didn't care if I never owned a home or got rich. My dream was to solo the Pacific!

Finally, at 19, after years of dreaming, planning and working at everything from being a tree planter to a deckhand on a trawler I purchased the *Ondine*, a 27-foot handyman special with sails for $15,000, along with high school friend Dan Audet. I had told few people of our plans, because I quickly learned the world is full of naysayers. The one I remember best was a sailor of indeterminate age at the local yacht club who pontificated, while breathing Scotch fumes from a face charted with broken capillaries, that I had neither the experience nor the finances and that my venture was utterly doomed from the outset. "I'll put it out of my head immediately!" I piped up. I certainly didn't want to be the one to upset his limited presumptions. But I knew what would make me *happy*—and it was to strike out into the unknown.

We took a three-day sailing course and then sailed away from Vancouver Island. Our route took us down the coast of the U.S.A. to Mexico and then across to French Polynesia. There, Dan accepted a job as a deckhand on a yacht and I continued sailing solo towards Australia, visiting Tonga, the Cook Islands, Fiji, New Caledonia and New Zealand .

In total I spent five years living my dream of being a pirate on the high seas. I finally sold the *Ondine* in Papua New Guinea. This journey was never meant to be an expedition; it merely fulfilled my childhood ambition to explore the world from the vantage of a sailboat. My years on the sea opened my eyes to the fact that there are infinite ways to travel the world and experience its wonders.

My youthful years on the Pacific Ocean kindled my desire to continue exploring and taught me that careful planning and disciplined teamwork can yield incredible results. My next adventure was a complete descent of the Amazon River in a whitewater raft, a feat I achieved with Ben Kozel and Scott Borthwick. Only one other group had succeeded in this quest, although there had been many attempts—all with tragic outcomes. On this five-month journey over 1999 and 2000—which included the entire crossing of South America by manpower alone—we almost died of thirst in Peru's desert altiplano searching for the Amazon's source, were pummelled by class V+ whitewater in the Amazon's upper gorges and were shot at by Shining Path guerrillas in the cloud forest. The journey was just a warm-up for the Big One (though I didn't know it at the time).

I prepared for my next expedition in 2001: the first descent of the Yenisey River through Mongolia and Siberia, with Ben again, Tim Cope and Remy Quinter. The Yenisey, the world's fifth-longest river, had never previously been navigated from source to sea. Our small team had a five-month ice-free window to complete this journey, which took us through some of the most remote regions on the planet, finishing at the Arctic Ocean.

Then, in the summer of 2002, I learned during a Google search that nobody had ever circumnavigated the planet using muscle power alone!

Julie's moment: As a young girl I dreamed of exploring remote places. My father, an engineer in the Canadian Air Force, fuelled my fantasies with stories from his travels and my parents took me with them when they visited their home countries of Germany and Syria. But it wasn't until a Girl Guides camping trip outside of Edmonton, when we were in the midst of identifying the bugs we collected, that I decided I wanted to explore our world through science! From that point on I made sure every decision I made would bring me to this quest. I completed a master's degree in molecular biology and moved to the West Coast to be near the mountains and the sea.

It is a privilege to live in a place of ancient rainforests, rugged mountains and expansive coastline and it inspires me to experience more remote places in intimate ways. For me the moment of deciding my life's path has stretched over decades but it is the beauty of the world around me that has always whispered clues.

Our story: We first met in 2002 at a presentation in which Colin described his rafting journey down the entirety of the Amazon. Julie was impressed by his implacable determination and bought his book to support his next shoestring budget expedition. When he signed it, we spoke briefly and made a lasting impression on each other. That would have been it, if not for a chance meeting eight months later. It was the morning of the annual Vancouver Sun Run and we were both en route to the race, waiting for a bus at the same stop! Ten months later we were engaged.

We both love the outdoors and exploring wild places, and are passionate about doing what we can to preserve and protect our environment. Our relationship grew as we hiked together in the coastal mountains and spent time canoeing. We have partnered with the Trans Canada Trail to raise money and awareness on one of our speaking tours to help build the longest trail system in the world.

When we left on the circumnavigation, we felt confident our relationship was strong enough to weather most challenges. Five months together in a rowboat has been the ultimate test of our relationship and we were wed in August 2007.

COLIN ANGUS was born in Victoria, B.C., in 1971 and JULIE WAFAEI in Toronto, Ontario, in 1974.

Colin is a filmmaker, best-selling author and adventurer who has chronicled his expeditions in three books, *Amazon Extreme*, *Lost in Mongolia* and *Beyond the Horizon*, and has written for many publications, including *The Globe and Mail, Reader's Digest* and *Cruising World*. He has co-produced three documentaries that have collectively won ten awards, including Best Adventure Film at the Taos and Telluride Film Festivals and been broadcast internationally by *National Geographic*. Colin was honoured in 2006 by *Outside* magazine, along with Al Gore, as one of 25 "bold visionaries with world-changing dreams" for his efforts in combatting climate change. *Outside* described the circumnavigation as "one of the last great challenges."

Julie has two undergraduate degrees with honours from McMaster University (biology and psychology) and a graduate degree in molecular biology from the University of Victoria. She spent over a decade studying and developing treatments for heart disease, cancer and genetic ailments before focusing completely on examining the natural world through exploration. She has explored over 30 countries and cycled 15,000 kilometres through more than half of those. Julie has also written for several publications, including *Venus* and *The Ring,* and is writing a book, *Rowboat in a Hurricane*, about her part in the circumnavigation adventure. Her photography has appeared in *Outside, Explore, The Globe and Mail* and *BC Busines*s. She co-produced the award-winning documentary *Beyond the Horizon* with Colin.

They jointly received the 2006 "Adventurer of the Year" award from *National Geographic Adventure*. Julie and Colin live near Courtenay on Vancouver Island, B.C., where they are able to enjoy the mountains, ocean and ancient rainforests.

22 Poles Apart

*We're all adventurers here,
I suppose, and doing wild
things in wild countries
appeals to us as nothing
else could do. It is
good to know there
remain wild corners
of this dreadfully
civilized world.*

—ROBERT FALCON SCOTT,
EN ROUTE TO THE SOUTH
POLE, 1912

Hugh single-handedly moving the South Pole. HUGH DOWNS COLLECTION

One of America's Broadcasters

On December 10, 1982, at what would be 6:10 p.m. Eastern Standard Time, I picked up the actual South Pole and set it in its new and proper place. It wasn't the barber pole we see in pictures, but rather a 15-foot bamboo pole with a tattered green flag at the top—and it was then several hundred yards away from the actual position of the earth's axis. Being at that long-coveted location fulfilled a dream born in my childhood.

"Some people explore because they want to compete against their fellows. Some compete only against past accomplishments—to set records. But to me the real explorer is one who wants to expand human knowledge. To go into latitudes and spaces not yet reached or understood; and these are driven not by ego, but by a deep desire that humanity will ultimately benefit from the new knowledge."

You see, Admiral Byrd established Little America on the Ross Ice Shelf in Antarctica in 1928 when I was seven years old. We lived in Lima, Ohio, where my father worked at the Lima Locomotive Works. He also built radios as a hobby in those days, and I heard the news on a headset frying with static. I remember the thrill of knowing I was hearing people and program material actually talking and coming from a distant city. Magic. On hearing about the continent where the south end of the Earth's axis comes out through the ice, my dual dream was born of one day getting to the Pole myself—and reporting on events from there.

The excitement generated by that new knowledge stimulated me to pursue my media career and all my other adventures.

In 1982 I had an opportunity to mount a TV feature for my ABC program 20/20, when I learned that new polar satellite data had made it possible for a much more accurate positioning of the Pole itself. I called John Slaughter, then head of the National Science Foundation, to ask when they planned to move the Pole to a corrected position. He told me this would take place in December. I asked (only half seriously) if I could be the one to move it. Two weeks later he called me back and said he had discussed this with the scientists at Pole Station and they thought it would be a good idea.

Just being there after all that time was the fulfillment of that long-ago dream; to be given the honor to reposition the Pole itself was a thrill beyond description. This enabled me to mark off a little under eight feet up the Greenwich Meridian, and then walk around the world in 24 steps, each one in a different time zone. I was the first to do this. My brother Wallace did the same thing. We may not be the first brothers at the Pole, but are probably the only ones who moved the Pole to a corrected position.

HUGH DOWNS, anchor of ABC Television's primetime news magazine *20/20* for 21 years until 1999, is one of the most familiar figures in the history of U.S. broadcasting. In 1985 the *Guinness Book of World Records* certified him as holding the record for the greatest number of hours on network commercial television. In his career he has broadcast from every continent and both Poles.

Hugh has received six Emmys. He hosted PBS's *Live From Lincoln Center* for a decade. He launched his career as the announcer on *Sid Caesar's Hour*; helped launch NBC's *Tonight Show* in 1957 as Jack Parr's sidekick; anchored *The Today Show* from 1962 to 1971, and has broadcast numerous specials and documentaries. He has received the Broadcaster of the Year Award from the International Radio and Television Society; and the Lowell Thomas Broadcast Journalism Award.

Hugh is a pilot, with several ratings from multi-engine to hot-air balloon. He qualified for participation in the space training John Glenn took in 1998 to return to space. He has authored 12 books, including *On Camera: My 10,000 Hours on Television*. Hugh also received a Certificate in Geriatric Medicine for Continuing Medical Education; Geriatrics Review Course at Mt. Sinai Hospital, New York; and has a post master's degree in social gerontology. Since 1982 he has also served as a member of the Board of Overseers of the Brookdale Center on Aging of Hunter College. From 1978 to 1998 he was Chair of the U.S. Committee (now Fund) for UNICEF and is still Chair Emeritus. He has been an advisor to NASA and is currently the Board Chair of the National Space Society's Board of Governors.

In 1999, Arizona State University upgraded its Communications Department into a school bearing the name the Hugh Downs School Of Human Communication. He's a frequent visitor and enjoys lecturing on a variety of subjects.

Hugh and wife Ruth live in Arizona. They have two children, Hugh Raymond and Deirdre Lynn, two grandchildren, Lia Downs Harb and Cameron Black, and as of April 2005, two great-grandsons, Alexander William Black and Nathan Harb.

MAREK KAMINSKI

"Exploration is crossing barriers, both external and internal—and crossing internal barriers is more important and difficult."

Perfect weather for skiing to a pole. MAREK KAMINSKI

A Pole to the Poles

In 1995, I became the first man to reach both the North and South Poles by land in the same year. In 2004, I did a similar trip with a 17-year-old disabled boy— Jasiek Mela.

These journey are most remarkable not only because of the hardness of the expedition, but also because I am the first one to dream and to realize it. I can't draw any lesson from anyone, I have to find my own way. It made the preparation process more difficult than other expeditions.

Also, since I am going with a young boy who no one believe he can reach the Pole, I have to ensure his safety. My sense of responsibility made this journey more unique. I am really glad that we ended the trip with a huge success, as it opens ways for others, showing that people can achieve their goal if they dream about it, despite how difficult it seem to be.

I start to dream about traveling to the moon when I was a child, I had so many imagination about making such a trip. I read a lot of books about explorations; I found the world inside books is more realistic and fascinating than the outside world. And second was a series of Polish cult comics by very popular artist Papcio Chmiel. *Tytus, Romek i Atomek* described various adventures of three friends. Then when I was about eight years old, I broke my arm and I had to stay in hospital alone for a long time. This gave me a chance to think—and there I read *Twenty Thousand Leagues Under the Sea*, by Jules Verne. My imagination of being an explorer started to blossom at this point.

The best way to realize our dream is to making the first step. I believe, by making many small steps, solving small problems, eventually we can reach our destination. Of course, good planning and organizations are needed. To me, my first step was taken when I was 14 in 1978. I got on a cargo ship to Denmark on my own. Next year, I got on another cargo ship, but this time, I went to Africa. These two expeditions strengthen my belief and faith to become an explorer.

I didn't want to spend all my life at university so I started to attend to Military Academy. I understood that it wasn't for me once a colonel—my teacher—told me that he would teach me not to ask questions (as a reply to my question). I decided to live in a tent and prepare a trip around the world.

MAREK KAMINSKI was born in Gdansk, Poland, in 1964. He studied philosophy and physics at Warsaw University and speaks English, German, Italian, Russian, Spanish and Japanese. Marek has a long history of serving the community, particularly by lecturing to young people. In 1996 he set up the Marek Kaminski Foundation not only to support exploration but to offer aid to disabled and ill children. He is the recipient of numerous awards, including the Man of the Year 1995 from the daily newspaper Đycie Warszawy; for "Outstanding Achievement in Promoting Poland all over the world" presented by Foreign Minister Adam Daniel Rotfeld; and he was named the Hans Christian Andersen Ambassador 2005.

He has completed numerous expeditions, including: the first-ever Polish crossing of Greenland on skis, 600 kilometres in 35 days; the North Pole from Ward Hunt Island by skis without support, 880 kilometres in 72 days; the South Pole from Berkner Island, alone, on skis, without support, 1,400 kilometres in 53 days; attempted solo unsupported crossing of Antarctica, 1,450 kilometres in 54 days; crossing Antarctica's Ellsworth Mountains, and climbing Mt. Vinson; first-ever crossing of Australia's Gibson Desert with an international team, 670 kilometres in 46 days; crossing the Atlantic by yacht, then by catamaran in 15 days (a qualification race for The Race 2000); crossing Greenland with parasails, 600 kilometres in 13 days; and a scientific expedition to the source of the Amazon, with the National Geographic Society, Smithsonian Institution and The Explorers Club. Marek made many of these expeditions into films and books.

He has been seen on the Discovery channel, included in National Geographic Poland and National Geographic, and was one of the explorers, photographers and travelers featured in the Polish anthology Between Heaven and Hell.

Marek lives with his wife, Katarzyna, and daughter, Pola, in Sopot on the Polish coast.

JEFFREY MANTEL

Beth,
Wishing you a life filled with adventure!
Jeff

Literally on top of the world: Jeff at the North Pole. RICHARD WEBER

"The essence of exploration is an insatiable curiosity, an overwhelming desire to experience for oneself and a willingness to take serious risks."

Waking Up Happy at 50 Below Zero

After twice falling through the Polar Ice Cap into the Arctic Ocean, I reached the North Pole April 1, 1994, traveling on foot with the famous duo of Richard Weber of Canada and Dr. Mikhail Malakhov of Russia.

I was a bit of a loner as a kid, wandering around the woods near home, looking under every log and rock. My dad owned a civil engineering firm and my mother was a regional health planner. I have always been athletic, having played minor league soccer for six years and been a professional league referee for 12.

But it was 1969, at the age of 21, before I was bitten with the exploration bug. I spent three months in the East African bush doing construction work and exploring the remote areas of Kenya and Tanzania on foot. It was then that I had an epiphany; I remember it as if it were yesterday. In late August, I was standing on the floor of Ngorongoro Crater in northern Tanzania with the game warden looking at a herd of wildebeest being stalked by a pride of lions. When I turned around, there were hippos in a pond, not more than 50 meters away. About the same distance from us was a mother rhino with its baby—and mama was not looking too pleased to see us so close. We backed away slowly, and after my heart rate slowed to about 200 beats per minute, I took photos. I knew then that I enjoyed taking the risks necessary to experience the thrills of exploring such wild and forbidding places.

The events leading up to my intimate connection with the high Arctic started during the first of three ski trips to New Zealand in 1990. I spent time with guides climbing glaciers on the South Island. I fell in love with the ice. Finally, in 1993, I connected with the Weber-Malakhov North Pole Expedition for my first North Pole expedition and have been in love with the Arctic ever since. Not only is the animal life extraordinary but learning how to survive and thrive living in unheated tents in wind chills that can reach 170 degrees below zero is incredibly fascinating. Despite suffering torn cartilage in both knees, a ruptured disk, cracked teeth, a broken foot and a torn rotator cuff, I continue to heed the call of the Arctic. It has become as much a necessity in my life as breathing.

I have continued my association with Weber and Malakhov on a total of seven Arctic expeditions thus far. We have explored the remotest areas of the Arctic, such as Baffin Island, Ellesmere Island, Ward Hunt Island, northwestern Greenland and the Polar Ice Cap. In 1999, Richard and I incorporated in Canada and I became a major shareholder. Our company is licensed as outfitters and guides and we now own the northernmost wilderness lodge in the world, on Somerset Island, 600 miles north of the Arctic Circle.

JEFFREY HUNT MANTEL, PH.D., of Florham Park, New Jersey, was born in 1948, has lived all over the U.S. and owns a financial technology consulting company. His career path took him from mathematics professor, to actuary, to minor league soccer player to professional soccer league referee, to Wall Street derivatives trader and to financial technology consulting. Jeff has published articles in numerous financial technology magazines and has given talks about his Arctic exploits to various Explorers Club chapters and academic institutions.

In his 36-year love affair with exploration, he has traveled on foot across the Polar Ice Cap to the North Pole four times, traversed for the first time an unnamed glacier abutting Mt. Wordie on Baffin Island in Nunavut Territory, climbed the Greenland Ice Cap and trekked across the Clement Markham and Diebitsch glaciers. During a trek across the sea ice from Ellesmere Island to Greenland, Jeff made landfall at the exact spot where Dr. Frederick Cook had landed in his North Pole attempt of 1907-1908, and found the remains of the cabin where Cook over-wintered.

Jeff was married to Shane Kelley and has two stepsons living in Canada, Damian and Devin.

23 The Cutting Edge of Exploration

Some men see things as they are and ask why. Others dream things that never were and ask why not.

—GEORGE BERNARD SHAW

CHARLES H. TOWNES

Where Charles does his best thinking ... on a park bench. KIRSTIE TWEED

The Birth of the Laser

The most remarkable moment in my life was early one morning in 1951 when, sitting on a bench in Franklin Park in Washington, D.C., with beautiful flowers all around, I suddenly recognized how to amplify electromagnetic waves with molecules or atoms—the origin of the maser and laser.

I had been working hard at trying to find a way to produce waves shorter than what electronics could do—as short and shorter than one millimeter. In Washington, I was chairing the last meeting of a national committee to investigate how to

"I believe there is no long-range question more important than exploring the purpose and meaning of our lives and our universe. In this exploration, I find no conflict between science and religion."

do this, and we had not been successful. I woke up early in the morning worrying over our lack of success, went out and sat in the park puzzling over the problem, and suddenly the idea hit me.

As a youngster, I grew up on a farm and always enjoyed natural history, exploring and finding birds, insects, fish, and looking at the stars. That's when my curiosity to try to understand what this universe is and how it works was aroused. My first course in physics at Furman University locked me into research—I was immediately fascinated by the beautifully logical structure of physics.

While at Furman, my interest in the natural world continued and I served as curator of the museum and worked summers as a collector for Furman's biology camp. In addition, I was occupied with other activities, such as the swimming team, the college newspaper and the football band.

I wanted to stay in academia but the Depression prevented that path. In 1939 I took a job in New York with Bell Labs. With World War II starting, I was assigned to work on radar, which wasn't initially pleasing. But after the war, I turned my attention to applying the microwave technique of wartime radar research to spectroscopy, which I saw as a potentially powerful new tool for the study of the structure of atoms and molecules and as a new basis for controlling electromagnetic waves. I wanted to find a way to amplify and produce pure electromagnetic waves of high frequency to help in my exploration to explain the natural world, and indeed the laser has. The maser or the laser has been a critical instrument in about a dozen Nobel Prizes in science.

I'm not now working on lasers anymore because once a field becomes important and good people are working on it, I'm not needed. I like to explore an area I think is being neglected, which has lead me to radio astronomy and now infrared astronomy, where I have made a system for seeing details of the behavior and changes of stars.

Interestingly, the bench where I had my epiphany was just across the street from where Alexander Graham Bell experimented with sending messages on beams of light. I wonder if he had any of his *Eureka!* moments on this same bench!

Nobel Laureate CHARLES H. TOWNES of Berkeley, California, was born in 1915 in Greenville, South Carolina, and attended Furman University in his hometown, where his mother and father had also gone. He completed a joint B.S. in Physics and B.A. in Modern Languages, graduating *summa cum laude* in 1935 at the age of 19. Two years later, he received his M.A. in Physics from Duke and, in 1939, his Ph.D. from the California Institute of Technology with a thesis on isotope separation and nuclear spins. He has a number of patents in related technology for his work on radar at Bell Labs, where he was employed from 1933 to 1947. He has been on the staff of Columbia University, MIT and the University of California, and has also been active in advising the government on issues involving science and technology.

Charles' work on lasers resulted in the Nobel Prize in 1964 and nearly 125 other awards and honorary degrees, including the Templeton Prize, as well as basic patents on the maser and laser. The laser opened the door for a multi-billion dollar explosion of inventions in telecommunications, computers, electronics, medicine, and other areas now in common use around the world. His book, *How the Laser Happened: Adventures of a Scientist*, was published in 1999.

Charles and his wife Frances have four daughters, Linda Rosenwein, Ellen Anderson, Carla Lumsden and Holly Townes..

24 The Mountain Men (and Women)

We knocked the bastard off.

—ED HILLARY

"*Exploration is going
where no one has ever
been before—it's a
much misused word.
A climber doing
a new route is an
explorer—someone
going to the North
or South Pole by a
route others have
been before is most
definitely not.*"

Have rope, will climb. Dario Rodrigues

Discovering Climbing

The high point of my climbing career was making the first ascent of the 'last great problem'—the southwest face of Everest. I led members of the British Everest Expedition to success in 1975, after an attempt in 1972.

I was 16 in 1951 when I went on holiday with my grandfather who lived on the outskirts of Dublin. The railway line to Holyhead, the ferry port to Ireland, skirts the Welsh coast, and the hills thrust onto the very shore. I gazed out of the carriage window, enthralled. There was something strangely exciting about the way the deep-cut, utterly desolate valleys wound their way into the mountains. There were no crags, just big rounded hills that gave a feeling of emptiness, of the unknown.

When I reached Dublin, I found that my grandfather's house was on the doorstep of the Wicklow Hills. These had not got quite the atmosphere of the mountains I had seen from the train but they were still exciting. I wanted to explore them, to find out more about them, but at the same time I was frightened by their size and my own lack of experience.

On the way back from Ireland, at the tail end of the summer holiday, I stayed with my great aunt Polly in the flat suburbia of Wallasey in the Wirral Peninsula. One night we called on some of her friends and while they talked I idly picked up a book of photographs of the Highlands of Scotland.

Suddenly, my imagination was jolted in a way I had never previously experienced. The book was full of photographs of mountains: the Cairngorms, huge and rounded; the Cuillins of Skye, all jagged rock and sinuous ridges; but what impressed me most of all was a picture taken from the summit of Bidean nam Bian in Glen Coe, with the serried folds of the hills and valleys merging into a blur on the horizon. To me it was wild, virgin country and yet it was just within my reach: I could imagine exploring these hills for myself. A book of Alpine or Himalayan peaks could never have had the same effect.

From that moment I was hooked on mountains.

While still in my teens, I attained a high level of climbing skills. After University College School and the Royal Military Academy at Sandhurst, in 1956 I was commissioned in the Royal Tank Regiment and was in charge of a tank troop in Germany for three years, followed by two at the Army Outward Bound School as a mountaineering instructor. It was then I launched into serious climbing: in 1958 I made the first British ascent of the Southwest Pillar of Les Drus in the Alps; and in 1961 the first ascent of the Central Pillar of Freney on the south side of Mount Blanc.

On leaving the army in 1961 I joined Unilever as a management trainer but found I could never combine a conventional career with my love of mountaineering. Since 1962 I have followed a career as a writer, photographer and mountaineer. That year I made the first British ascent of the North Wall of the Eiger. My fast-developing career as an adventure photojournalist reached a climax in 1968 when I accompanied Colonel John Blashford-Snell making the first-ever descent of the Blue Nile. On the expedition, I felt too much of a voyeur, though, and returned to something I understood and loved: mountaineering.

In 1970 members of the team I led ascended the South Face of Annapurna. At this time no Himalayan wall had been tried. Tackling the huge 12,000-foot wall was a step into the unknown.

SIR CHRISTIAN BONINGTON, CBE, DL, of Nether Row in the English Lake District was born in 1934 in Hampstead and is the U.K.'s leading mountaineer. He has been climbing for over 50 years, making first ascents in his home country of the British Isles, the Alps, the Andes and the Himalayas. He has been honoured with the Patron's Medal of the Royal Geographical Society, the Livingstone Medal of the Royal Scottish Geographical Society, the CBE, a knighthood and numerous other awards. He is currently Chancellor of Lancaster University and the recipient of numerous honorary appointments. He has authored 20 books, including *Chris Bonington's Everest.* He has been involved with several television documentaries. Chris is still climbing actively, if at a gentler level.

He's married to Wendy, a freelance illustrator of children's books. They have two sons, Daniel and Rupert.

CATHY O'DOWD

The calm before the storm: on the Lhotse Face, 1996. 1ST SOUTH AFRICA EVEREST EXPEDITION

Reaching for the Heights

On a perfect day in 1999, I stood on the summit of Everest for a second time. Four of us were the only climbers around and the world spread out below in a complex tapestry of silvery peaks and tawny plains. I had just become the first woman to climb Everest from both its south and north sides. It was the culmination not just of a peak, but of years of planning, preparing, attempting, failing and returning; an exploration not just of a mountain but of myself and all that I was capable of. I felt fulfilled.

"Exploration is a voyage of discovery, of both an outer landscape and an inner topography. It is the fulfillment of a curiosity about life, about the wilder aspects of the world and about how we cope in those conditions."

I had come to Everest from unlikely origins. While being brought up to be a little lady at an all-girls school in Johannesburg, South Africa, I had hated the physical activity on offer, the thunder thighs of the hockey team and vicious back-hands of the tennis girls. I retreated into wild fantasy adventures in my parents' huge garden and roamed the dusty veld on my bicycle. Always there was a sense of something missing, a part of me unfulfilled by suburban life, by the wide flat grasslands and unchanging blue sky.

At 14 I was shipped off to a summer camp in South Africa's Drakensberg mountains. A range of adventure activities were offered—including one morning of rock climbing. We were only in the foothills of the range, and climbing on an overgrown boulder, but I was entranced. I loved the size of it all, the vast peaks that touched the sky, the clouds that enfolded them, the ageless grandeur. I loved the activity of climbing, the mental puzzle of fitting my body to the random possibilities of this surface. I was filled with curiosity. What would it be like to look beyond the highest peaks, to climb the towering rock pinnacles? This I could learn to love.

I finally escaped school to discover that the University of the Witwatersrand had a rock-climbing club. A wildfire passion for climbing, and an attractive blond lad in the club, made for several happy years exploring in southern Africa. But the curiosity still burned. What would it be like to go higher, colder, more remote?

I found out at 21, on my first mountaineering expedition to the Ruwenzori in central Africa. I was trudging wearily back along a muddy trail in search of equipment that had dropped off an overloaded pack. The mountain range was expunged by cloud, as if it had never existed. Then a misty gap opened, framing a floating vision of dusky peaks with ice-blue glaciers cascading like layered lace between spiked ridges.

I knew the reality of that landscape, the frustration of navigating in unrelenting mist, the toil of scrambling up scree-choked gullies, the fear of descending glass-hard ice. And the depression of realizing we were seriously short of food. I knew mountaineering was neither glamorous nor easy nor achieved a great deal. Standing on a summit was no more of a 'conquest' than an ant perched on top of a refrigerator. However, as the scene floated in mist, I was entranced. Bewitched by the wild beauty of it, the mingling of earth and sky in these cold and remote heights of the world. This I had to have more of.

I continued to explore as best I could from South Africa until, while completing a master's degree and lecturing in media studies, I saw an advertisement looking for a woman to join the first South African Everest Expedition in 1996. I made the team, and was still there when it made the summit. The expedition revealed not just the majesty of the world's highest mountains, but also the complex interplay of the best and worst of human behaviours.

More expeditions followed, including an ascent of Lhotse, a second ascent of Everest, this time from the north, and an attempt to climb a new route on Everest's east side.

CATHY O'DOWD was born in 1968, grew up in South Africa, lives in Andorra and is married to Ian Woodall. She has climbed across the planet, on rock, snow and ice. She is the author of *Just for the Love of It*, an account of her Everest experiences.

Her experiences, particularly with teams on Everest, brought a new fascination with how people react under the pressure involved in reaching the planet's high peaks. She developed a career as a professional speaker, speaking to corporations about the behaviours found in teams under stress and ways to improve them, illustrated with examples from the world's wild places.

> *"Travelling from the bottom of the world to the highest monastery in the world and meeting someone or something from the past, exemplifies the journeys all explorers must take."*

Can you hear the roar?: at Angel Falls, Venezuela. LAUREN SHULMAN

Antarctic Dreaming

Standing at the South Pole where Amundsen and Scott stood in 1911–1912 is my greatest achievement. I was travelling in an old Cessna with the pilot, Max Wenden, and an explorer from New Zealand, Ian Ford, to the South Pole. On the way, we made a hazardous landing to refuel at the White Fields fuel dump; the left ski on the Cessna had developed a dangerous wobble! Immediately on landing Max asks me—no instructs me—to help him correct it. It's not very scientific but he intends to reverse the ski, hoping that will cure or lessen the wobble. The ski is surprisingly only connected by a small, twisted-wire cotter pin. Max will lift up the ski, whilst I straighten the pin and pull it out. We will then together reverse the ski and, with Max holding the ski, I will need to insert the pin quickly back into the tiny hole and twist the end again to refasten it.

The pin is so small I have to remove my mittens and gloves to do the job. My hands are absolutely freezing and I'm terrified I will drop the pin in the snow where it would vanish without a trace. The nearest rescue would be from the Scott-Amundsen Station at the South Pole. It could take two weeks to look for and find us ....

My dreams of exploration were inspired by this place, the coldest, windiest, most remote on Earth: the Antarctic. As a schoolboy I had two heroes, Admiral Horatio Nelson and Captain Robert Scott. Nelson fought many glorious and extraordinary campaigns and died at the Battle of Trafalgar, surrounded by fellow sailors and his many admirers. Scott tragically died in the bleakest of environments, in a snow-swept tent with just a few good men dying next to him. Nelson knew he had been victorious but Scott thought he had failed. Instead, he succeeded in inspiring a multitude of youngsters to fight on against the odds, myself included.

I read avidly Scott's journals and many polar stories. Posters and photos of him, Amundsen and other polar heroes covered a whole wall of my bedroom. I've managed to keep some of them still, tattered and yellowed, but full of memories, promises, and a schoolboy's dreams. I just never thought I would ever be able to follow in Scott's polar footsteps, but amazingly, nearly 40 years later, I was able first to travel to the North Pole. Then there was no choice but to plan an expedition to the South Pole.

And there we almost ended up like my childhood hero. Well, somehow I didn't drop the cotter pin and the Cessna lifted off. And in January 1997—I was finally and fortunately able to stand at that Pole where my hero Robert Falcon Scott had stood 85 years before on January 17, 1912.

So my youthful dream … which almost became a nightmare … became an adult reality.

Some years later I am climbing from Tibet in the Himalayas and eventually make my way to the Everest Base Camp. Sited on the north side of the remote mighty Everest is the Buddhist Rongbuk (Rongphu) Monastery, the highest in the world. I enter to pay my respects. In the corner of a dimly lit prayer room I can make out the shadowy figure of a bulky, bearded figure studying some wooden carvings. Unbelievably it turns out to be Ian Ford, with whom I've had no contact since the Antarctic! He was about to leave, so another hour and we would have never known we had both been at this ancient monastery.

NEVILLE SHULMAN of London, U.K., is a Fellow of both The Explorers Club and the Royal Geographical Society and a member of the Bhutan Society. He works in theatre, film and the arts and is Chair of the Theatre Forum, Director of the International Theatre Institute, and has written several books about his explorations and mountain climbing, including *Some Like It Cold* and *Zen Explorations in Remotest New Guinea*. His latest is called *Climbing the Equator*. He has climbed mountains on several continents and launched expeditions to Ecuador, Peru, Venezuela, Brazil, Tanzania, Kenya, Vietnam, New Guinea, the Arctic and the Antarctic. Most of his expeditions are undertaken to raise funds for children's and international charities. Neville covers all expedition costs himself. He has received a number of honours, including the CBE from Her Majesty Queen Elizabeth in 2005. He was previously awarded the OBE in 1990.

"Exploration is the process of overcoming fear."

Helen with best friend Charlie.
THE THAYER COLLECTION

A Life of Challenge

In 1987 I became the first woman to travel alone to the magnetic North Pole. At age 50 I skied 364 miles in a month, facing polar bears, storms and broken ice. Although I was the first woman to solo either of the world's Poles, to be first was unimportant. It was the challenge of surviving the journey alone; what I learned about myself; the severe environment; what it does to a human. After this expedition I walked 2,400 miles across the Sahara and at age 63 walked the 1,500-mile Gobi Desert, both firsts for a woman. In a unique study with my husband, I lived 100 feet from a den of wild wolves for a year. There have been many more expeditions, but these captured the most challenge and intrigue.

I was born in 1937 and raised in Auckland, New Zealand. My dream, my thirst for adventure began at nine years old in 1946 when I climbed Mount Taranaki, 8,261 feet, in mid-winter with my parents. Although my young legs felt like lead weights and my lungs approached the bursting point, I was determined to make it. Standing on the summit I felt like the queen of the world! But that was just the start!

The defining moment that pushed me to unlimited horizons was when I first met Sir Edmund Hillary. I was introduced by our headmaster, himself an accomplished Himalayan climber. It was Sir Edmund Hillary (Ed Hillary to us Kiwis) who encouraged me to set lofty goals, challenge myself and look to distant horizons of achievement. Throughout my childhood he was my hero, my mentor. His determination to reach goals inspired me to never give up on my outdoor ambitions.

I continued to climb higher and more technical routes in New Zealand's Alps until later I travelled overseas to climb mountains including Mount McKinley, Alaska (20,320 feet); Aconcagua, Argentina (22,834); Lenin Peak, Tajikistan (23,405); and Ismail Semari, Tajikistan (24,590). I also climbed in China and Mexico.

When I stood on the summit of Ismail Semari (formerly Communism Peak) looking down at a sea of magnificent peaks I knew I should turn my future expeditions into educational programs and share this world with students and teachers.

It on was on that peak in 1986 that I resolved to take the four corners of the world into the classroom. On the descent, by the time I reached 22,000 feet, a storm had engulfed the mountain. I continued downward in the grey gloom of a powerful wind. As darkness locked the mountain in a black veil I arrived at an unfamiliar ridge. On the ascent I had taken compass bearings at key turns and now I followed the magnetic needle of my compass downward hoping my calculations would enable me to reach base camp safely in the pitch black night. Finally, safe in my sleeping bag with a cup of hot chocolate, I realized my magnetic needle had shown me the way. I decided that my next expedition and the first program in Adventure Classroom would be a solo journey to the magnetic North Pole. I had a long-standing fascination with polar bears and was anxious to find the Pole my compass needle pointed to.

However, my journey would be different than most modern polar expeditions. I would be 50 years old, travel alone on foot, pulling my own 160-pound sled with no dog teams, snowmobiles or any resupply or support.

Those who take on adventures into wild and dangerous places often face fear. Although fear is not something I seek, it has often stalked me as I walked to the Pole, walked across deserts or kayaked rain forests. But I've learned to acknowledge fear, know that it is fine to be afraid, as long as I face it squarely with confidence that I will survive. This realization has given me a quiet confidence that I can continue regardless of obstacles strewn across my path.

HELEN THAYER is the author of *Three Among the Wolves* and the best selling *Polar Dream*. Her many awards include being named by National Geographic Society/National Public Radio as "One of the Great Explorers of the 20th Century." In addition to exploration of the world's remote places for education, Helen represented three countries' national teams in track and field and was the United States national luge champion. Adding to a long career in mountain climbing and extreme expeditions, she was a kayak and ski racer in international races.

She and her husband live in Washington's Cascade Mountains and continue to train for more exploration.

25 Himalaya Cha Cha

When you wish upon a star....

—NED WASHINGTON

EDWARD MIGDALSKI

Overlooking the magical, mysterious Kathmandu Valley, 1947. S. Dillon Ripley

The Museum Man

The year was 1947 and after a grueling ascent from India, I sat on my pony looking down, exhausted but exhilarated, into the Kathmandu Valley. I was 30 and on one of the first expeditions to the Forbidden Kingdom—and among the first lucky 100 outsiders allowed in! I felt like I was living a magic dream ....

I was fortunate to have parents who loved the great outdoors and who nurtured me in that direction. One day I saw an advertisement in *Field & Stream* magazine titled *Become a Taxidermist in Your Spare Time*. I became a student-by-mail.

During junior year in high school, my main interests, aside from girls, were athletics and taxidermy. So, while fidgeting in my classroom seat, I was less than impressed by the looks of Mr. Harriman, the biology teacher. "He is a wimp," I thought. His appearance was opposite that of coaches—role models to the macho gang to which I qualified as a member of the football, basketball and track teams.

I was surprised, however, during a bird lecture when he withdrew a mounted blackbird from a cabinet. After explaining the structure of the wings, he expounded on the aerodynamics in the beats of the wings. I was awed. When I asked about

> *"Exploring, to me, is the investigation or examination of previously unknown facts or knowledge pertaining to any discipline."*

the blackbird and the others in the cabinet, he off-handedly suggested I visit him after class. To his surprise, I did. When I discovered that taxidermy was his hobby also, my feelings toward the "wimp" began to change. By graduation he had replaced football coach "Chick" Bowen as a role model.

It was that day with that biology instructor which sparked my life's work as a naturalist traveling the globe, experiencing exotic adventures and exploring while collecting specimens for Yale University's Peabody Museum of Natural History.

At one of our after-school sessions, Mr. Harriman opened a brochure depicting exhibits in the American Museum of Natural History. I vowed to visit. I stashed earnings from my spare time endeavors for train and subway fare to travel to the unknown hazards of New York and the famous American Museum of Natural History.

As I looked up at the colossal façade and walked through its massive doors, I was overwhelmed by the sight of mounted elephants dominating the rotunda, while the encircling dioramas of animal life created an illusion that the visitor was in Africa. When I read the label at the base of this phenomenal display, I learned that Carl Akeley, a famous explorer of Africa, was responsible. He became my idol.

It would have been beyond my fondest dreams to believe that in the future I would be studying exhibit preparation in this great museum. At the time, however, and I remember it distinctly, as I stood awestruck in that great African Hall named after Akeley, I thought, "I must become a museum man!"

Because I lived close to the Peabody, I spent many wonderful afternoons scrutinizing exhibits. During one, I built up my courage and walked with trepidation into an open door office where an attractive secretary was typing. I asked, "Where can I see the boss?" She chuckled and said, "Why do you want to see him?" I replied, "Because I want to be a museum man." From the inner office, Professor Richard Lull, a renowned paleontologist who overheard us, came out. He looked at me in my white wool sweater emblazoned with blue felt letters representing Hillhouse High School and asked, "How did you earn those?" I replied, "Football." In his office, he showed me a picture of Rutgers University football team, and he was on it! After discussing my reason for wanting to see him, he escorted me to a laboratory and introduced me to Tom James, an elderly, tobacco-chewing man skinning birds. "Tom, this young fellow wants to be a museum man. Could you use him as a volunteer assistant?" Tom James's face lit up. When the distinguished Lull left us, Mr. James turned to me and said, "You can start by sweeping the floor and emptying the wastebasket."

And that was the inauspicious start to my exploring years.

As a special student under Yale's program for returning World War II servicemen, EDWARD MIGDALSKI spent a month collecting birds and mammals in Nepal. In 1948, he returned as associate leader of a major scientific expedition sponsored jointly by *National Geographic*, the Smithsonian and Yale.

In the course of furthering his education in the natural sciences at Yale and Cornell universities with majors in ornithology, ichthyology and formal invitational visits to natural history museums throughout the world, Ed participated in more than 20 scientific expeditions. He was elected into The Explorers Club in 1949 and has authored nine books, including *Lure of the Wild: The Global Adventures of a Museum Naturalist,* and about 150 articles. A national leader and pioneer in outdoor recreation and club sports, Ed was responsible for initiating the Club Sports Program at Yale in the early 1960s.

Although retired, the museum man continues to serve Yale as a consultant.

Up on the roof: John in Ru-thok, Tibet. J. V. BELLEZZA

*"Exploration is the innate power to know the
world around us and to realize our ultimate destiny:
knowledge of the cosmos and the life it
has spawned upon this earth."*

High on the Himalayas

Although I had spent many years wandering around Tibet on foot, it was only
in 1999 that the Chinese authorities finally began to sanction my archaeological survey work in the uppermost reaches of the plateau. I had already spent five
months in the field that year and the fierce winter of the northern plains was drawing close. It was nearly time to return to Lhasa and plumb the significance of what

I had found that year. I was pleased with my work documenting a wide range of previously unknown Iron Age monuments and didn't expect to find much more. Yet, I kept roving, spurred on by my curiosity and the desire to see and learn as much as I could.

In the region of Rishi, reports came to me of an old Buddhist monastery and nunnery located high above the community of nomads. I was interested in the much rarer pre-Buddhist sites but I thought to myself, "You never really know what's there unless you look for yourself." I set out up the slopes to 16,000 feet to discover not the ruins of a Buddhist religious center—but the extraordinary Yul Khambu site, probably the largest Iron Age funerary pillar complex in all of Eurasia!

Yul Khambu belongs to the Zhang Zhung phase of Upper Tibetan civilization, when warlike tribes worshipped powerful territorial gods to subdue their neighbors, both human and spirit. The necropolis consists of six temple-tombs up to 200 feet in length with concourses of small menhirs set in rows aligned in the cardinal directions. Remarkably, 6,000 of the approximately 10,000 pillars originally erected were still standing. Tibetan literary sources indicate that these ritual structures were established to defeat the agents of death and lead the deceased to the celestial afterlife. Yul Khambu also appears to have had a potent social role welding the Zhang-zhung elite and able-bodied fighters into a firm pact that extended beyond the grave.

Since I can first remember, I wanted to be an explorer. I never liked to stay indoors and went outside whenever I could no matter what the weather. As a small child playing in New York City I would make believe I was venturing across far-flung corners of the globe looking for dinosaurs. The most seminal moment, however, occurred when I was six years old and living in northern California. I found myself inexorably drawn to the hills outside our town and would visit them on a frequent basis often alone. Most of my friends had no desire to go so far afield, happier instead with their bicycles, baseballs and televisions. This caused my parents considerable consternation and they would warn me that cougars prowled the wooded slopes.

But I felt little sense of fear. I was intrigued by the exuberance of the forest and the sheltered, secret aspect of its many nooks and crannies. Coming over each rise and encountering a new vista was always exhilarating. I learned to make myself invisible when I heard something big approaching and this resulted in an abiding sense of security and confidence. I passed untold hours happily observing insects, birds and other animals. In later childhood, in the cultivated forests of Germany and the Pine Barrens of New Jersey, I continued to spend much time in the natural world, now armed with a telescope, microscope, dissecting kit, field manuals and a rucksack full of camping equipment.

The first major turning point came when I dropped out of university, putting enormous pressure on me to figure out what I was doing with my life! Inevitably, I was attracted to the Himalaya, a region I had dreamed of since childhood. Arriving in India in 1983, I strangely felt at home. I immediately set out to learn Hindi and Urdu, and then Tibetan and a smattering of Himalayan languages. For a decade, I covered huge distances on foot in the Great Western Himalaya and Tibet, collecting data on the region's natural and cultural history. I decided to focus my attention on ancient Tibetan civilization, a subject that captivated my imagination and of which little was known.

JOHN VINCENT BELLEZZA, born in New York in 1957, has been exploring the Great Western Himalaya and Tibet since the 1980s. He is a visiting scholar at the University of Virginia, and has published numerous papers and books pertaining to the cultural history of High Asia. His latest tome, *Calling Down the Gods*, explores the ancient traditions of the shamans of Upper Tibet.
   He and his son Eli reside in Himachal Pradesh, India.

CATHERINE COOKE

Leeches and ice storms added challenges to Catherine's journey.
Brian Hanson

"To quote actor-activist Alan Alda: 'When you embark for strange places, don't leave any of yourself safely on shore … you have to leave the city of your comfort and go into the wilderness of your intuition …. What you will discover will be wonderful. What you will discover will be yourself.'"

Ghost Call

High in the Himalayas I made the greatest discovery any explorer can …. I hear birds screeching, followed by the rumble of distant thunder. A thick mist surrounds me and it is very difficult to see. Ice is falling from the sky like sharp shards of glass; I am very cold. I can barely discern a track of some sort, ghostly footsteps in the snow … I follow.

The dream has come again, both scary and seductive. I zip my sleeping bag so that just my face is exposed, in darkness so complete that the roof of my tent is invisible. I listen. Yes, the thunder is real. But a ghost has lured me to Nepal. Since I was eight years old in 1958, growing up in San Antonio and first laid eyes on a small silver-framed photo (which still sits in my bookshelves today), I was mesmerized by the pale blue eyes staring out from it. Forty years later I discovered his correspondence, now yellowed with time, in an old shed, giving me entry to a private world of dreams and adventure. Images have haunted me—snowy mountains, hidden valleys, dark and sacred caves, mysterious creatures. I could not resist the call to his mythical Shangri-La; like everyone who searches for dreams, I believe I might find answers just over that farthest horizon.

The "ghost" was my uncle, a remarkable explorer named Tom Slick, whose curiosity and spirit of discovery led him to create five non-profit scientific research foundations, engineer new breeds of cattle and grasses, invent new technologies for construction and oil production and travel the world in search of mystery ... all before his early death at 46 in 1962. In the Himalayas, he sought the elusive Yeti whose legend has inspired expeditions to Nepal, Bhutan and Tibet for more than 100 years.

Finally, in 2001, a group of six friends—boldly calling ourselves "21st century explorers"—organized an expedition to one of Nepal's remotest regions, where mountain gods still control the rain and snow and hidden *beyul* (valleys) hold the promise of grail-like discovery. East of Everest, in the shadow of Makalu, the world's-fifth highest peak, we mapped our route along the Arun Valley, along rocky paths once taken by the blue-eyed "ghost" nearly half a century ago.

Combining 21st century technology—including night-vision equipment and GPS—with ancient lore and Tom Slick's journal entries, we began our month-long trek to look for scientific evidence of the Yeti, chart hidden *beyul* and better understand how mysteries guide our life journeys and why the unknown pulls all of us like a powerful magnet.

Previous expeditions to New Guinea, to study "magical healing," Guatemala and Belize to discover and document Maya temple sites at Rio Azul and Caracol and to Bhutan to track the migration of the black-necked cranes had all been enriching, life-changing experiences with the degree of challenge, hardship and reward one would expect. But in 2001, after the first week of strenuous trekking into a world without roads, electricity or even radio contact, the Nepalese expedition took me to new heights—both literally and figuratively—of (self) exploration. Unexpected heavy rainstorms and a surprise blizzard, jungle leeches and clouded leopards, porters climbing barefoot in the snow, friendships forged that will last forever, and my own ultimate challenge—slithering through the tight tunnels of sacred Khembalung Cave—produced a transformation of sorts. We didn't find a Yeti, or even a skull or bone, but we discovered something in that faraway place that every explorer understands.

CATHERINE NIXON COOKE lives in San Antonio after long stints on both coasts. She served as an Explorers Club Director from 1999 until 2005. She has carried three Club flags on expeditions to Nepal, Bhutan and Belize. As president and CEO of The Mountain Institute 2001–2005, she worked in remote villages in the Andes and the Himalayas on conservation, cultural preservation and livelihood development projects, and was selected as Valedictorian at Celebrating Mountain Women in Bhutan in 2002. She was formerly editor-in-chief of *Coronet Magazine* and has published more than 100 articles. She earned a B.A. in Communications/Anthropology from Stanford and did graduate studies at Trinity. Catherine is currently a consultant for Lewa Wildlife Conservation Trust (Kenya) and is completing a biography about Tom Slick, entitled *Mystery Hunter*. She serves on the advisory boards of the Harte Research Institute for Gulf of Mexico Studies, the Center for Medical Humanities and Ethics and The Mountain Institute.

Mountains are us: Fritz in the Alps. Lee Elman

Brotherhood, Sealed in Blood

The closest I have come to exploration in a true sense was a journey through Inner Dolpo, Nepal, in 1999. It is a shut-off land reached by traveling over two 18,000-foot-plus passes. The scattered settlements of Tibetan-like people are to be found at the base of the Himalayas. They inhabit a *shas-yul*, Tibetan for "hidden land." They practice the ancient Bon religion, forerunner to Tibetan Buddhism. Many had never seen a Westerner and besieged us with requests for medicine and asked us to cure assorted ailments. We even discovered yak herders living in caves.

My heart and soul had been imbedded in the hills and mountains since childhood. I was born in 1938 and raised in an out-of-doors environment in the Black Forest of southern Germany and the Swiss Alps. My family's entertainment center

> *"Exploration means being first, and though the Earth's surface has been explored to a point where few unknown locations remain, it still exists under the seas, in space, in archaeology, paleontology and biology."*

was hiking trails and ski slopes. Early reading material described the world's wonders—faraway places with exotic names like Timbuktu, Khyber Pass, Bora Bora and Tanganyika. I vowed to locate myself into lands of my imagination when the opportunity presented itself.

The key contributor to these longings was my father. His gifts of books were meant to curtail my climbing of trees and wanderings about my hometown of Baden-Baden. I divided my hours in the town's castles of the 1600s with the volumes that formed my initial library.

One author in particular changed my life. He was German. Karl Friedrich May (1842–1912) was a favorite author of Albert Schweitzer, Albert Einstein and Herman Hesse. May's imagination ran rampant as he wrote of Winnetou, a noble American Indian chief and of Winnetou's virtuous German blood brother, Old Shatterhand. The latter would shoot six-shooters out of the hands of adversaries. Karl May expanded his fields to the deserts of North Africa and to the Orient.

When I was about nine, one passage in particular sparked my dream to learn the ways of indigenous people. Winnetou and Old Shatterhand met on the trail and fought with knives. The combat went one way, then the other, but there was no winner. Instead, in the end, they came to have great respect for each other. Winnetou demonstrated how Indians become blood brothers by making a small cut on his arm and asking his former opponent to do the same. They then let each other's blood flow into their veins. I thought this a memorable scene and an act of nobility.

I did not learn of this until adulthood, but May first went to the U.S. in 1908—*after* he wrote his Westerns! He had worked from imagination! Hesse called the novels "fiction as wish fulfillment." I was not the only reader who was hooked. Today 600,000 Germans annually attend Karl May events, often dressing up in feather headgear and Stetson hats!

But there was also a motion picture, the first I had ever seen, that left an indelible impression. I was 11. *Four Feathers*, set in the desert of the Anglo-Egyptian Sudan, told of the struggle in the late 1800s between a British Expeditionary force and a cast of hundreds of natives. There were Sudanese riding camels and they defeated the British regiment.

Thirty years later, when I was riding a camel around Egypt's Great Pyramid, it all came to life once more. I doubt that I would have visited the monuments on a camel if those books and that film had not opened my mind to this world.

But it was really Karl May who first sparked my adventurous imagination and carried me out of my small town and laid the foundation for my worldwide wanderings, curiosity … and explorations.

FREDERICK P. "FRITZ" SELBY is a New York City-based investment banker who has served on the boards of a number of public corporations. His early schooling took place in Germany, Switzerland and Scotland. After graduating in economics from Philadelphia's Wharton School, he spent 1960–1963 in Nepal with the U.S. State Department. Nine journeys to Nepal and Bhutan followed, including ascents to 23,500 feet. Fritz was the first foreign trekker to visit the Annapurna region; first to water-ski in Nepal; and the first to shoot and produce postcards of the country. He has also led expeditions to Kilimanjaro, summiting it three times, and the Altai Mountains of Mongolia. He has published articles about the Maasai, Sherpas and the alpine ski Haute Route from Chamonix to Zermatt.

26 Volcanic Passions

Life is ... a fatal adventure. It can have only one end. So why not make it as far-ranging and free as possible?

—ALEXANDER ELIOT

About to board a chopper to inspect Mt. Cayley, a young volcano just north of Vancouver, Canada. OSCAR CERRITOS, GEOLOGICAL SURVEY OF CANADA, NATURAL RESOURCES CANADA

Explosive Beginning

Shuddering; grey streaked with white, ochre and vermilion; seething and churning, Mt. St. Helens disintegrated before my eyes. Massive jets of steam, ash and rocks boiled, churned and cascaded upwards and outwards—crashing down the mountain's flanks, engulfing the forest in a 480 km/h stone wind. Awestruck, I watched the eruption transform the once-tranquil, snow-clad peak into a grey mass of fury. Exhilaration turned into cold-blooded fear—where was there to run? My then husband Paul and I had driven there merely out of curiosity, but we now jumped into our old Renault station wagon (our two terrified dogs diving in first!) and sped away, with me continuously shooting pictures from the car, my mind searching for answers as to what was happening behind and around us. Three hours later and safe, I tried to explain what had happened—what I had

*"Exploration is delving into the unknown,
whether it be the mysteries of science, uncharted forests
and mountains or the secrets of the mind. By challenging
the frontiers of what we know, pushing farther
and deeper than anyone has gone before,
we ultimately discover truth."*

seen. Words could not describe it, but I sketched the scene and noted features of the eruption on a scrap of paper—my hands still shaking. Returning home to Vancouver, Canada, the vision of the eruption kept appearing, filling me with the terror of those hours spent trying to escape its fury. But always I was trying to overcome the fear and understand what had actually happened.

On Sunday, May 18, 1980, at 8:32 a.m., my career in volcanology was launched (erupted?), catapulting me to discover that the stone wind was actually a gigantic explosion of superheated steam and magma (a pyroclastic surge), unleashed by the world's largest observed landslide. I was 25 and immediately changed courses at university; I had been planning a career in sedimentology, but I now specialized in volcanoes—how they interact with mammoth glaciers and how volcanoes and ice can shape the landscape. Always aware of their killing power, I have become involved in hazard mapping, emergency management and outreach to help people understand the hazards they face.

That October I returned to Mt. St. Helens to begin studies ultimately contributing to a better understanding of the eruption. There was no more dramatic way to launch myself into a career in volcanology than to witness, describe and then study one of the most scientifically influential eruptions in history. I was part of it. I realized this was what I had been waiting for all my life—this was my epiphany.

As a small child growing up in northern Alberta, I was always fascinated with the great outdoors. My father, an avid hunter and fisherman, often had my brother and me up before dawn to walk stealthily along stream banks in search of elusive trout. Or in the cold autumn chill, smelling the musty scent of wet leaves, straw and grain, we would sit in silence as dawn broke and the whistle of wings overhead announced the ducks' arrival and the beginning of the hunt. My mother encouraged my growing collections of bones, bugs and rocks. Always there were books to read. How my imagination flourished when I read of great archaeological investigations! I dreamed of being there, exploring and finding vanished civilizations. But this was not to be.

My early university life was spent doing anything but geology! Early visits to incredible sites like the Rockies, Grand Canyon, Yellowstone and Yosemite stuck in my brain and when an unassigned science credit had to be filled and geology was an option, I took it. I knew immediately that this was what I wanted to do. Understanding the incredible mysteries of mountains and river valleys captured my imagination. Only a short two years later, I witnessed nature's titanic power first-hand. The stage was set, the curtain had opened revealing the incredible world of volcanoes.

Born in 1955, CATHERINE HICKSON is a leader in her field, having studied volcanoes throughout Canada, the U.S., South America, Iceland and New Zealand. In addition to *Mt. St. Helens: Surviving the Stone Wind* and co-authoring with Trevor Goward *Nature Wells Gray*, she has published over 100 scientific papers. Cathie keeps scientifically active while fulfilling several demanding administrative positions. She had just stepped down as manager of a large natural hazard project in South America (Multinational Andean Project: Geoscience for Andean Communities) when, in 2005, she was invited to develop a new program within Natural Resources Canada called "Reducing Risk from Natural Hazards." She works hard to create a program that will enhance Canada's preparedness for natural hazards and hopefully, sometime in the future, save lives.

Cathie and Glenn Helmlinger live in Burnaby, British Columbia.

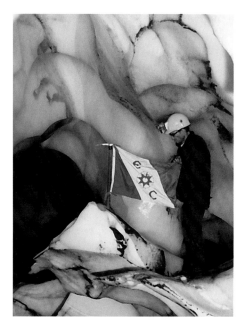

"Exploration is directly contributing to scientific knowledge in the field of geographical exploration or allied sciences; a quest to extend beyond their world and engage in self-directed learning. That's what I do."

The Explorers Club flag five miles inside Paradise Cave. Dr. Mark R. Dinning

Under the Volcano

On July 29, 2000, a helicopter dropped Chris Behrens and Bill Greninger and me on the 7,000-foot lip of Mt. St. Helen's volcano looking north. This gave us a spectacular view inside the lava dome. From this position we could watch in great detail the very active rock fall events. We found it hard to breathe with lots of rockslides and ash in the air. All day we did measurements deep down in the caves, then camped back on the lip. About 2:00 a.m. there was a huge rockslide on the west side of the crater that woke us. There were lots of rockslides around us. When we got out of the crater we found out that there were two earthquakes that night! One was 1.8 and one was 2.0 on the Richter Scale! I don't think we will camp below the lava dome again! This was the best adventure I have ever had!

The first time I went into a cave was when I was 10 years old, in July 1952 on a Cub Scout camp trip in Missouri. The Scout leader knew about the cave and had been in it. We went into the cave as a group. We used hard hats and carbide lamps and flashlights. This was a very big cave with lots of passages and you could get lost. If there was not one already, we made a mark on the wall showing our way out. There were lots of nice formations everywhere you looked. I remember so clear, this cave contained stalagmites, stalactites and flowstone in translucent shades of pink, green, blue and brown. Fragile minerals—"soda straws"—which had grown to several feet in length, hung serenely from the ceiling.

In this cave we found pits in front of us; some were about 50 feet deep. But we did not have rope or cable ladder with us and we had to stop going any farther. But everywhere we went in the cave, I wondered what was around the next bend or the next passage! I wanted to see the unknown parts of the cave. What is in the cave and how did this cave form and why?

On that day, I fell in love with caves and mountains. Little did I know that that cave would be the beginning of my life studying in caves, glaciers and volcanoes.

I started exploring caves and mountain climbing when I was around 15 years old. In 1966 I moved to Washington State and heard about the Stevens Glaciers and Paradise Ice Caves on Mount Rainier and started exploring them. There was very little information on them then, but I've done 320 descents into them now. The caves had lots of blue shades of color and some nice formations and went on for over 1,000 feet with no end in sight! By 1991 I had around 15 miles under the glacier. These descents really started my new science, being a glaciospeleologist!

My great love and work is at Mt. St. Helens volcano, which I've been studying since 1967. To date I have made 144 trips into the crater. Since the eruption in 1980, I've studied the redevelopment of the new glacier inside it. My investigation has taken me as far as 625 feet inside her glacier caves. Everyone says it's dangerous work, and I guess it is. Hardly anyone wants to join me. You've got hot magma under you and rocks falling out of the ice on top of you. Another danger is bad gas—sulphur dioxide you can smell, but not carbon dioxide. There's sometimes a potential for *lahar*, or volcanic debris flows. But you know what? It's exciting and reminds me of being a kid again in that first cave!

CHARLES H. "CHARLIE" ANDERSON of Federal Way, Washington, is Director of the International Glaciospeleological Survey (IGS), an organization he established in 1972 to explore, study and publish information about glacial caves. So new is this field science that he coined the name "glaciospeleology" himself. As a life member of the National Speleological Society, he has explored glacial caves as far afield as Canada, Iceland, Switzerland, France and Germany.

He is the 2003 recipient of The Explorers Club Pacific Northwest Chapter's Vancouver Award; holds degrees from the Colorado School of Mines in geology and the New York Institute of Photography; is the winner of many awards for cave photography; and has published considerably. He has participated in a Science Channel documentary, *Mount St. Helens: Forecast for Disaster*.

The volcanic personality at Kilauea, Hawaii.
BILL SMYTHE

"Exploration is being driven by one's curiosity to discover nature's wonders, big or small. We are all born explorers; some of us are lucky enough to turn our curious nature into careers."

My "It" Moment

I had the good fortune, from 1996 to 2001, to discover 71 previously unknown volcanoes on Jupiter's moon Io that the *Galileo* spacecraft observed, landing me in the *2006 Guinness Book of World Records* as "the discoverer of more active volcanoes on Io (or on Earth) than anyone else." I used an infrared instrument called NIMS, and was able to detect the heat of the active volcanoes. I thought I might find one or two during the mission—finding so many was truly unexpected!

My "It" moment is also my earliest memory. My dad was a real estate investor in Rio de Janeiro and my mother was a homemaker. I was a real girl from Ipanema— that's where we lived! I was four years old and I remember being in the kitchen where my family's cook, Josefina, busied herself at the stove. I spent a lot of time with Josefina, who adored me and used to buy me roses for every birthday. My parents came into the kitchen, very excited about something they had heard on the radio. Some Russian guy had gone into space. I didn't know what Russians were, but I had some vague notion about space—way, way up there in the sky. Dad asked me if I wanted to go into space when I grew up. By then, he said, people might even go to the moon. I replied with an emphatic "*Yes!*" I wanted to go into space, go to the moon! The idea planted itself in my mind at that moment and never left. I was not even deterred when Grandma Hilda came into the kitchen, having overheard the conversation. She said that God did not mean for us to fly into space and that He would send back anybody who tried to get to the moon. I adored Grandma Hilda, who in many ways was a woman ahead of her time, having studied when few women did and worked as a teacher when most women were homemakers. However, I understood even then that some of her ideas didn't make sense. Why shouldn't God want us to go to the moon?

By the time I started elementary school, I had decided to become an astronomer instead of an astronaut. I still desperately wanted to go into space but by then we had found out that I had incredibly bad eyesight. Added to being female and Brazilian, my odds as an astronaut candidate would not be good. I am not sure how I had the wisdom to figure that out at such an early age, but the path I choose has served me well.

In 1979 while in London studying astronomy, I went to Mt. Etna and saw my first eruption. I was hooked on active volcanoes. I finished my Ph.D. in Planetary Geology and Volcanology in 1985 and became a curator at the Science Museum in London, and later at the Old Royal Observatory at Greenwich. I became Acting Head of the Astronomy section and worked on a new collecting policy for the museum's astronomy collection. I went to the U.S. to the Jet Propulsion Laboratory in a postdoctoral program for two years in 1989, and then was offered a job on the Galileo mission in 1991.

I now explore space vicariously, through the eyes of spacecraft. I studied planetary geology and discovered the beauty of volcanoes on Earth, where my contact lenses are merely an annoyance. My parents accepted my strange career choice and encouraged me all the way. Grandma Hilda and Josefina are long gone, but I think they would be proud of me. I confess that I have not abandoned that first dream. Maybe the day will come when I can go into space—bad eyesight and all!

ROSALY LOPES, PH.D., was born in Rio in 1957 and is a Principal Scientist at the Jet Propulsion Laboratory, Lead Scientist for Geophysics and Planetary Geosciences and Investigation Scientist for the Cassini Titan Radar Mapper. Rosaly has visited many of the world's most fascinating volcanoes. Her work on planetary volcanism has included Mars, Io and Titan. She worked for several years on the Galileo mission studying the active volcanoes of Jupiter's moon Io. She currently works on the Cassini mission studying ice volcanism on Titan, Saturn's largest moon.

She has written numerous academic papers, as well as for popular publications. She is the editor of *Volcanic Worlds: Exploring the Solar System's Volcanoes* and the author of *The Volcano Adventure Guide*, the first travel guidebook to volcanoes. She is a member of several scientific societies, and in 2005 she was awarded the Carl Sagan Medal by the Division for Planetary Sciences of the American Astronomical Society.

Rosaly is divorced, has a son, Tommy, and lives in Pasadena, California.

27 The Cavemen

We grow great by dreams.
All big men are dreamers ...
Some of us let these great
dreams die, but others
nourish and protect
them; nurse them
through bad days till
they bring them to the
sunshine and light which
comes always to those
who sincerely hope
that their dreams
will come true.

—WOODROW WILSON,
28TH U.S. PRESIDENT

Following in Tom Sawyer's footsteps.
JAMES CUMMINS

"Exploration is a synergy of curiosity and action that leads to discovery— and can be done on a shoestring in one's own 'backyard'. It is not confined to wise and mature human beings who join The Explorers Club, but is characteristic of any life form that seeks knowledge beyond necessity."

The Aha! Moment

I nearly died in a cave in 1973—swinging at the end of a rope 100 feet off the floor under a hurricane of freezing water. Ironically, the most exciting moment in my 40 years of caving came not at the nexus of danger and discovery, but upon opening a letter that informed me that I had discovered a new species in a Montana cave. Where discovery treaded the dangerous edge, I had found new life; profoundly more satisfying and humbling to me than any physical or geographic first.

The birth of my caving began one fall 1962 afternoon, when Tom Sawyer climbed out of a sheaf of papers that lay on the dining room table and pulled up a chair beside me. Oh, we had met before, many times in fact. My nearby childhood copy of *The Adventures of Tom Sawyer* had, even then, been hard done by—read over and over and over, until its spine dropped off and the book's pages threatened to scatter like a flock of surprised birds.

I was never good at memorizing and quoting, so that afternoon I only generally remembered Twain's words as I studied the papers:

Presently they came to a place where a little stream of water, trickling over a ledge and carrying a limestone sediment with it, had, in the slow-dragging ages, formed a laced and ruffled Niagara in gleaming and imperishable stone. Tom squeezed his small body behind it in order to illuminate it for Becky's gratification. He found that it curtained a sort of steep natural stairway which was enclosed between narrow walls, and at once the ambition to be a discoverer seized him.

The papers were the *Montana Speleological Survey*, each page describing a Montana cave and how to find it. Spe'le-o-log'i-cal—a two-bit word for cave study—tangled tongue and teeth and required great care to slip it from my mouth. I tried it under my breath as I browsed the pages. The inventory of colorful names—Bottomless Pit, Hell's Half Acre, Skeleton Indian Cave, Hissing Well and The Black Hole of Calcutta—spawned Tom Sawyer imaginings. Flipping through the survey I was hooked by believe-it-or-not descriptions. "Indian artifacts have been found on the floor and there is evidence of Indian picture writing here." "Rumors of a giant hole have reached the Survey through contacts with prospectors and other mountain men." "The bottom is supposedly filled with the skeletons of many buffaloes." "This huge room is nearly 500 feet across and 1,500 feet in circumference."

Page by page, cave by cave, the ambition to be a discoverer seized ... *me*!

Forty-three years, 2,000 hours underground, 475 descents and 210 caves later, Tom Sawyer and I are still at it—only now I own a $75 annotated copy of Twain's book to go along with my old battered warrior of childhood adventure, the "spineless" *The Adventures of Tom Sawyer*.

On seeing, in 2005, a picture of that cave I was rescued in, I realized that my life's avocation was not a game, not an eco-challenge or adventure, not a resource inventory or gathering of data to grace a bureaucrat's file cabinet. It was exploration of the highest order and there were sacrifices to be made, including life.

JIM CHESTER of Eureka, Montana, is a weekend explorer. An eclectic streak led him down several career paths before settling in as a rural mail carrier with the U.S. Postal Service. He has kayaked nearly 2,000 ocean miles; dived thermal features in Yellowstone Lake; and rappelled into a 240-foot well in a European medieval castle. He also discovered a cave critter no bigger than the size of several periods at the end of this sentence: *Stygobromus glacialis*, named because it was discovered in a Glacier National Park cave, is a crustacean.

Jim's passion is cave exploration, specifically of the alpine wilderness cave systems of Montana. He is a Fellow of The National Speleological Society and is a holder of The Lew Bicking Award, the highest for U.S. cave exploration. He serves on the Board of Directors for The Alpine Karst Foundation and is a member of The U.S. Cave Exploration Committee of the NSS. He is past co-editor of *Alpine Karst;* authored The Boy Scouts of America *Orienteering* merit badge booklet; and was co-editor of *The 1977 National Cave Management Symposium Proceedings.* He has been interviewed by *The New York Times.* Jim is Chapters Editor of *The Explorers Log.*

If Bill would've become a coal miner he coulda been paid for this. BILL STEELE

"Exploration, in the case of caves, is to go where no man has gone before. Otherwise, exploration adds to the general knowledge about geographical areas. I believe that Christopher Columbus was an explorer, even though all lands he discovered were inhabited."

Gettin' Down

The exploration of the giant cave system at Sistema Huautla, southern Mexico, from 1976 to 1994 stands as my highest low point. My friends and I explored about 50 miles, which included hundreds of pits, and integrated a cave system almost 5,000 feet deep. It was the first outside of Europe to be explored to the landmark depth of 1,000 metres, and for a while, beginning with a major connection between two deep caves in 1987, stood as the second-deepest known cave.

I had two dreams as a kid. Among the books in the house as I was growing up was a copy of Thor Heyerdahl's *Kon-Tiki*. I read it at an early age and marveled at the story of determination through incredible hardship. Many times I stared at a photo in that book of Heyerdahl standing with polar explorer Peter Freuchen, looking at a huge globe in The Explorers Club. I dreamed of being an explorer of some kind and of someday becoming a member.

As a Boy Scout I went caving in Kentucky in the early 1960s. On my first trip we pushed ourselves through a maze of sharp-edged boulders and came up into a virgin cave passage! It thrilled me immensely when I realized that the soft dirt on the floor was devoid of footprints, and I threw out my arms like a school crosswalk-guard and suggested to my buddies that we should now go slowly in single-file and savor our first original exploration. I led the way and placed my footsteps softly, like each one meant something special. The others stepped in my footprints, and on the way out it looked like only one person had come in. After that, the only direction for me in life was down.

As I went caving through my teenage years and on into adulthood, I occasionally ran across mention of The Explorers Club. I read that Russ Gurnee, a former president of the National Speleological Society (NSS), which I had joined at 16, had also served The Explorers Club as president.

Caving remained my avocation through college, as I began a career, married and had kids. I was 29 during the 1978 NSS convention. Fellow caver Bill Stone and I had started the Huautla Project to explore the deep caves of that area. During the convention, Stone and I met Russ Gurnee and asked him to take a walk with us to talk about fundraising possibilities for our caving.

In the course of that walk, Gurnee urged us to join The Explorers Club! We were thrilled. He said it was very rare to have qualified applicants younger than 30 years old—but we qualified! After all, we had explored the deepest cave in the Western Hemisphere and many other significant caves. As an unexpected honor, we were elected as Fellows. Stone and I applied to carry The Explorers Club flag on our upcoming Huautla expedition and did so many more times through subsequent years.

I remember tingling all over the first time I visited The Club and stood before that big globe Heyerdahl used to plan his *Kon-Tiki* expedition. Thus, a young Boy Scout's dreams were doubly fulfilled.

And I'm still a Scout—though now as a national director of the Boy Scouts of America. In that capacity, I worked with The Explorers Club president to select 20 living American explorers to honor with camps named after them at the 2005 National Scout Jamboree. I was also a member of the Boy Scouts of America delegation sent to The Explorers Club Annual Dinner in 2005 to receive the Corporate Award for Support of Exploration.

C. WILLIAM "BILL" STEELE of Irving, Texas, has been described, along with Bill Stone, as one of the two Reinhold Messners of speleology. With over 2,000 descents, some to 5,000 feet, and having lived below ground for up to two weeks, it's no wonder. The National Speleological Society has honored him as a Fellow; awarded him their annual Lew Bicking Award for exemplary cave exploration; plus bestowed on him a Certificate of Merit. Besides exploring and mapping caves throughout the central United States (including Kentucky's Mammoth Cave, the world's longest), he was a primary explorer and surveyor of the longest caves in Texas, Oklahoma and Georgia, as well as the two deepest caves in the Western Hemisphere.

Bill's authored many chapters in books about caves and caving; wrote *Yochib: The River Cave, Huautla,* co-authored a chapter in *Encyclopedia of Caves* and published numerous articles.

SAM MEACHAM

Can't wait to dive Cenote Jade Pearl, Quintana Roo, Mexico, 2003. STEPHEN ALVAREZ

Diving into the Maya Underworld

In 2001, Christophe Le Maillot and I were wrapping up a survey of *cenotes* near the archeological site of Coba in Quintana Roo, Mexico. We descended into the darkness of a dry cave, unsure, as always, of what we might find. With our lights, we soon came across rudimentary stone steps leading down and shortly came to the cave's terminus, which ended in a crystal clear pool of water. We noticed that the floor was littered with pottery fragments and that the stairway continued along the wall and onto a ledge in the water. We were soon in the water with our masks and submersible lights. Almost immediately Christophe summoned me to where the stairway met the water. Wedged under the stairway was a human skull and nearby were other bones and sherds. As we moved into the center of the pool we looked down 10 metres and began to see shapes taking form on the floor. We immediately sent runners to bring my cave diving gear. Once geared up, I descended. Quickly, the shapes came into focus. I felt like I'd touched electricity! Over 30

"Exploration has many faces. The essence of exploration is the experience of discovery. As the adage goes, 'It isn't the gold, it's finding it.' Most people relate to the tangible discoveries, yet sometimes and more importantly, the discovery is found within. Finding the mental or physical strength to carry on when you are drained, or the courage to know your own limitations and turn back are essential. Ultimately, exploration gives us perspective and teaches us humility. The further we explore the limits of our world, solar system and universe, the more we come to realize how lucky we are to be here at all."

intact Maya ceramics lay strewn about, and in and around them six human skeletons in a jumble. The ceramics were from the Maya Classic Period, making them 1,200–1,800 years old!

The vision is clear although the dates are fuzzy. At Eanes Elementary School in Austin, Texas, in the mid-1970s we were visited by a classmate's father, a commercial diver in the Gulf of Mexico. I remember staring transfixed at his Kirby Morgan dive helmet and the scale model of an offshore oil platform he had brought. I don't remember the name of my classmate, and I'm unsure what grade we were in—all I remember was that from that moment on I wanted to breathe underwater.

I grew up largely without television and while I resented it at the time, I now realize that it is one of the greatest gifts that my parents ever gave me. Instead of *The Brady Bunch*, I was read to and encouraged to read from a young age. I developed an insatiable curiosity and an extremely healthy imagination. Ask me who my exploration heroes are and many are fictional. The exploits of Bilbo Baggins, Tintin, John Blackthorne and Jim Hawkins filled me with the desire for adventure and exploration.

As I grew older, other experiences reinforced my desire. A wonderful summer camp in the backwoods of Maine gave me skills and an appreciation of the outdoors, reinforced as a teenager by a semester in Africa with the National Outdoor Leadership School. Visits to the British Museum, the Egyptian Museum in Cairo and the Valley of the Kings spurred my imagination further. Always, I wondered, what would it be like to discover something as fantastic as a mummy or an ancient king? Propitiously, the first time I dived, at 16, was in Quintana Roo.

SAMUEL S. MEACHAM was born in 1967 and brought up in Austin and Casco Bay, Maine. He has a B.A. in Asian Studies from the University of Vermont and is the Director of the Mexican non-profit association Centro Investigador del Sistema Acuífero de Quintana Roo. Having lived in Northern Quintana Roo since 1994, Sam maintains great passion toward understanding the area's aquifer and the history, nature and people affected by it. He makes presentations in Mexico and internationally to raise public awareness about ongoing exploration of the area's flooded cave systems and the need for their protection. He's led many expeditions in the area. In the Ox Bel Ha cave system, the team he led added 50,000 feet of new passageway, making it, at over 80 miles, the ninth-longest cave on the planet, all underwater.

His articles have been widely published. He's also appeared on Mexican and NHK television, and starred with Steve Bogaerts in the BBC documentaries *Secrets of the Maya Underworld* and *Planet Earth*. Besides English, he speaks Spanish, French, Japanese and Mayan.

Sam and his wife Orane have twin sons Benjamin and Matteo. Their daughter, Margot, has sadly passed on.

28　A Scattering of Ologies

We shall not cease from exploration and the end of all our exploring will be to arrive where we started and know the place for the first time.

—T.S. ELIOT

KEVIN HALL

Collecting thermal data on San rock art at Giants Castle, Drakensberg Mountains, South Africa. ALIDA HALL

Having Fun—but Trying to Do Some Good

My greatest exploration moment would probably be in 1992–1993 working with a friend, Ian Meiklejohn, then my student, in a remote area of Antarctica and finding new areas, landforms and lifelike endolithic mites that live inside rocks, and being able to name Natal Ridge, where we did most of our work, after our university. It was exciting beyond the science and I think we felt like 'real explorers' as we lived in a tent for more than a month with no one else within hundreds of kilometres. We were dependent upon each other for survival—but had such great fun working on so many new things and in new places (including the crevasses we seemed to have a knack of 'finding').

The day 'it all began' would probably be at the age of 10 in the cathedral city of Wells, England, when my parents bought me the *Observers Book of Geology* for the grand price of five shillings. We then drove through Cheddar Gorge and I just loved looking at the rocks and the caves. Somehow, rocks and landscapes seemed to make sense to me, and I pursued this direction at school and at every opportunity there was for fieldwork.

This led me to a 'defining' time in the summer of 1968 when I was chosen to be a member of the British Schools Exploring Society expedition to Svalbard, the archipelago in the Arctic north of Europe, where I worked with Cambridge University mapping western Svalbard's geology. This determined my future direction would be 'cold environment studies.'

"Undertaking science in remote places where there is an element of personal 'effort' to make new scientific finds in remote field sites is the essence of 'exploration.'"

The 'calling' finally came on the day, in a geomorphology lecture at Swansea University, when Dr. Gillian Groom said, "So, you can see, we do not have many answers! It's now up to you to go find those answers!!" I was stunned. Here was a university professor saying how little we knew—not how much—and that we needed to go find the answers! Precociously, that really stimulated my desire to 'try and find out' regarding landforms and processes in as many cold places as I could get to.

My main turning point, really allowing the fulfillment of my hopes, was being given the opportunity to work for the Institute of Environmental Studies in the Antarctic for South Africa over three years starting in 1974. It opened the door to many other areas of Antarctica with wonderful people from several nations.

A later, perhaps more mature, restructuring of that desire 'to find out' came when standing in a San rock art shelter in the Drakensberg Mountains in southern Africa and seeing the incredible paintings on rock walls in 1984. It was the melding of science and exploration with art and a social conscience. They were a legacy of the original peoples and, despite the remoteness of many sites, they need to be recognized and preserved in situ. It generated a change in focus for me, from a fairly selfish one to that of work aimed at preserving this legacy for future generations; a change in focus to try to use science for 'good' instead of 'just for the fun.'

With hindsight, South Africa provided the perfect meld—satisfying both the youthful need for excitement and now the mature (geriatric?) desire to do some good. I also 'found' a terrifically patient and understanding South African wife, Alida, and we have two daughters, Kathryn and Lyndl, in whom the love for Africa runs deep.

KEVIN HALL, PH.D., was born in Hampshire, U.K., in 1949. He has also led an expedition to Arctic Norway, which led to crossing the Juneau Icefield in Alaska twice. Work on South Africa's sub-Antarctic Marion Island led to Antarctic opportunities on Kerguelen with France, the McMurdo region with New Zealand, Livingston, Signy and Alexander islands with Britain and Terra Nova Bay with Italy. In between he has done exploration in the Andes, Ellesmere Island, Tibet, and the Namib and Gobi deserts. He has explored southern Africa's mountains on several occasions.

Kevin has written over 130 scientific papers, and is a professor of geography at the University of Northern British Columbia in Prince George.

IAN MACINTYRE

"Exploration is discovering the unknown, whether it is a place, an organism or a process."

How many people can actually make a living beachcombing? Ian is one such lucky one.
RICHARD B. ARONSON

Island in the Sun

My greatest discovery was in the early 1970s when I discovered the location of submerged, relict coral reefs off most of the islands in the eastern Caribbean. These submerged coral reefs were stranded in deeper water by the rising seas caused by the melting of the Pleistocene ice sheets. Even now, after 40 years of marine research, I still have a sense of excitement with every scuba dive I make. We still have so much more to discover.

Not surprisingly, the focus of my exploration is the sea. You see, I spent the early years of my life, from age four to 11, on the island of Barbados, arriving in 1939 and being trapped there by German U-boats. What a place for a boy to be trapped! Our house was next to a golf course where I collected bird's eggs and butterflies. My father showed me how to carefully drill a hole on one side of the eggs and insert a fine glass tube to blow out the contents. This gave an intact egg when it was placed in my collection on the side with the hole. Butterflies were knocked out with a little lighter fluid and mounted on pins with their wings spread out.

Our house was also close to the ocean, where I spent many hours diving up sea-shells. Most of my shell collection consisted of the Sunrise Tellin bivalve mollusc, called "auroras" because of their radiating colour patterns. I spent many hours pumping the sand in shallow back-reef areas to try to feel these slippery shells and dive them up. When they are slit open with a razor blade and allowed to dry out they resemble butterflies. I was darned proud of my tidy collections. But I learned there was an even bigger one on the island ....

My father was the manager of a small oil company. Dr. Alfred Senn was a geologist who worked with him. After school, waiting for my father, I used to spend time watching Dr. Senn in his laboratory studying *his* numerous collections of microfossils, all in neat little vials. He radiated a contagious sense of excitement when he studied them, which were mostly foraminifera. He explained to me how they helped him understand the history of the island of the Barbados—a history well beyond any time scale that I had ever heard of before.

I thought his were the *ultimate* in collections and decided then and there that I would become a geologist, too.

After my carefree, formative years in the Barbados, I was sent to a boarding school in Scotland. In 1953 I immigrated to Canada and obtained a degree in geological engineering from Queen's University. I then spent six years in western Canada exploring for oil with Shell. On a Shell field trip to the Florida Cays and the Bahamas to see modern coral reefs (to compare them with fossil reef oil reservoirs I was drilling), I decided I would like to get back to my first love—the ocean. I obtained a Ph.D. in Marine Geology from McGill University, then did three years at Duke Marine Laboratory, which led directly to the Smithsonian Institution's National Museum of Natural History in Washington, D.C.

IAN MACINTYRE of Falls Church, Virginia, has been with the Smithsonian Institution since 1970, studying the geological history of coral reefs in the Caribbean and the Eastern Pacific, seeking to understand how coral reefs survived the post-glacial rise in sea levels, related to the melting of the ice sheets. Much of the work involves collecting cores from the reefs. In 1996, in recognition of his numerous research publications, the International Society for Reef Studies awarded him the Darwin Medal.

BERTIL NORDENSTAM

"Exploration, discovery and adventure are nearly synonymous, meaning memorable and sometimes unforgettable encounters with the unknown or unexpected, be they places, people, animals or plants. Such encounters are indeed highlights in life."

In Sanetti Plateau, Ethiopia, 2003, collecting the rare Euryops prostrates *which Bertil had described 42 years earlier.* ALISON STRUGNELL

Exploring Eden

On May 31, 1963, I looked around a dramatic mountainous landscape. Down below was the Namib desert with the Atlantic coastline barely visible. I was on top of the Brandberg, highest mountain of Namibia. On the way up I had found many strange and beautiful plants new to science. A dream since my boyhood was fulfilled.

I was 14 in 1950 when our school in Gothenburg, Sweden, invited Sven Hedin, the famous Central Asian explorer, to lecture. I made the posters announcing the event, with camels and sand dunes. The old man with failing eyesight told fascinating stories, sparking a desire to explore and discover—not territories, but plants—already my great hobby. I was familiar with Scandinavian flora, but in other parts of the world there would be unknown flowers awaiting discovery and naming.

My encounter with Hedin must have been similar to his own experience when he at 15 witnessed the triumphant return of Nordenskiöld after the successful North-East Passage. That moment was decisive for Hedin's career.

I studied botany at the University of Lund and completed a master's degree in biology and chemistry. A three-month botanical odyssey in the Aegean on a small fishing boat was good training for more exotic countries.

Like some Linnaean disciples, I was attracted to South Africa, where the Cape of Good Hope alone housed more flowering plants than all of Scandinavia. I got a grant from South Africa for two years of botanical research and a free voyage by cargo ship to Cape Town. In South Africa I travelled widely in my Volvo Duett and often slept in the open by a campfire. After half a year I found an adventurous Swede as companion. We ventured to the interior of Basutoland on horseback and rambled widely in South West Africa.

In Windhoek I asked the leading botanist why he had not investigated the flora of the Brandberg. He said, "There is probably nothing up there that isn't down below." The 2,573-metre Brandberg was first climbed and measured by Germans in World War I. A second ascent was made in 1943 by a native mountaineer, and an expedition in 1955 discovered much of archaeological and geological interest, but had no botanist along. I decided to be the first to explore the mountain.

We carried heavy packs with food enough for 10 days, plant presses and sleeping bags. After we passed the famous White Lady rock painting, the terrain became rough with huge boulders and steep slopes. We slept near waterholes, where leopards left footprints and a pregnant smell in the air. At higher altitudes we found a rich flora! Among 10 new species was a handsome aster shrub, which I named *Felicia gunillae*, using the names of my family. A botanical Eden had been found! That magic moment on the summit has not been quite equalled on later trips to wonderful mountains such as Chimborazo, Jamaica's Blue Mountains, Mount Kinabalu or Kilimanjaro.

I remembered my obligation to Sven Hedin when I crossed the Taklamakan desert in 1992, finding the little pool that saved his life.

BERTIL NORDENSTAM is Professor Emeritus of the Swedish Museum of Natural History in Stockholm, Sweden, where he held various positions between 1969 and 2001 as Head Curator, Director of Botany, Head of Research and Deputy Museum Director. Born in 1936, he matriculated in Gothenburg in 1954, then studied in Lund for a B.S., M.S., Ph.D. and D.S.

Bertil specializes in the daisy family, *Compositae*, which is the largest of flowering plant families, with a worldwide distribution. He has done extensive fieldwork in all continents except Antarctica (too few plants). In Africa he has spent altogether almost three years, especially in southern Africa, but also in tropical Africa and Ethiopia. He has published about 200 scientific papers and several books or book chapters, and runs an international journal, the *Compositae Newsletter*. He has described about 30 new plant genera and 100 new species. Other authors have named about 10 species in his honour.

Besides being a member of many boards and societies, Bertil has been active in the Royal Swedish Academy of Sciences since 1984. He was vice-president , then president of the Travellers Club in Stockholm for 14 years.

Bertil has been married to Gunilla for 40 years. They have a daughter, Felicia, and two grandchildren.

TOM REIMCHEN

"As with most researchers, exploration to me is doing deductive science—testing established ideas about the real world—but of greater importance to me, exploration is more about inductive science, trying to formulate new ideas about how the world works."

Nature Boy. Miwako Nicol

The Grizzly Connection

For a Canadian prairie boy, the return migration of salmon to hundreds of streams and rivers was dramatic. In 1992, I spent five weeks at one remote, pristine salmon stream documenting all of the species that fed on salmon and collecting fundamental data on predator/prey interactions. The richness of wildlife associated with the migrating salmon was striking: sea lions, seals, bears, otters, eagles, ravens and thousands of gulls. However, I was not prepared for what I would soon learn—or that this would set me in a new research direction.

It was the simple act of sitting where the stream entered the ocean and, in the dim evening light, watching black bears capture salmon and carry them into the ancient forest. While I was much too nervous to follow the bears during darkness, at dawn I retraced their movements and found hundreds of partially eaten salmon carcasses scattered throughout the mossy forest floor. A rich assemblage of crows, ravens, bald eagles, pine martens and many soil insects feasted on the remnants. Over several weeks, I determined that the bears had transferred over 3,000 salmon into the luxuriant woods adjacent to the stream. I suspected this might represent the single largest yearly source of nutrients for the forest.

Perhaps it was no coincidence that giant trees grew beside the streams if these salmon nutrients were a common feature. Perhaps, embedded in the annual rings of these 500-year-old trees, was a history of salmon abundance? These observations provided the impetus for 10 years of investigating most of the last pristine watersheds on Canada's West Coast, assessing what proved to be the remarkable cycling of salmon nutrients—particularly nitrogen—initially sequestered from the open Pacific to the canopies of the ancient forests.

I was brought up on a small farm in central Alberta. My parents, of German extraction, were very strict, as was the fundamentalist church I attended three times weekly. Perhaps it was fortunate that I was the youngest of three siblings, for much of my first eight years were spent with my mother doing farm chores, including cutting hay and collecting berries in the forests adjacent to the stream that flowed through the farm. It's difficult to identify any single event that was to structure my later career other than my young anger for the authoritarian church, its attitude of intolerance and its slavish following of Biblical creationism, when I intuitively suspected otherwise.

I think it was the contrast between this hard religious intolerance and the joy of sitting with my dog in a berry patch that set in motion my later decisions to study biology, in particular animal behaviour and how predator and prey interactions led to evolutionary adaptation.

Much of my professional career from 1975 to 1997 played out from a small log cabin in Haida Gwaii, the mist-shrouded archipelago formerly known as the Queen Charlotte Islands, 100 miles off British Columbia's West Coast. I had chosen a slightly different path than my urban colleagues and decided to undertake a long-term research program on a very unusual form of three-spine stickleback, a common small freshwater fish. The stickleback from Haida Gwaii were particularly unusual, as each of the remote lakes we explored contained a unique form, akin to Darwin's finches of the Galapagos, where each island has a unique form. Over a 20-year period, my partner, Sheila Douglas, and I sampled 700 lakes on Zodiac expeditions. It was then that my interests in conservation and marine protected areas began to develop—and when I became fascinated with salmon.

My career choice of studying evolutionary biology was finally embraced by my parents, although my shift to a full secular view of the world has always remained an impassable gulf between us.

TOM REIMCHEN was born in 1946 in Wetaskiwin, Alberta, and received his Ph.D. in 1974 from the University of Liverpool. He has published extensively on a diverse range of interests, including the evolution of stickleback, glacial refugia of western North America, the nocturnal behaviour of black and grizzly bears and the global incidence of human colour blindness. His research on nutrient cycling between ocean and forest has been the subject of articles in periodicals including *Equinox, Ecologist, BBC Wildlife* and *Natural History*. He's been the focus of three Canadian and two Japanese television documentaries.

In 1997, Tom and Sheila moved to Victoria, British Columbia. He is an adjunct professor and lecturer at the University of Victoria.

NAT RUTTER

Studying climate change in Antarctica, 2005. MARIA RUTTER

System Earth

The greatest discovery or enlightenment of my career was, I suppose, obvious—the earth operates as a dynamic, integrated system. As a Quaternary geologist (earth history of the last 2.5 million years or so), I have focused my research on past climate changes, with the view of aiding the prediction and causes of future climate change by studying what happened in the past.

My most rewarding exploration achievement started in 1987. Along with an international team, I was able to spend several field seasons in the Loess Plateau of Central China investigating probably the most complete sequence of terrestrial sediments of the relatively recent past found anywhere in the world. The sediments contained alternating beds of loess (wind-blown dust) and paleosols (soils in the agricultural sense) that together stored a wealth of paleoclimate information, such as pollen and faunal remains. The results of this interdisciplinary study included a better understanding of terrestrial environments, climate, and causes and timing

"Exploration, research and travel are synonymous.
If one dominates, aspects of the other two are always
there. It is the curiosity about the unknown that has
driven me and continues to do so."

of climate changes in this region for the last 2.5 million years, during which time there's been 37 major climate shifts.

Using computer models, these results could then be extrapolated to other parts of the globe, thus treating the earth as a system—a change here causes a change there. It is evident that dramatic climatic change is ongoing but it appears that we're accelerating the trend, at least in the short term.

My moment came during the summer of 1953, after my first year geology professor selected me to be a student observer on the resupply mission to the joint U.S./Canada weather stations in the Canadian Arctic. Having little experience outside the relatively sheltered life of New England, being cast into the remote Arctic Islands and Greenland was an entirely new experience that changed my direction. I had now caught the travel bug and through the persuasion and influence of my mentor and professor, decided to leave the pre-law program and major in geology—hoping to continue field research and travel.

My choice was quickly confirmed by my first job. Upon graduation in 1955, I went to work for an oil company and was assigned geological field mapping in the jungles of Venezuela and Colombia and a few months later in the Kurdish region of southeast Turkey. My interest in geology only increased with this experience. However, I knew that if I wanted to pursue original research in areas of my interest, I would have to attend graduate school. In the process I developed an interest in past climate change and the influence of climate change on terrestrial environments. This led me to an M.Sc. at the University of Alaska in the physics of glacial flow and a Ph.D. at the University of Alberta on the glacial history of the Banff area.

After a few years with the Geological Survey of Canada investigating various aspects of the glacial history of western and northern Canada, I joined the University of Alberta Department of Geology and continued investigations in glacial and engineering geology and archeology, but now with a bevy of keen graduate students. Having never tired of travelling, and wanting to explore and investigate other Quaternary deposits, I was able to undertake projects with international colleagues on every continent. As important as exploration is to me, it's the people who I have been able to work with that make my career so satisfying.

NAT RUTTER was born in 1932 in Omaha, Nebraska, and brought up outside of Boston, Massachusetts. He is Professor Emeritus of Earth and Atmospheric Sciences, University of Alberta. He also spent a term as Environmental Advisor to the National Energy Board in Ottawa and served as the U of A's Chairman of the Department of Geology. He is the author of over 300 scientific publications, has edited several books and co-authored the outstanding *Climate Change and Landscape in the Canadian Rocky Mountains*.

He has led or been a member of many scientific committees and organizations, including President of the International Union for Quaternary Research, member of the Scientific Board (geology) of UNESCO, and one of the founding members of the International Council of Scientific Union's program on past global change. He was the founder and first editor of the scientific journal *Quaternary International*. His numerous honours include election as a Fellow of the Royal Society of Canada, Officer of the Order of Canada, Honorary Doctor of Science and Honorary Professor of the Chinese Academy of Sciences. He has been a recipient of distinguished career awards from the Geological Association of Canada, the Canadian Quaternary Association and the Geological Society of America.

He and Marie live in Stony Plain, Alberta. Todd and Christopher are their kids

29 With Pen, Paint and Camera

For lust of knowing ...
We take the Golden Road
to Samarkand.

—*THE GOLDEN ROAD TO*
SAMARKAND,
JAMES FLECKER

In Death Valley on the set of The Sum of all Fears. MARK FELLMAN

"Exploration is the insatiable need to fathom the unknown ... and to further understand the known. There is an innate need in humans to explore and understand."

The Hollywood Dreamer

We had been filming *The Mosquito Coast* in 1985. The weather was hot ... very hot. At one location near the border with Guatemala we had cleared away the jungle in order to construct our sets. Back in Belize, where major photography was taking place, I had heard of an amazing jade head that had been discovered near Altun Ha, and, having a bit of free time in Guatemala, decided to explore the area. I plodded around for a day or so, and then noticed a hillock that appeared to be in an unnatural area. I cut through the brush—and discovered a small, densely overgrown pyramid! Omigod, could this be real? We had been constructing realistic sets in the jungle but this had an aura ... an aura of an ancient culture. I cleared some of the brush and it *was* real! The local authorities were notified, but, sadly, we had to leave to film in the States before serious archaeology began. I've always lived with feet in two fascinating fields.

My inquisitiveness into science and exploration started at nine. My older brother Louis had gone off to school, leaving behind his chemistry set. It provided numerous experiments, often at the expense of my parents' patience when they went awry. Another seminal moment was at 12. Dr. Wernher von Braun spoke in our hometown of Savannah, Georgia. Because of my interest in science (I had already read every book on science, space exploration and science fiction the library offered) my dad took me. I vividly remember von Braun in his brown suit. His talk was about the need to explore space. When I met him after his talk, that did it. I was hooked. I *had* to travel to the stars!

But as a nine-year-old (or so), I had had another earlier—and competing— Eureka moment. My father owned Leopold's Ice Cream, a Savannah tradition, and a favorite customer was Johnny Mercer, whose childhood home was a block away. I exactly remember Dad calling me over to meet him. Johnny had on a snap-brim hat, tweaked my cheek, and smiled. I knew he was famous, lived in Hollywood—and was in the movies! To a child, this was touching fame … the Holy Grail! Meeting Johnny sparked urges for another quest … the motion picture business. I struggled to fuse these wildly divergent fields: science and exploration with movies!

At the local military high school, I was accepted into the national Westinghouse Science Talent search. It introduced me to Alec Ormond, a scientist with the Union Camp Corp. Alec and I conducted rocketry experiments in his backyard. We constructed a simple rocket tube with interchangeable sizes of venturi openings and nacelles. The rocket was placed in our version of a static test stand that had a cable running to our hiding place behind a concrete slab. These were idyllic years.

Then Robert Mitchum was in Savannah to film *Cape Fear,* the first one, released in 1962. I was a 15-year-old freshman and the filming was near our drill field. I remember the lights, camera, Mr. Mitchum (who kindly autographed our hats) and the euphoric feeling. I was being stretched in two directions like toffee....

I began college but my scientific desires had evolved into inner space. I became a zoology major. My father's death kept me from medical school and subsequent research, since I was left to run the business. But during these years I was involved in several local explorations, from mosquito studies to the accents of indigenous residents of barrier islands. Pat Conroy later, in 1974, explored the same topic in *Conrack* with Jon Voight. Science and film converged!

I left Savannah at 25 seeking my future. In Atlanta, I met Sandy Fuller and started work on documentaries. He has had (and continues to have) an exciting life … dug with Leakey, dove with Cousteau, flew with Fairbanks, all primarily for *National Geographic.*

The film business has taken me to the far corners of the Earth. At every location I strive to explore the area, making weekend trips into the field. I would love to document the tribes I saw along the Amazon and I yearn to return to documentaries. I've reopened Leopolds and when my movie star friends drop around, or I'm around a bar with them in New York, exploration is the subject.

As a motion picture producer and Paramount's Executive Vice President for Production, STRATTON LEOPOLD has produced such movies as Tom Cruise's *Mission: Impossible III,* *Star Trek* XI, Terry Gilliam's *The Adventures of Baron Munchausen,* and *The Sum of All Fears* with Morgan Freeman and Ben Affleck.

Stratton and Mary live in Savannah, where they can often be found dishing ice cream at Leopold's Ice Cream. Among the 30 or so homemade flavors, they are especially proud of Stratton's father's signature creation—tutti-frutti.

ROBERT BATEMAN

Salt Spring Island's landmark Mt. Maxwell, behind Bob, has featured in his remarkable paintings—his way of exploring nature. Birgit Freybe Bateman

"Exploring is a very broad term. It involves discovering a place or its aspects for oneself rather than reading about it. The field may be large or intimate but it is increasingly difficult to find large areas for original exploration."

An Artist-Naturalist

In the 20th century it became less and less possible to set foot on dry land that had never before been explored. I was privileged to be part of a small geological field party of four "white" men and two Inuit during the summer of 1953. We were mapping iron deposits for Fenimore Iron Mines in Arctic Quebec, an area known as Ungava. We were walking on ground the two Inuit said had never been visited by their people. We knew no European explorers had been there.

The land was magnificent, rolling tundra ridges with heather and harebells reminiscent of Scotland. We named the lakes that are now gazetted on the official maps, as well as spectacular waterfalls. Bird life was at a peak: we saw nests belonging to rough-legged hawks, peregrine falcons, a golden eagle and a gyrfalcon. It was a fisherman's paradise: abundant speckled trout, and Arctic char so common we had one on the line every third cast. Finger Lake is the largest lake we named. It is now the base area for international fly-in fishing trips.

My dreams were born in St. Clement's Public Library in north Toronto. I devoured the books of naturalists Ernest Thompson Seton, Ivan T. Sanderson and Gerald Durrell. Inspired by Seton's *Two Little Savages*, exploring began for me at 12 in the thickets at the bottom of our garden in the old Belt Line ravine, a tributary of the Don River. The other two authors explored more exotic, mostly tropical lands, and as an adult I have had the chance to more or less follow in their footsteps. Especially for a young person, exploring can be very local and intimate. When we moved to the wilder areas of Haliburton county, north of Toronto, I bought topographic maps and with a compass set off to explore remote, roadless areas and visit lakes and follow rivers.

Everybody's a nature lover, I am one step more intense—a naturalist. I took geography at the University of Toronto in order to get summer fieldwork in the wilderness so that I could paint it and bird watch as well as collect small mammals for various museums. I have small mammals in the collections of the Royal Ontario Museum, National Museum of Canada, Chicago Field Museum, the American Museum of Natural History and the British Museum in London. Geology or fisheries research was my work; the painting and collecting were serious but spare-time activities.

A very important event in my life was in 1957 when my biologist friend Dr. Bristol Foster said to me, "Let's go around the world in a Land Rover. Tomorrow, give me three reasons why we shouldn't." The next day I couldn't think of one, so in 1957–1958, we drove across equatorial Africa, northern India, Nepal, Sikkim, Burma, Thailand, Malaya and Australia. I returned to Nigeria to teach high school from 1963 to 1965. In 1985 Bristol talked me into moving to Salt Spring Island. I don't know what he's going to talk me into next!

I can't conceive of anything being more varied and rich and handsome than the planet Earth. Its crowning beauty is the natural world. I want to observe it and to understand it as well as I can. And then I'd like to put it together and express it in my painting. This is the way I want to dedicate my life.

ROBERT BATEMAN is one of the world's greatest artists depicting the natural world. Born in Toronto in 1930, he was a high-school art and geography teacher in Ontario for 20 years, but by the mid-1970s his art had attracted such an enormous following that he began to pursue it full time.

His paintings appear in the collections of many art museums as well as in those of HRHS Prince Philip, Prince Charles, the late Princess Grace of Monaco, and Bernhard, Prince of the Netherlands. He has had a huge number of shows, the most spectacular of which drew record-breaking crowds at the Smithsonian Institution. He has been the subject of several films and biographies, has had three schools named after him, been awarded 10 honorary degrees, the Order of Canada and the Order of British Columbia, and is the author of numerous best-selling art books, including *Bateman's Backyard Birds*.

Since the early 1960s Bob has been an active member of over 30 naturalists clubs and conservation organizations. This involvement has reached a global scale, as he has become a spokesperson for many environmental, preservation and political issues. He has used his artwork and limited-edition prints in fundraising efforts that have provided millions of dollars for these worthy causes.

Bob and photographer Birgit have two children, Christopher and Rob. Alan, Sarah and John are children from his previous marriage. He and Birgit live on Salt Spring Island, British Columbia.

MICHAEL "CHARLIE" BROWN

"The really interesting exploration landscape is the human spirit, and it gets more interesting as we take it to extremes."

On top of the world: "Charlie Brown" filming in the Himalayas. ACE KVALE

Escaping Dungeons, Slaying Dragons

To date, my career highlight has been taking the first high-definition camera to the top of Mount Everest while filming the award-winning *Farther than the Eye Can See*, featuring a remarkable blind man, Erik Weihenmayer. Erik placed great trust in us as his team; he taught us that believing is seeing.

In elementary school I was unpopular. I was skinny with greasy hair, the last one picked for the team, the one wearing glasses whom the bullies liked to pick on. Gym class was the worst part of every day. I didn't want to shower with the others. There are so many ways the kids could be cruel, especially to a kid from a poor family wearing dirty clothes. Their favorite was to break my glasses with fast basketball passes. To make it worse I was nicknamed for the comic character Charlie Brown. I hated it at the time.

I escaped into the world of Dungeons and Dragons—and I still remember the rush of adventure I got playing it. I liked making up wild places and having pretend adventures. The best part was making maps with high mountain passes, wildernesses full of monsters and relics of an ancient age. I loved to add fine details, and even included meticulous weather data. Mountains and glaciers were the most intriguing. I wouldn't know where to draw in a glacier until I had worked out the details of the mountain and climate. I liked to include fantastically high peaks and rivers that traveled through caves. These make believe expeditions were very real and 30 years later those imaginary places still exist vividly in memory.

By the time I graduated from college in 1990 I was passionate about science, especially meteorology. My fantasy was to photograph a tornado and live through a hurricane. I even had dreams where I could reach out and put my hand inside a tornado. But I started bartending because meteorology would require more school and I didn't have the stomach for more of it.

Then Dad and my brothers badly needed help. They had a ski film project in Colorado and a kayaking one in the Mexican jungle in development for the National Geographic channel. These projects seemed interesting, so I agreed to give it a try.

My first real journey away from home was to Chiapas, Mexico. As I exited the plane I was met by a hot blast of heavy, humid air. By the time I descended the stairs, I had three mosquito bites. It was magical and I was hooked, though the cameras intimidated me. When a kayaker was going to run a big rapid we needed every camera rolling. Loading film inside a black bag was bad enough, I didn't like all the setting and focus rings. I was afraid that I would just waste film, but my older brother Gordon encouraged me. The first time he set the camera for me and all I had to do was point and shoot. When I saw one of those shots on television it was a mystical experience! I wanted more.

The first expeditions were frustrating for another reason. I had very limited skill in adventure sports. I could barely roll a kayak in a swimming pool, let alone in white water, and knew nothing about climbing. In an adventure setting I was a liability. Time and time again I was left behind while the more skilled athletes did the exciting parts of the adventure.

The frustration of being held back led to boldness. I resolved to learn how to kayak and climb—and started scaring people. Duckies (inflatable kayaks) became my favorite watercraft. I started dropping into the biggest rapids and somehow survived. In climbing I would just go fast and head for the top. Slowly the skill began to catch up with my boldness and people began to accept me as part of the team. Still today, all of these experiences and the demons that go with them define my adventures.

MICHAEL "CHARLIE" BROWN of Boulder, Colorado, was born in 1966 and is an adventure filmmaker who has won three Emmys. His Serac Adventure Films have also won 24 international film festival awards. He has reached the summit of Mt. Everest four times from Nepal and Tibet, made numerous other first ascents, explored unseen caves and made several first descents of wild rivers in Asia and South and Central America. He has participated in over 30 expeditions to every continent. Michael holds a B.A., with a major in geography, from the University of Colorado. Meteorology was an area of focus.

Charlie is still single. This one-time ugly duckling has too many pretty women flocking around him to consider settling down.

LIEUTENANT (NAVY) JOSEPH FREY

At Wright Valley, calling in a chopper from Antarctica New Zealand's Scott Base on Ross Island. NATALIE CADENHEAD, ANTARCTICA NEW ZEALAND.

Exploration Is the Meaning of Life

I was one of only seven international journalists picked to go to the Antarctic during the 2001–2002 research season. Operating out of New Zealand's Scott Base, I interviewed many of the world's pre-eminent polar scientists. While pursuing my own research on paleoclimatology and climate change, the historian in me was drawn to the three intact huts used by Scott and Shackleton in their respective quests to the South Pole.

But it was while camping out in Wright Valley, one of the dry valleys used by NASA to simulate Mars, that I made one of my most important discoveries, if only significant to me: that not only was Sir Charles Seymour Wright a native Torontonian like me, but he also found Scott's frozen remains in 1912. He also led the British team that invented radar. Wright was nevertheless a virtual unknown in Canada, and I made it my mission to publicize Wright's achievements. I published articles on him in *Time* as well as in other publications.

"Always curious, and wanting to see what is over the next hill, exploration to me has become the physical expression of intellectual curiosity."

During March 2007 while on Salt Spring Island, British Columbia, where Wright died in 1975, I met with an author who was inspired by my writings on Sir Charles and is now writing a book on the Canadian I admire the most. And it all started in a cold, frozen, windswept valley in the Antarctic.

I was never a good student. Sitting still in an elementary classroom almost drove me insane. I couldn't wait for weekends to escape, eagerly anticipating the moments I would spend listening to my father's childhood stories from his native Hungary, where as a boy he'd crawl through the ruins of Turkish fortifications.

Joseph, my dad, would also reminisce about his beloved maternal grandfather and father, both of whom had served with the Austro-Hungarian army in Imperial Russia during the First World War. Or his own experience during the Second World War with the Hungarian army in Yugoslavia, and in the Soviet Union at the Battle of Stalingrad. It was through my father that I developed my passion for history, but at the time I didn't know it.

Similarly my mother, Ottilia, would talk about how her father's oxen team had crashed through the ceiling of a forgotten cellar on one of the family's vineyards, revealing historic relics from the Ottoman Empire. This was my first exposure to archaeology.

Speaking in Hungarian and German, she would recall her family's travels along the Danube to visit relatives in Budapest and how her maternal grandfather was on garrison duty in Sarajevo the day that Archduke Franz Ferdinand was assassinated. Or of the bleakest period in her life, when she and her father were sent in cattle cars deep into the Soviet Union to a labour camp, where he died. She would always mention place names and make references to maps. Enthralled, in my mind I'd picture the majestic Danube winding its way to the Black Sea.

But the moment that it all came together—my love of history, geography and exploration—was in my grade three reader. I hated to read up until that point. "Dick, Jane and Spot" numbed my imagination. Thumbing through the book, I came across two images, one of two men carrying muskets, battling their way through a winter storm, and another of Iroquois warriors attacking French woodsmen. I couldn't believe it: Dick, Jane and Spot weren't part of the story! As it turned out these men were French explorers, Pierre Radisson and Médard des Groseilliers. The challenge of battling the elements and exploring uncharted territory enthralled me. Excited, I read the entire story. I savoured every word, feeling the cold winter winds of northern Ontario and imagining the morning mist rising off the Ottawa River.

I just couldn't get enough; I actually started seeking out more stories of French explorers in North America. I pored over maps of French colonial possessions in North America.

Discovering that the ruins of Sainte Marie among the Hurons, a French Jesuit mission, were near our family cottage on Georgian Bay, I talked my father into driving me to it. Even though there wasn't much to see on the surface, just stone markers showing the outlines of French buildings, Huron longhouses and Algonkin wigwams, I was captivated.

Shortly thereafter, another Frenchman, Jacques Cousteau, would influence my life, and by the end of the 1960s my horizons expanded even further afield as Neil Armstrong and Buzz Aldrin proved there weren't limits to human exploration.

My parents' struggle for survival gave me the spirit needed for hard-core expeditions.Encouraged by my wife, Diane, the summer of 2005 I took our 13-year-old son Jonathan on his first palaeontology dig with Philip Currie and Eva Koppelhus. Hopefully this becomes his moment of inspiration, just as reading that story of Radisson and Groseilliers had been mine.

Lieutenant (Navy) JOSEPH G. FREY, C.D., F.R.G.S., is Chairman of The Explorers Club Canadian Chapter, a recipient of the Canadian Forces Decoration, and a Fellow of the Royal Geographical Society. Under his leadership, it won the Club's "Best Chapter Award" in 2004.

An accomplished science writer, Joe has been published in Canada, Britain and the United States in such publications as *Time*, *The Globe and Mail*, the *Medical Post* and the *National Post*, as well as contributing research to *Science*, *The Economist* and three books on polar issues. His archaeological activities focus on aboriginal and European sites dating to the French Régime in North America (1603-1763). His interest in paleoclimatology and paleoglaciology has taken him to the Antarctic, Greenland and the Canadian High Arctic.

Joe's currently a serving officer in the Canadian Forces and has also been employed by the Ontario government's International Division. He has operated two businesses, with offices in Toronto, Hong Kong and Riga, Latvia. He's travelled to over 60 countries and administrative territories on all seven continents. Joe is a sailor and scuba diver, a graduate of both York University and the University of Toronto, and the recipient of The Explorers Club Citation of Merit in 2006 for outstanding leadership.

He and Diane and son Jonathan live in Toronto.

JOHN GEIGER

"The goal of all exploration is to open worlds and minds, not necessarily in that order."

Solving the puzzle: At the 1845–46 Franklin Expedition Beechey Island grave site. DANIEL J. CATT

I Was Two People in Two Places

I'm best known for my work with Owen Beattie in providing an account of the 1845 British Arctic Expedition commanded by Sir John Franklin, and the role that lead poisoning from their tinned food supply played in their destruction. But I'm just as proud of my role in debunking the long-accepted interpretation of the fate of the 1719 expedition commanded by Capt. James Knight, which ended in mass disaster on Marble Island, a desolate outcrop in Hudson Bay. Knight's men were purported to have been extinguished by slow, lingering deaths of scurvy and starvation after becoming marooned there, but our research proved they had adequate food, seaworthy ships and small whale boats, suggesting a very different fate, possibly involving conflict with the natives.

To this day Marble Island is approached with either apprehension or reverence by the Inuit of Rankin Inlet, the nearest settlement. Before landing by boat in 1989 for the first of our three field seasons there, my colleagues and I were warned by an elder to crawl up the stone beach as if to assuage unquiet spirits. This we did, but were still greeted by fearsome lightning storms, hypothermia, plagues of insects, marauding polar bears—in other words, all the usual terrors of the Arctic. One season on the island, the weather turned and we found ourselves hopelessly stranded. We couldn't establish radio communication. Suddenly we contemplated not solving the mystery of the fate of Knight and his men but replicating it. I then experienced something I had felt only once before, during my childhood, yet something I had always wanted to experience again.

At age seven I was on a field trip with my father, K. W. Geiger, who was working for the Research Council of Alberta, surveying the bedrock topography of southern Alberta. It was a sweltering summer day, and we were walking along a fringe of uncultivated land near the top bank of the Oldman River. At one point we had to climb up a steep embankment. I was following my father, when I was stopped dead in my tracks by a rattlesnake, coiled and ready to strike.

I remember what happened next very clearly, as if it happened yesterday. There was a moment of sheer terror and extreme stress. Then, suddenly, there was a physiological shift of perspective. I felt detached from my immediate situation and surveyed the scene from another, impossible angle. I was two people in two places at one time. I saw my father and I saw a child, a child who could only have been me. If not me, then who? Yet I was seeing it all unfold from a distance, as an observer. Time seemed to slow. And yet it was all over in an instant. My father grabbed the boy with one arm and with what seemed like superhuman strength, pitched him over his shoulder and out of danger.

It was an unforgettable experience—one that could not possibly have ever happened as I remember it. Or could it? All I know is that, in my memory of the incident, when I count, there are not two, but three people there. More than anything I wanted it to happen again.

It did—22 years later, on Marble Island. I was in my tent, wet and chilled to the bone, unable to get warm, shivering almost rhythmically. Suddenly there was a physiological shift of perspective. I felt detached from my immediate situation and saw the scene from a different angle in time/space. It seemed like the exact experience that had haunted me from childhood. Exploration is, ultimately, a head game, its success measured in part by an ability to transcend psychologically the terror—or the abject discomfort—of the moment. There are neurological mechanisms to aid this, to offer that passage of escape.

JOHN GEIGER, F.R.C.G.S., was born in Ithaca, N.Y., and studied history at the University of Alberta. He is co-author of the international bestseller *Frozen in Time: The Fate of the Franklin Expedition*. From 1989 to 1992, Geiger was historical investigator for the Knight Expedition Archaeological Project. This research was published as *Dead Silence* in 1993. He has also authored *Chapel of Extreme Experience* (2003), and two other books.

He is a Governor of the Royal Canadian Geographical Society and Chairman of the society's Expeditions Committee. He is a Member of the Canadian Advisory Council for the International Polar Year, a Member of the Advisory Board of Wings Worldquest and was St. Clair Balfour Fellow at Massey College. He received the Queen's Golden Jubilee Medal and Alberta Centennial Medal.

He is Editorial Board Editor for *The Globe and Mail* and lives in Toronto with his wife, Marina Jiménez, and son, John Alvaro.

MONIKA ROGOZINSKA

"Exploration means to cross the border of the known, to go beyond the limits and to describe it. It also means to describe with new tools in a new way something seemingly well known."

Reporting on the Nanga Parbat winter expedition in the Pakistani Himalayas, 1977–78. MONIKA ROGOZINSKA COLLECTION

Calendars from behind the Iron Curtain

My greatest exploration achievement is being able to describe the world through my writing—and most particularly human behaviour as it faces the most extreme challenges imaginable in exceedingly harsh conditions on the world's highest mountains in winter.

Growing up in communist Warsaw I spent many nights sitting on my bed crying. My brother, a physician, brought calendars from his clinic sent by a Western pharmaceutical company. I pinned to the walls pictures ripped from them, read books about heroes of exploration, mysteries of the world, and gazing into the maps, I imagined that I was travelling. I wanted so much to do so! But I was 20 and a prisoner in my own country!

There was not much on TV apart from Soviet war movies. The streets were gloomy and shabby and the people were sad and tired. Books were censored and printed on low-quality paper, the pictures inside grey. But the calendars showed a different world! Brightly coloured and beautiful! Here was the Matterhorn reflecting in the lake, alpine meadows dotted with flowers, Monte Rosa purple-lit from the setting sun, slender Aiguilles of Chamonix, fairy-like villages and smiling people! I knew very well the history of conquest of those mountains. I wanted to be there so much!

History dictated my family's travels. Grandmother Emilia, escaping the Bolshevik Revolution, crossed Russia by Trans-Siberian Railway, then by ship back to Poland through Japan, the Suez, London and Gdansk. Under her bed she kept a small suitcase in which she had piles of postcards. She bought them at each train station and in each port. I stared wide-eyed at pictures of Novonikolajevsk and the house of merchant Ipatiev where the Tzar's family was shot; ornamental openings of Manchurian houses; stunning gardens in Nagasaki; rocky Hong Kong; elegant residencies of Crimea ....

Grandfather Julian, a Polish Army officer during World War I and a professor at Warsaw University, took her from the mayhem of revolution. He used to send postcards as well. Their son Jerzy, a Polish Home Army soldier during World War II, who later became a professor at American universities, saw Russia from behind the barbed wire of Gulag camps. After World War II, Poles were closed in prisons or in their own country without right to leave.

And so I was sitting on my bed, browsing through the calendars, reading books about exploration and dreaming ... dreaming ....

Finally, in the 1970s Poland's borders opened and as a student of 22 at Warsaw University I had three months of vacation! I flew to London with $20 (U.S.) in my pocket (my mother earned little more monthly as a physician). The first days of this holiday still haunt me in nightmares. I was robbed on my first night in a youth hostel. But I found work and after two months stood in amazement in front of the Chamonix Aiguilles and Mont Blanc, then on the summit of Monte Rosa, Europe's second-highest mountain.

I was sitting with two Austrians admiring the setting sun over the Matterhorn and Monte Rosa when one said: "You know, the idea to come here was excellent. It looks much more beautiful than on the photos of the pharmaceutical company's calendar which is in our office."

MONIKA ROGOZINSKA was born in Warsaw in 1954 and completed an M.A. in Polish Literature and Cultural Studies at Warsaw University. After losing a fight with censorship in Polish radio, she moved to Tatras in the Carpathians, where she became a member of the mountain rescue service and a guide. After a dozen years she returned to Warsaw and worked at the Mickiewicz Literary Society. When Poland was freed after 1989, she became a journalist, stringing for Polish radio and TVand writing for *Rzeczpospolita*—the most respected national daily newspaper—as well as for magazines, covering exploration, science, travel and history. Her passion is mountains and following ancient civilizations.

Monika has been an editor, co-author or consultant on several books. She has climbed in the Tatras and the Alps and hiked in the Andes. She has helped organize expeditions to the Himalayas and Karakorum, and was a correspondent on several 8,000-metre climbs in winter. During the Nanga Parbat expedition she was a witness to an earthquake, participating in a rescue operation for a comrade. On the K2 expedition of 2002–2003, the first-ever from the Chinese side in winter, she sent film and news reports that were seen by four million viewers on Polish TV.

In 1993, Monika co-founded the Polish Chapter of The Explorers Club, and has served as its secretary. She has two sons and lives in Warsaw.

STAN SPIELMAN

That's Stan on the left. MARGARETHA E.
SPIELMAN

"Exploration is a persistent quest for new knowledge that takes one into the natural world or field. The exact circumstance of the effort is usually uncertain, associated with a degree of risk and/or discomfort requiring unusual resourcefulness and fortitude."

Born to Explore

My greatest achievement has been to visit numerous remote villages during the past 35 years, documenting unique images of endangered tribal people with oil portraits while providing medical care.

My dreams were born during childhood and were cultivated until they blossomed into a moment of epiphany as an adult. Growing up in Pennsylvania I had an innate, intense curiosity about the natural world. It manifested itself in exploration of a nearby forest and its fascinating creatures. I climbed tall trees, collected frogs and snakes and learned to identify bird calls and animal tracks in the snow. I dreamed of living in the world of Tarzan movies and fantasized about trekking through Africa and meeting exotic tribal people as portrayed in the movie *King Solomon's Mines*. I assumed that these people had long disappeared and continued only as imaginary subjects of stories and movies. My early dreams took me on adventures that eventually led to my moment of inspiration in Africa.

I also had visions of exploring the ocean's mysteries. I carved fish in hardwood and painted them with oils. Under the influence of my father, a consummate portrait painter, I learned the skills of wood crafting and oil painting. In medical school I became a part-time medical illustrator. When my family moved to

Atlantic City, New Jersey, I designed and hand-built a fishing boat, *Harpoon,* and as a charter boat captain, took parties deep-sea fishing.

I later moved to Miami on *Harpoon* and began my practice in ophthalmology. With the University of Miami I conducted shark vision research—fitted contact lenses and refracted shark eyes underwater to answer the question Do sharks need glasses? (No.) I also researched shark attacks, prevention and treatment. While the dream to explore the ocean was becoming a reality, another was about to launch.

In Tanzania on my honeymoon in 1970, I met the Maasai and became captivated with the incredible picture they presented. Tall and lean, their hair was colored red, beads adorned their necks and they were draped in characteristic rusty-hued cloaks. Men carried spears and colorful cowhide shields. They were the most picturesque of any people I had ever encountered. They displayed a majestic grace and embodied the exotic images of my dreams. I considered the Masai as much a symbol of Africa as the more popular game animals.

On a clear sunny day in the Ngorongoro Crater, Tanzania, I was illuminated by the proverbial lightning bolt! I realized that I had an opportunity to paint portraits of traditional tribal people and it could be a lifelong project.

My passion was heightened when I learned that tribal cultures, having survived thousands of years, were rapidly vanishing. Their portraits were seldom displayed in U.S. art museums and their fantastic images were generally overlooked by the art community. I was particularly inspired to paint my first portrait, an elegant and proud Masai mother, closely holding her child within her cloak.

An entire world lay before me and was mine to explore. Thus began the adventure that continues today, taking me from Africa and the Amazon Basin to the New Guinea Highlands. I live my dreams. I climb tall trees and explore the ocean's depths. My soul is enriched.

STANLEY SPIELMAN, M.D., of Miami, Florida, was awarded first place in art at Atlantic City High School. In 1972 anthropologist Margaret Mead recognized the superb quality of his "very handsome paintings" and encouraged him to visit the Yanomamö Indians of Venezuela (where he narrowly averted an ambush). Pan American World Airways sponsored a one-man show in 1984. In Washington, D.C., the Smithsonian Institution of American Art judged his bronze sculpture "Spirit of Serengeti" Best of Show.

Stan has carried Explorers Club flags on two shark research expeditions (Brazil) and four to indigenous tribes. In 2005 he visited the Cat People of the remote Javari Valley, of Peru and Brazil. With the University of Miami he participated in 40 research cruises funded by the National Science Foundation and The Bureau of Naval Research. He's piloted ultra-light aircraft to survey shark populations and was featured in National Geographic television shows and on Wild Kingdom as "The Shark Doctor." He has also appeared on the Today Show, NBC Prime Time News, 20/20 and MSNBC's Time and Again. Stan's work has been documented in publications including *National Geographic, Encyclopedia Britannica, World Book Encyclopedia, The Journal of Brazil* and *The Explorers Journal.*

Stan's wife is Margaretha and they have three children—Anneli, Eric and Tina—all of whom have graduated college.

Say coconut! Filming the women of the Arowe Tribe, Papua New Guinea. Karen Huntt

*"Exploration is not always about climbing peaks,
soaring to space or descending to the depths of the ocean.
For me, it was made clear that exploring our past and
those of others that can be equally rewarding."*

Through a Lens Brightly

The young Papua New Guinean news reporter looked at me, tears filling his eyes. It was at the end of a two-month long expedition, "Headhunt Revisited—Charting Cultural Change in Melanesia," and we were at a reception at the U.S. Embassy in Port Moresby. He said, "I want to thank you for photographing my people with beauty, dignity and pride." As a photographer on the adventure of her life, that was the moment I knew I had succeeded beyond my wildest dreams.

As a child growing up in the 1950s and 1960s, the norm was for little girls to plan schooling and activities around becoming the perfect housewife and mother. An important profession, but tomboys don't seem to hold an interest in such domestic activities—and I was best at being the perfect tomboy! My attention span lasted longest when listening to my father share his Navy adventures in the South Pacific or describing how he made an emergency exit from a fighter jet while on a test flight with the pilot. My parents, against voices of criticism for not forcing me to behave like a proper young girl, encouraged me to explore what I was interested in. It may have included the wildlife in the forests on our trips or collecting and observing creatures from my own home territory. But only when I was able to spend time with my Uncle Paul, who had such varied successes in his Air Force career, did I realize that there were no boundaries. Paul Albert was not only a pilot but an accomplished engineer in the space program *and* a biochemist. When I was eight I set my sights on becoming a biologist, studying animal life in far-flung places.

However, I did a complete 180 when I married and divorced quite young, then entered corporate real estate for 22 years. In the back of my mind, though, was always the idea of getting back to my love for the outdoors and trying new adventures. Instead of being forced to parachute from an airplane, I chose to make it a hobby. Instead of looking through a microscope, I discovered the camera. Instead of walking through the forests of North America, I dived the beautiful waters of the Florida Keys. It was a combination of experiences that led me to the most gratifying part of my life—capturing life of all kinds with a camera in some of the most intriguing locations on the globe.

Today my specialty is Melanesia, more particularly, Papua New Guinea. I've been traveling there for 14 years and recently completed a marvelous expedition that will become a book, documentary film and lecture series. The goal of this project is to raise awareness of cultural preservation—images with passion and purpose.

MICHELE WESTMORLAND has never been one for sitting still. She was born in 1949—a Navy brat with a taste for seeing new places. She became a scuba diver in 1984 and became obsessed with photographing and studying marine life. Her travels to remote locations, however, gave her a fascination for more terrestrial subjects: people. Learning how to understand the behavior of many living subjects allowed her to capture images that elevated her into the world of publication. Career Number Two started in 1995 and shortly thereafter she met her husband, Stuart, also a photographer. Together they have an incredible life discovering new locations and subjects to document and write about.

Michele's work has been published in many books and in periodicals such as *National Geographic Adventure* and *Traveler, Outside, Condé Naste, Nature's Best, Sport Diver, Scuba Diving* and *Fathoms*, and she is the author of *Ocean Duets*. Her memberships include The Explorers Club, Society of Woman Geographers, North American Nature Photography Association, American Society of Media Photographers and American Society of Picture Professionals. She lives in Seattle, Washington.

30 A Spiritual Explorer

To die will be an awfully

big adventure.

—PETER PAN,
SIR J. M. BARRIE

ALAN NICHOLS

Making friends with a Kazak atop Monster Rock Pass, Kyrgyzstan. SHAN NICHOLS

Mountain Dreams

My "firsts" reflect, in most cases, overpowering lifelong interests: biking the entire Silk Web (known erroneously as the Silk Road) from Istanbul to Xian, China's old capital; bicycling across Xinjiang province from Urumchi to Lhasa; circumambulating the holy mountain of Kailash and Lake Manasarovar in southwestern Tibet right after China opened Tibet to the West; and writing a book, *To Climb a Sacred Mountain*, about the role of sacred mountains in religions.

I was named for my uncle Alan. When I was around seven, my dad gave me a framed certificate in French of a *Croix de Guerre* awarded posthumously for Uncle Alan's heroism as a World War I pilot in the French Army. In a dogfight he had shot down two German planes but was wounded in the stomach. He landed safely but died in the front line hospital from blood loss. My uncle had a passion

> *"Exploration is not just an attempt to find some new interesting or even challenging place. For me it is an obsession with discovery ... physically, mentally, emotionally, spiritually ... unraveling a personal mystery. In other words unraveling the Mystery often called God."*

for exploration and adventure, especially for a cause he believed in, so he joined the French Army before the U.S. came into the war. This certificate hung on the wall facing my bed. One night, just before going to sleep, I vowed to myself that I would live out my uncle's dreams, since he died at only 19. I've been trying to live up to that vow my whole life.

I also remember a very specific dream in 1968, when I was 38, that launched my sacred mountain quest, in turn introducing me to the Silk Web. For two weeks I had been trying a lawsuit in Arizona. When I wasn't thinking about the case, I thought about a movie I was making about Mt. Lassen in California as a tribal totem. I had been staying in a hotel room:

> *There's a mountain in front of me, probably in the deserts of Idaho; for some reason I know it is Mt. Analogue. I'm taking a group of people to climb it to find out why it's so important and why no one can find it. I want to climb it but can't do it by myself. Suddenly it erupts into a flash of light.*

I woke suddenly to sunrise across the desert outside my window. I jumped out of bed and wrote a poem about sacred mountains directly from my dream.

When I finally returned home after the trial, to my surprise there was virtually no literature on the role of sacred mountains in religions! Here was an opportunity to add to the world's knowledge, to bring together all the disparate religions and philosophies as they relate to sacred mountains, to travel, to experience the personal spiritual effects of them and to immerse myself in the history of religions. Sacred mountains became a lifetime exploration.

My first expedition on this theme was a journey around the world in 1969, followed by expeditions to sacred mountains all over the world. Because of their proximity, my experiences at Mt. Kailash led to my first Silk Web cycling expedition in 1989. Over the following years, until finishing in 2005, I bicycled the rest of the Silk Web from Istanbul, across Turkey and Iran, Turkmenistan, Uzbekistan, Tajikistan, Kyrgyzstan, Kazakhstan and finally from Kashgar across China.

For me, God is a mystery, while Spirit is experience. My epiphanies are linear more than sudden events—like peace with my own death as a Shungendō at the Fifth Shugyo on Mt. Omine-San, Japan. And my transformation in gratitude from cycling in and out of the Taklamakan desert where it is said, "All who enter never return."

ALAN NICHOLS was born in Palo Alto, California, in 1930 and brought up in Pocatello, Idaho, and Seattle. Upon receiving his law degree from Stanford in 1955, he practiced in California, founding three law firms, as well as working as a real estate developer. He's also a Tibetologist and Archaeological Investigator (Spiritual Site Layering). He's the author of 10 books, poetry and plays, has produced two movies screened at lectures, written many articles about his explorations and staged photography exhibits. *Journey, A Bicycle Odyssey through Central Asia* tells the story of his Silk Web adventure.

He's a member of the Royal Geographic Society and the Stanford Faculty Club.

Alan and Becky live in Belvedere, California. Their combined families consist of Alan, Sharon, Shan, Mike, Charlotte and Jenny.

31 Conservation – the New Frontier of Exploration

Who will speak for planet Earth?

—CARL SAGAN

JEAN-MICHEL COUSTEAU

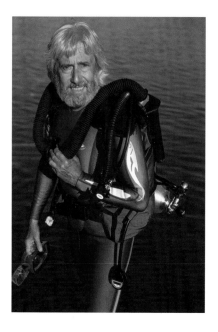

"The point of exploration is to satisfy your curiosity— to always find out what's on the other side of the hill."

Diving headfirst into the family business.
TOM ORDWAY, OCEAN FUTURES SOCIETY

Dreams from the Sea

Having had the privilege of exploring so many different parts of the world, my greatest achievement is to know with certainty that everything is connected and much of that because of our global water system. My good fortune is to have my different dreams converge.

My passion began at age seven when my soon-to-be-famous father, Jacques Cousteau, pushed me overboard wearing his pioneering scuba gear. With my younger brother, Philippe, we started to live a dream as the first children to enter the world under water. I only realized much later, as an adult, what a privilege it was to share the dream of my father.

And although exploring the world under water became my passion, and making sense of it my mission, I did have another dream that seemed unrelated—that took almost 50 years to come true.

The other dream was to become a member of the Olympic track team. My youth was spent dreaming of crossing the finish line under the intertwined Olympic circles. I trained as a runner in private school in Normandy, France, and specialized in the 1,500-metre race. As I competed and began to win, my dream of the Olympics grew. I gave it my all, and after nearly every competition I was the one on the sidelines losing my breakfast.

Finally, the Olympic trials for the French team were within my reach. I placed sixth in the trials. The first three qualified. I was devastated. For years and years.

But my life passion was clear and I worked with my father on what quickly became our shared mission—to protect what we loved: the sea and its vital connection to all life on this planet, including ourselves. My race became one of educating people in time to the effects of our behaviour on the sea, and my track became every road I could travel with that message: protect the ocean and you protect yourself. My education as an architect, and my dream of running in the Olympics, faded far into the background.

Then one day a few years ago, the phone rang with a confidential message: I had been selected to represent the Environment and to carry the Olympic flag in the Opening Ceremonies of the 2002 Winter Olympics in Salt Lake City. It was confidential because the Environment for the first time joined Sports, Culture and the Five Continents as pillars supporting the spirit of the games.

As the music swelled and I carried my corner of the Olympic flag into the Opening Ceremony, I had to marvel at how dreams evolve—I was an Olympics participant at last, and in a way that meant far more to me than as the young athlete I once was. My presence that moment represented everything my father and I had worked all our lives for: a recognition, to 1.2 billion people, of the importance of the natural system and our life-sustaining environment.

That was a dream come true so far beyond, and so much bigger than, my original dream and a moment for which I will always be grateful. And then the dream took another turn.

In the 2004 Olympic Games in Athens, birthplace of the Olympics, I was invited to carry the Olympic flame for a portion of the long road leading up to the games, and I ran like a kid.

Explorer, environmentalist, educator, film producer—for over four decades JEAN-MICHEL COUSTEAU of Santa Barbara, California, has travelled the globe communicating his love and concern for our water planet to people of all nations. *Jean-Michel Cousteau's Ocean Adventures* is seen on PBS. He was born in 1938.

The son of Jacques Cousteau, Jean-Michel has explored the world's oceans aboard *Calypso* and *Alcyone*. Honouring his heritage, he founded Ocean Futures Society to carry on this pioneering work through television specials, multimedia educational programs, web-based marine content, books, magazines and newspaper columns and public lectures, reaching millions of people.

Jean-Michel meets with leaders both at the grassroots level and at the highest echelons of government and business. He is dedicated to educating young people, documenting stories of change and hope and lending support to energize alliances for positive change.

For over 30 years, Jean-Michel and his team have conducted a hands-on environmental education program, called Ambassadors of the Environment, in over seven countries. In 2004, he launched the Sustainable Reefs Program, a package of materials including a CD-ROM, cartoon book, and video on sustainable management of the coral reef. These materials are distributed at no cost to communities bordering coral reefs around the world.

LEE TALBOT

Sharing a joke on their way to Angel Falls, Venezuela, in the 1990s. Lee Talbot

Living History and New Horizons

One hot afternoon in 1956 car trouble brought my ecological survey of the Serengeti Plain to a temporary halt. I climbed a small rocky hill and sitting in the sparse shade of a thorn tree I could see 50 miles of unbroken grassland. Herds of wildebeests, zebras and gazelles dotted the plains until they disappeared in the afternoon haze. A pair of jackals trotted across the foreground and vultures wheeled hopefully in the hot sky. I suddenly felt that I had stepped back in history. The wildebeest could have been bison on the long-lost American prairie, and the gazelle and zebra their nearly extinct counterparts on the former Syrian plains. Plainslands with abundant wildlife were an important part of man's environment worldwide, but increasing human populations and land use had relegated almost all these to history, long before research could define what they were and how they worked. I realized here was the chance—perhaps the last one—to study living history and learn about it directly. My resulting research focus on the Serengeti region has led to a lifelong involvement with Africa.

Perhaps most explorers have a defining moment when their dreams of exploration were born but I can remember no such epiphany. I believe those dreams were born with me. From my earliest recollections, exploration, travel and adventure were simply what one did and what one dreamed that one would do throughout life. My grandfather, C. Hart Merriam, was founder of the U.S. Biological Survey, an explorer of the West and the Arctic, organizer and scientific head of the Harriman Alaskan Expedition. My mother was an adventurous biologist and ethnologist. Dad was a pioneering forest and range ecologist, a distinguished professor and administrator and an outdoorsman—a superb

"Exploration means finding new horizons, learning and developing new information about what is over them, and using that information to make a positive and lasting difference."

horseman and a dead shot. Our house was full of books, paintings, cultural objects and other exploration collections. Exploring new horizons, geographic and intellectual, was taken for granted as a central part of life.

I grew up in Berkeley, in the outdoors, hiking, camping, backpacking, riding, wildlife watching and mountain climbing. So it seemed only natural that my central interests were and still are in the environment. I have designed my career to try to obtain experience with as much of the world as possible, as well as to have the greatest impact I could on environmental conservation and management. Exploration is an integral part of this.

LEE M. TALBOT was born in 1930 and studied at Deep Springs College and Berkeley (B.A., M.A., Ph.D.). He's a Professor of Environmental Science, International Affairs and Public Policy at George Mason University in Fairfax, Virginia, and senior environmental advisor to governments, the World Bank and the U.N. An ecologist and geographer, he has over 50 years experience in environmental affairs in 128 countries. His former positions have included, among others, Chief Scientist and Foreign Affairs Director for the White House Council on Environmental Quality for three U.S. Presidents (Nixon, Ford and Carter); head of Environmental Sciences for the Smithsonian; and Director-General of IUCN—the World Conservation Union. He has been a member of over 20 committees and panels of the U.S. National Academy of Sciences.

Lee is the author of over 270 scientific, technical and popular publications, including 17 books and monographs. Besides having written for *National Geographic*, he's been a consulting editor for their books and other materials, such as the endangered species map of Africa. He was cited as "an acknowledged leader in the shaping of national and international environmental policies and principles" when receiving the Distinguished Scientist Award, the highest recognition of the American Institute of Biological Sciences.

His pioneering fieldwork in remote areas of five continents has often required him to organize and lead (or perform solo) expeditions. Lee has led over 130 expeditions and participated in dozens of others.

Since 1959 he has often worked in the field with his wife, Marty, who is a biologist, conservationist, fellow member of The Explorers Club and a member of the Society of Women Geographers. Together they have spent over six years on research safari in the Serengeti-Mara region of East Africa, and have backpacked, dived, whitewater rafted and mountain climbed throughout the world.

For over 50 years, parallel with his scientific fieldwork, Lee has driven in national and international championship automobile racing on four continents. He still competes and wins.

Lee and Marty have sons Lawrence and Russell and live in McLean, Virginia.

The closer to the source, the sweeter the water: the mighty Yangtze as a trickle. WANG CHIH HONG

Fragile Antique China

I first discovered a source for the Yangtze in 1985 following three *National Geographic* expeditions of many months and thousands of miles across Tibet's rugged plateau. But in 2005, the latest satellite and radar technology from space gave me the chance to discover a definitive, *longer* source. We reached it a second time in one month. As I fell to my knees and drank from it, the water was freezing, but it warmed my heart.

The deeds of Italian Father Matteo Ricci—the Sage of the West—a pioneer to China in 1582, fascinated and inspired me as a boy. I am introduced to him around the age of 15 when I attended Wah Yan College, the Irish Jesuit High School, in Hong Kong. In his 28 years there he had to exercise great prudence and tenac-

> *"Exploration is seeking the unknown and broadening man's quest for knowledge."*

ity. He pioneered the delicate connection between East and West, introducing Western thought and science as well as Christianity, in his last years spent in the Emperor's court. But I am also influenced by martial art storybooks that were later made into local TV shows and movies. Though fictional, they were integrated with some true history and were very popular when I was growing up in the 1960s. They left me spellbound with descriptions of their carefree life roaming over great mountains and the distant land of remote China!

At my Jesuit high school, discipline and academics were both very important. Conforming to rules was rewarded, and denying them, punished. I held out being baptized. I never take "no" as an answer, always probing the grey area of permissiveness. This often landed me in detention. But I learned early on that if I could afford the consequences, I go ahead and do things my way. Also, good Catholics go to confession and I learned early that it is easier to ask for forgiveness than permission. Later on, when I worked in China with all its red tape, I was able to apply this motto with skill and grace. This led to my years in exploring remote China, where the official line is always a "No" but the reality is actually a "No, but ..." Learning to fill in the dotted line, I generally accomplish what I set out to do.

My dream was really born when I finished a journalism and arts degree in 1973 at the University of Wisconsin and began exploring China in 1974. Everywhere I went I encountered people and customs that were going to vanish almost as soon as I'd photographed them. I realized that to be an explorer in today's world, you can't escape becoming a conservationist. This is especially true of China, where rapid modernization threatens its rich heritage.

I was hired by *National Geographic* in 1982–1986 to lead expeditions to China's remote border regions and photograph them. In 1986 I founded the China Exploration and Research Society. CERS operates several centers and theme museums and manages about two dozen projects in remote parts of the country. Its major theme is preserving China's natural and cultural heritage. One involves a campaign to end the slaughter of chiru, whose fur makes shahtoosh shawls. Another aims at restoring a tiny Tibetan nunnery's frescoes. Using space shuttle imaging, we seek out ancient cities along the Silk Road. We also identified the world's most northerly rain forest, in eastern Tibet.

WONG HOW MAN was born in Hong Kong in 1949. In 2002 *Time Magazine* chose him as one of its 25 Asian Heroes and "China's most accomplished living explorer." He has led six major expeditions for *National Geographic* and dozens more for CERS.

How Man is the author of several books, including *From Manchuria to Tibet,* which won the prestigious Lowell Thomas Travel Journalism Gold Award. His CD-ROMs *Exploring the Yangtze* and *Tibet,* won 11 and five international awards respectively. His research and documentary on the mysterious hanging coffins of China won him an award for Best Documentary in Asia. His documentary work has been featured on Discovery and National Geographic channels, BBC, CNN, ABC, CNBC and CCTV.

He has also received numerous awards for conservation. CERS has helped preserve over a dozen wildlife species in China, including the wild yak, Asiatic beaver, golden monkey, Tibetan antelope, wild ass, argali sheep, river otter and Black-Necked Crane.

How Man is a Research Fellow of the Academia Sinica's Beijing Institute of Geography, and the Yunnan Institute of Geography; an advisor to the United Nations' 50th Anniversary Community Awards; Chief Advisor of the Arjin Mountain Nature Reserve, Xinjiang; adviser to the Aksay Kazak Autonomous County, Gansu; and Environmental Advisor to the City of Panzhihua, Sichuan.

How Man lives in Hong Kong.

32 The Future of Exploration

After sleeping though a hundred million centuries we have finally opened our eyes on a sumptuous planet, sparkling with colour, bountiful with life. Within decades we must close our eyes again. Isn't it a noble, an enlightened way of spending our brief time in the sun, to work at understanding the universe and how we have come to wake up in it?

—RICHARD DAWKINS

EVE D'VINCENT

"Exploration involves a fearlessness and willingness to experience life's miracles, regardless of the consequences."

Hardly a glacial stare: Eve at Tracy Arm in southeast Alaska. Cynthia D'Vincent

A Life Beyond Limits

There is a hunter who lives on the edge of the Bahia, Brazil, forest whom we interviewed to determine if he had seen the highly endangered yellow-breasted capuchin monkeys. He said he hadn't, just as multitudes of others before him. We had no choice but to take him at his word. His house is about seven by seven feet and the floor is dirt. There is a small circle outside where he cooks his dinners. I look at the fire pit and notice bones, which seem the same size as an adult monkey. I did not feel betrayed, but instead felt sympathy for the starving man: a sympathy that was not only overwhelming but confusing. Here I was trying to protect the capuchin and yet I could not hate this man that hunted it.

Few people forget their first real communication with nature, and I will never forget mine. This event brought my dreams into focus, and made indelible in my mind the necessity for conservation. It was a sunny afternoon in Alaska and my mother and I were in a 17-foot Boston Whaler. I was eight years old, watching a humpback whale calf play in a kelp forest while its mother swam nearby, grazing on krill. With a rebellious little snort the calf turned and swam directly towards us. I watched in amazement as it swam underneath the boat, its white flippers ghosting by on either side. The calf surfaced right next to me, raised its head and looked me directly in the eye. It then rolled on its side, gently arced a long, slender pectoral fin over the railing as if reaching for me—and I reached out and touched the very tip of its flipper. That is the exact moment when I decided to devote my life to helping animals through conservation of threatened habitats.

I spent much of my childhood aboard research vessels. At least three months each year were spent in the pristine wilderness of Alaska. My mother studies whales and she took my brother and me on every expedition. My earliest memories are of whales, bears and exploring the wilderness. I fell in love with the life of an adventurer, and that of a scientist. I became fascinated with temperate rainforest habitats in Alaska, then extended my research from temperate to tropical rainforest biology.

My first summer in Brazil, in 2001, was preoccupied with establishing a research program for amphibians. I became intrigued with living on bare necessities in an environment with minimal human impact. The contrast is especially poignant when I visit large cities or wealthy neighborhoods. I learned Portuguese quickly, which was critical in conveying the essence of the project to local hunters, whose actions impact the lives of thousands of endangered animals. The forest, with its macaws, would soon become a part of the fast-food chain as cow pastures encroached. That summer, I recognized the urgency of my generation.

In collaboration with Conservation International, I returned to conduct a capuchin survey, consisting of hiking miles through impassable jungle, cutting our way with machetes while balancing a cluster of green bananas on our backs to leave in target areas. The chatter of monkeys immediately alleviated my discomfort and made me forget the incessant mosquitoes. I craned my face, dripping with sweat, up into the canopy for a glimpse of the capuchin.

I returned again in 2002, working with Duke University researchers. We did a census of two rare species: the Rio Branco antbird and the hoary-throated spinetail. We used mist-nets and playback equipment to locate and band the birds. In 2004, I conducted research on Kauai, Hawai'i restoring the beach habitat of green sea turtles to encourage nesting. I also reintroduced endemic plant species.

EVE D'VINCENT was born in 1985 and studies cultural anthropology at Duke University, Durham, North Carolina, U.S.A. She has assisted in humpback whale studies aboard Intersea Foundation research vessels in Alaska and has designed and implemented an amphibian study in Brazil in collaboration with the Reserva Ecológica de Guapi Açu. With Conservation International, she conducted a three-month study on endangered primates in Brazil. As a researcher with Duke University, she undertook research on endangered birds in Amazonas, Brazil. In alliance with the National Tropical Botanical Garden, she has repaired nesting habitat for endangered sea turtles. A recipient of five scholarships from The Explorers Club for her research, Eve has published seven articles and contributed to three publications.

She was featured on Discovery channel's *In Search of Big Mama*. She lives in Carmel, California.

DALIA AMOR AND FERNANDO COLCHERO

Dalia and Fernando putting the collar on a jaguar. HELIOT ZARZA

From a Dream to a Way of Life

D alia's moment: It was 4:00 a.m. and we could hear dogs barking in the jungle. "They got it. *Yes*! They got it!" We took the darting equipment and the GPS radio collar and we started running, trying not to fall because of lianas. We found the dogs barking around a zapote tree. There, in the top, we saw the captivating eyes—a big jaguar! We looked at each other, and in that moment we knew we had everything we wanted in life.

Fernando's moment: There we were at 1:00 a.m. bouncing like an old buoy, the little boat's engine broken and the anchor barely keeping us from flipping over in the waters of the well-named Infiernillo Channel (Little Hell) in the Gulf of California. Dalia was safely in San Diego but here the wind felt like a thousand freezing needles, finding its way through our meagre coats. The boat had died two hours earlier while we were trying to keep the expedition going by bringing food and water back to the island to feed the crew. The only thing I could do was keep the s.o.s. light shining to the mainland and to the little Navy base on the island. No one answered. At that time I was finishing a bachelor's degree in biology and had been working on the project for three years. Although my entire body was

> *"There is not a better way to find the essence and flavor of life than through exploration, which often starts from an early dream inspired by the stories of a former explorer."*

numb and I couldn't feel my hands, my mind kept going back to the time when all this started ....

Dalia's dream: My passion for the outdoors, life, nature and the cultural diversity of my country, Mexico, changed the course of my life. When I was a little girl in our little apartment in Mexico City, *National Geographic* magazines were at home. I cannot forget the image on the cover of one of Biruté Galdikas' baby sharing a bath with an orangutan! (June 1980, with son Binti). I must have been six when my father read me Galdikas' article. In that moment I began my dream to explore in the most isolated tropical forests in the world. But my dream of exploring jungles got a meaning beyond what I ever imagined ....

It was while studying population genetics at the National Autonomous University of Mexico (UNAM), when all my exploration plans changed. I managed to escape from my genetic studies when I started working in the mountains of Oaxaca and the jungles of Chiapas, and when I joined the UNAM geography research team to climb my favorite volcano in Mexico, the 5,700-meter Popocatépetl. Those expeditions went beyond fulfilling my curiosity; they brought me closer to my country's reality: the fast depletion of our natural resources, which is strongly correlated with the loss of our cultural diversity and the extreme poverty of the indigenous communities. It was then when my trips started to have many purposes.

In 1999 the indigenous communities in Oaxaca asked me to participate as an observer for the democratic election process. The Mazatecos indigenous assembly won for the first time their autonomy, without violence, after years of struggle. The indigenous assembly had many projects to improve their community, to maintain their cultural traditions and natural resources. After many trips they knew that Fernando and I loved nature and that we were studying natural sciences. The assembly asked us to advise them on how to settle a protected area and to conserve their remnant forests. I had never felt so ignorant in my life. I knew about DNA sequencing and population genetics, but I did not have the tools and knowledge to help them. This was the exact moment that I decided to change my life.

I finished my dissertation on genetics, knowing I was not going to continue in that path.

Fernando's dream: By the time I graduated from high school I had decided to study biology, despite my family's expectations that I would become a renowned physician like my father. Actually my father knew that I was not fitted for spending the rest of my life working in a hospital. As he once told me, I spent all my childhood devouring our old animal encyclopedia and bringing home any kind of exotic animals that made my mom jump out of her chair. I couldn't miss a chance to go into the woods around Mexico City, or to go to people's ranches and ride horses, no matter how hard I fell off.

So there I went, fascinated with my new school, the National Autonomous University of Mexico, the largest university in Latin America. People of all backgrounds crowded its classrooms; a real taste of Mexico. It was all a little too much for me. I immediately joined an invertebrate physiology lab and started spending too much time making friends, playing guitar and harassing crayfish. I wasn't able to find my real passion. I decided to try my luck playing guitar. I met many wonderful people before leaving school, the most important being the woman that a few years later changed my life for good. Dalia had started her first year biology when I met her in 1994, the most beautiful and bright girl I had met. However, our paths were not meant to meet quite yet.

In a bold move, I joined a flamenco guitar school and a band. I even convinced myself that I wasn't made to study. The only thing that I couldn't take out of my mind was Dalia. Three years passed until one day I heard from a friend that that really attractive young lady from school did not have a boyfriend, believe it or not! I did not think twice; I called her and, after going out a couple of times, I was able to convince her that despite my bohemian life, I was the right guy for her.

Dalia had joined a conservation biology lab and was about to leave on a trip to the Chihuahuan desert to survey pronghorn antelopes. My mind spun with the idea of being out there, working with large mammals, camping in the desert .... I immediately understood that exploration was my absolute passion. After her trip I announced to Dalia that I had decided to return to school. I joined the same lab and was lucky enough to get involved in a project with her on an island in the Gulf of California.

My job was to study the population dynamics of an introduced population of desert bighorn sheep, working with an indigenous community, the Seris or Kon Kaak as they call themselves. I spent three years doing aerial surveys, capturing bighorn sheep to repopulate their historical ranges and walking across the island understanding the vegetation and its relationship with the sheep. This brings me back to the beginning of my story ....

As part of a conservation strategy, the Mexican government and the Seri community allowed two hunting expeditions a year. Our boat misadventure happened during one of those. Fortunately, at 5:00 a.m. a Seri boat pulled us back to the mainland.

After that I kept working on the project and joined another one with Dalia in Chihuahua mapping habitat for pronghorn antelope. Eventually I did my thesis on this last project and graduated in 2001. After that, Dalia and her overwhelming conviction persuaded me that we needed to do a Ph.D., that we couldn't just stop there.

Our future story: We were married in 2004. By this time we have worked on numerous conservation projects together, including the reintroduction of pronghorn antelope to areas of Mexico; bighorn sheep on Tiburon Island with the Seri indigenous community of Sonora; jaguars in Mexico, Guatemala and Belize; and India's Melghat tiger reserve.

We had been planning to go to the U.S. to do doctorates in ecology, but now my, Dalia's, goal was to work in the field of natural science, but from a different perspective. I want my research to be used to propose conservation alternatives that include the human aspect. What I did not expect is that my research and explorations led me to understand patterns of biodiversity loss not only in Mexico, but around the world, including Kenya's Masai Mara reserve; and across all of Southern Africa as part of an elephant research team. My early expeditions not only gave a different meaning to my life, they gave it a mission.

We are pursuing our Ph.D.s at Duke University in North Carolina. Our interests and goals being so similar, we plan to work as a team in the future. Our goal is to find a job in which we can both keep doing research and conservation worldwide but particularly in Mexico and Latin America.

DALIA AMOR was born in Baja California, Mexico, in 1974. She is studying patterns and causes of deforestation in the Mayan jungles, its environmental and political basis and its effects on jaguar populations. In 2002 the American Association of University Women honoured Dalia for her academic achievement and her work in the Mazateco indigenous communities. In 2003 she received the L. Ron Hubbard Young Explorers Award for her jaguar conservation expedition. In 2005 she was given the Wings Women of Discovery Field Research Award, underwritten by a gift from Rolex. She was also elected a W.P. Carey Fellow.

FERNANDO COLCHERO was born in 1972 in Mexico City. His research focuses on the effects of environmental changes on bird and mammal population dynamics. He is currently working on the effects of ocean warming on the breeding behaviour of sooty terns at the Dry Tortugas in Florida. The results of his conservationist projects are being used as the basis for the national bighorn sheep recovery plan in Mexico.

TED GILLILAND

The Duke exploring the jungles of Costa Rica. CLINTON JENKINS

Up on the Roof

I was sitting cross-legged with a group of villagers inside a mud hut in north-western Madagascar. As we picked apart small cooked fish with our fingers and shared a large communal rice bowl with one spoon, I said to one of the head villagers, "Mitsiaro be ny sakafo, misaotra betsika." (The food is delicious, thank you.) She looked up from her bowl and through the curling smoke from the oil lamp between us replied, "Gasy ianao," which means, "You are Malagasy." At that moment, I probably should have been thinking what an honor it was to have been invited to eat with one of the head villagers and having been accepted into the group so much as to be considered one of the Malagasy, but all I could think of was the rooftop of my suburban home in Cleveland, Ohio.

To explain how or why I ended up in a village in northwestern Madagascar I have to start right back to that very rooftop in Cleveland and to what happened on May 5, 1998. Bored and tired in my seventh-grade history class the day before, I managed to turn the scribbles on the side of my paper into a design for a bird

*"Exploration has always been a way to
delve into the natural world in order to observe,
understand and appreciate it."*

feeder. That evening, having pieced together the feeder and filled it with seed, I placed it on a branch high enough that I had to jump to reach it. The sun had already set by then, and when I turned around to take a glimpse at the feeder, I could see that a female cardinal had already perched on it and was feeding in the evening light. Although I didn't make much of it, I decided I would sit on my rooftop the next day after school and observe what frequented the feeder. The next day was May 5th, which serendipitously is the peak of spring bird migration in Cleveland. There were incredible birds of all colors and shapes everywhere. I was entirely overwhelmed with a sensation of fascination and completely hooked, for good. I was 13 years old and I had realized that exploration was a way to delve into the natural world.

As time went on I didn't have to jump to refill the bird feeder anymore and I began to go on weekend expeditions into the field instead of simply sitting on my roof. I began to investigate the natural history and ecology of birds through field research and quickly developed the dream of investigating birds and the environment in tropical countries around the world. I started out just dreaming of these expeditions, and it was birds themselves that eventually led me to them.

While my 16-year-old peers sneered at the idea of squandering an entire spring vacation bird-watching, I grabbed my pack and headed to Florida with my parents in search of that same sensation I felt for the first time on my roof. On a boat heading for a few mud islands out in the Gulf of Mexico, birds quickly became the subject of conversation between another passenger and me. As we discussed birds and the environment, it became apparent that this man was Stuart Pimm, a well-known conservationist. By the end of our day of bird-watching together, he posited me this: "We have field research stations all over the world. We work in Brazil, Mexico, southern Africa, Madagascar ... would you like to come work with us?" I leapt at the chance and chose Madagascar.

I have moved from watching birds atop my roof in Cleveland to mountain peaks in Costa Rica and the tops of Mayan temples above the canopy of the Guatemalan jungle, but the sensation in all these places has remained the same. Although my dreams have carried me from my seventh-grade history classroom to villages in Madagascar and the rainforests of Central America, my sensation of utter fascination with the natural world and my passionate desire to explore it has remained the same as it was when I started on my rooftop in suburban Ohio in May of 1998.

TED GILLILAND was born in 1985 and is a student at Duke University where he studies environmental sciences. He has been the recipient of two Expedition Grants from The Explorers Club Youth Activity Fund for his work in Madagascar and the Mayan Rainforest of southern Mexico, Guatemala and Belize. In addition to his interest in exploration and birds, he is dedicated to the conservation of the environment, its biodiversity and the services it provides to humans.

POST-EXPEDITION NOTES

During the course of compiling this anthology and prior to publication, four contributors ventured on to that higher exploration.

One was Norman Vaughan, who had turned 100 just six days before. In my one meeting, in New York, and two telephone conversations with Norm, the latter in some depth, I was greatly impressed by his obvious love of life and adventure. Enthusiasm bubbled from him as from a spring. The boy was still very much alive and running around behind his twinkling eyes, happy smile and upbeat voice.

The second was Bradford Washburn, at 96. The last time I spoke to him, by phone, I couldn't help but comment about the field photo he submitted for this book, capturing him and his wife Barbara atop Mt. McKinley in 1947: "Man, Brad, you have this great life—and you even got the beautiful woman!" He was pleased with that. I think Barbara was too. She was still bright and vivacious when I talked to her then, a delight, with a quick mind and a wonderful, light sense of fun.

Bill Burnham was the third. Born in 1947, he died of brain cancer in the fall of 2006, eight months after being diagnosed. His is one of the most inspirational stories in this book—an academic washout and tradesman so strongly motivated he drove himself to achieve that all-important Ph.D. in the exploration field he strived to belong to. He was intensely focused on conservation, and his legacy is the powerful conservation society he built, which will continue to protect his beloved raptors.

The fourth was Peter Lewin, a gentle, kind, sensitive soul respected by all who knew him, and I'm proud to say I made his acquaintance as well. He was on his final sick bed when we worked on his contribution via email. It took almost three weeks to finalize, and he moved on to that last expedition less than two weeks later. I knew he had end-stage cancer but I never mentioned it, nor did he. Recalling the exciting birth of his love for archaeology—and his unique contribution to it—was his last act as an explorer, and he knew it. With his contribution to this book, we both silently knew he was leaving a small blaze on a tree, his legacy to exploration.

Closing in on a century of full living, Norm and Brad well knew this too, that they couldn't be around forever. For these reasons, their contributions remain, their words taking on greater meaning than if they were still among us.

JASON SCHOONOVER

Jason with ex-headhunting Ifugao friends in Banaue, Philippines. Su Hattori

> *"Exploration is the grand adventure of following one's curiosity to discover."*

About the Author

Jason Schoonover has been a writer and an ethnological field collector since the 1970s. His collections are found in museums around the world, as well as in private collections. South and Southeast Asia, including the Himalayas, are his main areas of interest. A one-time columnist, he's widely published in newspapers and magazines, and has a background as an announcer and writer/director/producer in radio and stage.

He was profiled in Jerry Hopkins' *Bangkok Babylon: The Real-Life Exploits Of Bangkok's Legendary Expatriates Are often Stranger than Fiction*. Jason is a Fellow of The Explorers Club and a member of the Foreign Correspondents Club of Thailand. He and Su Hattori divide their time between Bangkok, Thailand; Saskatoon, Saskatchewan, Canada; and the rest of the world. Exploring old fur trade and exploration routes by canoe is a favourite passion.

Jason's motto is Follow Your Dreams. He can be reached at jasonschoonover.com.